Foundations of Modern Management:
Marketing

Volume 8

Edited with a new Introduction by
Morgen Witzel

OVERSTONE

Marketing

Edited and Introduced by Morgen Witzel

Volume 1
The Economics of Marketing and Advertising (1923)
William D. Moriarty

Volume 2
The Marketing Problem: How it is Being Tackled in U.S.A (1926)
Edward T. Elbourne

Volume 3
Scientific Sales Management Today (1929)
Charles W. Hoyt

Volume 4
Cases on Industrial Marketing (1930)
Melvin T. Copeland

Volume 5
The Psychology of Advertising (1932)
Walter D. Scott

Volume 6
Marketing Research Technique (1931)
Percival White

Volumes 7 and 8
Collected Articles and Chapters

Printed in England by Antony Rowe Ltd., Chippenham

Collected Articles and Chapters

II

THOEMMES PRESS

KYOKUTO SHOTEN LTD

This edition co-published in 2000 by

THOEMMES PRESS
11 Great George Street, Bristol BS1 5RR, United Kingdom

KYOKUTO SHOTEN LTD
12, Kanda-Jimbocho 2-Chome, Chiyoda-Ku, Tokyo, Japan

www.thoemmes.com

MARKETING
8 volumes : ISBN 1 85506 628 9

PUBLISHER'S NOTE

The publisher has gone to great lengths to ensure the quality of this reprint but points out that some imperfections in the original book may be apparent.
This book is printed on acid-free paper, sewn, and cased in a durable buckram cloth.

- Overstone is an imprint of Thoemmes Press.

Contents

The Relation of Consumers' Buying Habits To Marketing Methods[1]

Melvin T. Copeland

From the standpoint of consumers' buying habits, merchandise sold in retail stores can be divided roughly into three classes: (1) convenience goods; (2) shopping goods; (3) specialty goods. Using this classification, one of the initial steps in laying out a sales or advertising plan is to determine whether the article to be sold will be purchased by consumers ordinarily with shopping or without shopping, at points of immediate convenience or in central trading districts, with insistence on an individual brand, with merely brand preference, or with indifference to brand.

This preliminary analysis facilitates the determination of the kind of store through which the market for the specific product should be sought, the density of distribution required, the methods of wholesale distribution to be preferred, the relations to be established with dealers, and, in general, the sales burden which the advertising must carry.

Convenience Goods

Convenience goods are those customarily purchased at easily accessible stores; examples are canned soup, tobacco products, electric light bulbs, safety razor blades, shoe polish, laundry soap, crackers, popular magazines, confectionery, and tooth paste. The consumer is familiar with these articles; and as soon as he recognizes the want, the demand usually becomes clearly defined in his mind. Furthermore, he usually desires the prompt satisfaction of the want. The unit price for most articles in this class is too small to justify the consumer's going far out of his way or incurring the

[1] From *Harvard Business Review*, vol. I, no. 3 (April, 1923), pp. 282–89; reprinted in F.E. Clark (ed.), *Readings in Marketing*, New York: Macmillan, 1923, pp. 233–41.

expense of a street-car fare in order to procure a special brand. It is for such reasons as these that a product subject to this type of demand gains a large sales advantage when it is purveyed in numerous stores located at points easily accessible to consumers. The consumer is in the habit of purchasing convenience goods at stores located conveniently near his residence, near his place of employment, at a point that can be visited easily on the road to and from his place of employment, or on a route traveled regularly for purposes other than buying trips. In sparsely settled districts, to be sure, the distance a consumer must travel to reach a store carrying convenience goods necessarily is greater than in densely populated districts, but fundamentally the buying habits are the same in all districts. Convenience goods, moreover, are purchased at frequent intervals by the average consumer, and these "repeat" purchases enable the stores handling such wares to secure adequate patronage with reasonably small investments in stocks of merchandise.

Typical retail establishments carrying convenience goods are grocery stores, drug stores, and hardware stores. A majority of these stores are unit stores, but it is in the trade in convenience goods that chain store systems have shown the greatest development.

Because of the desire of consumers to purchase this type of merchandise at easily accessible stores, the manufacturer of a convenience article must aim to secure distribution of his product through a large number of stores in each territory. Many of the retail outlets commonly utilized for this purpose at the present time are small unit stores; consequently, to obtain this widespread distribution it is customary for most convenience goods to be sold through wholesalers. Whenever a manufacturer of a product in this category elects to sell directly to unit stores, he must develop a large sales organization and arrange for his salesmen to visit the retailers at frequent intervals.

Shopping Goods

Shopping goods are those for which the consumer desires to compare prices, quality, and style at the time of purchase. Usually the consumer wishes to make this comparison in several stores. Typical shopping goods are gingham cloth, women's gloves, chinaware and novelty articles. The typical shopping institution is the department store. Shopping goods are purchased largely by women. Ordinarily a special trip is made to the shopping center for the purpose of buying such merchandise. As a rule, however, the specific store in which the purchase is to be made is not determined until after the offerings of at least two or three institutions have been inspected. The exact nature of the merchandise wanted may not be clearly defined in advance in the mind of the shopper; this is in contrast to the usual attitude in purchasing convenience goods. The purchase of shopping goods, furthermore, usually can be delayed for a time after the existence of the need has been recognized; the immediate satisfaction of the want is not so essential as in the case of most convenience goods. Because of the variety of merchandise which must be carried to satisfy the shopper and the relative infrequency of purchases of shopping articles by the average consumer, the store catering to the shopping trade must have a central location which attracts shoppers from a wide territory. In order to justify the expenses of operation in such a location, the volume of sales must be large. Conversely, it follows that the type of store which handles convenience goods ordinarily cannot carry a large enough variety and range of products to offer an attractive opportunity for shopping.

A store location suitable for trade in shopping goods usually is not adapted to the convenience goods trade; for the rental is high and the delivery interval inconvenient to consumers. It is seldom that a department store, for example, has found it possible to operate a grocery department at a profit. The factors of location, organization, and consumers' buying habits, which enable a department store to cater effectively to the shopping trade, handicap it in developing a business in convenience goods. When a manufacturer is laying out his marketing plans, therefore, he ordinarily finds it inconsistent to attempt to distribute his product through both department stores and scattered unit stores or through both department stores and chain stores. The type of store selected depends upon whether it is a shopping line, a convenience line, or a specialty line.

The number of stores selling shopping goods, furthermore, is much smaller than the number of convenience stores. The average size of the shopping store is large and its credit generally strong. This facilitates the marketing of shopping goods directly from manufacturer to retailer.

Specialty Goods

Specialty goods are those which have some particular attraction for the consumer, other than price, which induces him to put forth special effort to visit the store in which they are sold and to make the purchase without shopping. In purchasing specialty goods, the consumer determines in advance the nature of the goods to be bought and the store in which the purchase is to be made, provided a satisfactory selection of merchandise can be effected in that store. Whereas convenience goods are purchased at stores that are easily accessible, it ordinarily is necessary for the consumer to put forth special effort to reach the store selling specialty goods. As in the case of shopping goods, the actual purchase of a specialty article may be postponed for a time after the specific need has been felt by the consumer. Examples of specialty goods are men's clothing, men's shoes, high grade furniture, vacuum cleaners, and phonographs. Specialty goods are purchased by both men and women, but men's purchases of specialty lines are a larger proportion of the total sales of such merchandise than in the case of shopping goods.

For specialty goods the manufacturer's brand, the retailer's brand, or the general reputation of the retail store for quality and service stands out prominently in the mind of the consumer. It is because of distinctive characteristics associated with the brand or the store that the consumer is prepared to rely upon the service, quality, and prices of merchandise offered by that store as generally being fair and to accept the merchandise without shopping. In numerous lines of specialty goods, such as men's shoes and clothing, the consumer prefers to deal with a store offering an attractive variety of styles and sizes from which to select. Purchases are made by each individual customer at infrequent intervals. Consequently, a specialty store generally is located at a point to which customers can be drawn from a wide area.

From the manufacturer's standpoint, a specialty line calls for selected distribution, in contrast to the general distribution essential for convenience goods. The dealers who are to handle the specialty line must be carefully selected on the basis of their ability to attract the class of customers to whom the product will appeal. Retailers must be chosen who can be relied upon to use aggressive selling methods in attracting customers to their stores. Frequently, exclusive agencies are granted to retailers for the distribution of specialty goods. An exclusive agency is seldom, if ever, justified for any line which is not a specialty line. It is only in the marketing of specialty goods, furthermore, that manufacturers have found it practical to operate retail branches.

Because of the part which each individual retail store handling the merchandise plays in the sale of the specialty goods, the care with which these stores must be selected, and the methods of co-operation which are essential between the manufacturer and the dealer, specialty goods are especially suited to distribution by direct sale from manufacturer to retailers. The manufacturer of specialty goods who works out his plan of distribution systematically on this basis also often finds it advisable, through his national or local advertising, to assume part of the burden of focusing the demand on individual stores.

In case of several commodities, the articles tend to fall into more than one of these three categories. Staple groceries, for example, are clearly convenience goods; fancy groceries, on the other hand, are specialty goods. In each city there usually are from one to three stores which have a high reputation for specialties in groceries. Although these stores also sell staple groceries, their patronage is secured primarily on the basis of the specialties that they carry. Because of the limited market for such specialties and the volume of business necessary to justify carrying such a stock, ordinarily only one or perhaps two or three stores in a city can obtain enough business on these goods to warrant taking on a line of fancy groceries; in the same city, anywhere from one hundred to several hundred grocery stores are carrying convenience goods.

In the shoe trade, medium- and high-priced shoes for both men and women are specialty goods. Women's shoes which feature style novelties border on the shopping classification. The common grades of work shoes, on the other hand, border on the classification of convenience goods.

The manufacturer of women's novelty shoes, for example, cannot advisedly leave the shopping institutions out of consideration in planning his sales program. The manufacturer of cheap work shoes, however, ordinarily must place his product in a larger number of stores than would be required were he selling medium-grade dress shoes for men.

Although women's ready-to-wear suits generally are shopping goods, a few manufacturers recently have been developing standard trade-marked lines, which tend to fall into the class of specialties. Several retail stores also have developed specialty reputations for women's ready-to-wear. In view of the conditions in the women's ready-to-wear field and also in several other fields, the average department store now seems to be faced definitely with the question of whether its merchandising should be primarily on a shopping basis or whether at least some of its departments should be developed on a specialty basis. The piece goods departments are likely to remain shopping departments. Shoes, men's clothing, women's ready-to-wear, furniture, silverware, and numerous other departments are being developed in several department stores as specialty departments, but generally without a conscious, well-coordinated policy for a store as a whole. In these specialty departments the emphasis is shifted from comparative prices and comparative styles to the special qualities and characteristics of the merchandise carried. In other department stores the merchandising is still almost entirely on a shopping basis, with the featuring of prices and bargains that are supposed to appeal to the shopper. In so far as department stores develop specialty departments, they will afford attractive outlets for manufacturers whose distribution otherwise would be through specialty stores.

Relation of brands to buying habits

Convenience, shopping, and specialty goods are sold both branded and unbranded. Because of the differences in the buying habits of consumers in purchasing these classes of goods, brands do not play the same part in the merchandising plans for all three classes, and the advertising problems of manufacturers are quite dissimilar for shopping, convenience, and specialty merchandise.

A brand is a means of identifying the product of an individual manufacturer or the merchandise purveyed by an individual wholesaler or retailer. The real demand for any commodity is the quantity which consumers will buy at a specific price. If a product is unbranded, the volume of the demand ordinarily depends upon the quantity that consumers elect to buy, either entirely upon their own initiative or as a result of the sales efforts of the retailers by whom it is sold. When sugar was sold in bulk, for example, the demand depended upon the amount consumers wished to purchase or were induced to purchase by retailers who featured the article; sales were not directly stimulated by the sugar refiner.

For an unbranded product, the individual manufacturer seldom can afford to assume the burden of stimulating demand which can not be specifically directed to the product of his own factory. For such an unbranded product the manufacturer must rely chiefly upon his ability to produce cheaply, in order to be able to offer low prices, and he must pursue merely passive selling methods, or, at most, direct his sales efforts chiefly toward wholesale and retail merchants. If the product is branded, on the other hand, the manufacturer can undertake not only to direct the active demand to his particular product, but also to arouse latent demand by stimulating a larger number of consumers to want his product or by making previous consumers desire to use more of his product at a specific price. When the American Sugar Refining Company, in 1912, for example, began to put out sugar in packages bearing the company's trade-mark, the company not only was in a position where it could inform the consumer regarding the merits of that particular brand, but it also could practically undertake to induce consumers to use more sugar, as, for instance, in canning fruit.

With the development of the package trade, the tendency during recent years has been for an increasing proportion of convenience goods to he branded. The increase in the sale of crackers in packages, for example, in contrast to the former bulk sales, has given greater significance to brands of crackers and has facilitated the use of aggressive sales methods by cracker manufacturers. Among shopping goods there has been some increase in the number of brands, but large quantities of merchandise in this class still are sold unbranded. Specialty goods are all branded, except in a few cases where retail stores have reputations which practically render it unnecessary for them to have brands placed on the merchandise which they sell.

When a manufacturer undertakes to focus the potential demand upon his product with brand identification, he must consider the attitude in which the consumer ordinarily approaches the purchase of such an article. The attitude of the consumer may be that of: (1) recognition, (2) preference, or (3) insistence.

Consumer Recognition

When a brand has any significance at all, it serves primarily as a cause for recognition. If the consumer's previous acquaintance with the brand has been favorable, or if the manufacturer's or dealer's advertising has made a favorable impression, other things being equal, the recognized brand will be selected from among other unrecognized brands or from among unbranded merchandise. For some products—such as silk goods, ginghams, and women's suits—pattern, style, and price are considered by the consumer, before brand. When the selection narrows down to a choice between articles of this sort approximately equal in pattern, style, and price, the recognition of a known brand sways the choice. The manufacturer of such goods, however, cannot hope ordinarily to secure many sales merely because of brand, if his product is higher in price or less popular in pattern and style than directly competing goods shown in other stores.

Consumer recognition—an acquaintance with the general standing of the brand—probably is the only attitude toward that brand which the manufacturer of a typical shopping line ordinarily can establish in the mind of the average purchaser by means of advertising and sales efforts. If the product has some special feature, as, for example, cotton fabrics dyed in fast colors or fast-colored silk goods loaded with a minimum of tetra-chloride of tin, it occasionally is possible to arouse the interest of the consumer to a point of preference.

A family brand, by which is meant a brand or trade-mark that is applied commonly to a group of different products turned out by a single manufacturer, serves primarily to establish consumer recognition for all products in the group as soon as the consumer becomes acquainted with one article bearing the common brand. The experience of retail dealers indicates that for shopping and convenience goods the common brand aids in promoting consumer recognition. If it is a specialty line, the experience of the consumer with one article bearing the brand is likely to establish in the minds of consumers at least an attitude of preference for other articles bearing the same brand. It is unsafe, however, for the manufacturer to count upon the family brand to develop more than consumer recognition without the presentation of sales arguments for each article bearing the brand.

Consumer Preference

Consumer recognition soon shades into consumer preference. When several brands of merchandise, which are similar in general qualities and in external appearance, are offered to the consumer by a retail salesman, the one for which previous experience, advertising, or perhaps the retailer's recommendation has created a preference, is chosen. The strength of the brand depends upon the degree of preference in the mind of the consumer. In purchasing convenience goods, for example, the consumer often approaches the retailer with the question, "Have you the X brand?" If the retailer does not have that brand in stock, another brand ordinarily is accepted by the consumer, or, if the retailer specifically urges another brand in the place of the one called for, a substitute may be taken by the consumer. This practice of asking for brands is common for many consumers in the purchase of convenience articles. The brand comes first in the consumer's mind and signifies to him the quality, style, or pattern of article, or the type of container that he wishes to obtain. In such cases the consumer has a preference for the brand asked for, but ordinarily it is not strong enough in this class of merchandise to make him insist on that brand to the point of visiting a less convenient store to make the purchase. It is because the consumer generally has merely the attitude of brand preference in purchasing convenience goods that it is essential for the manufacturer of such a product to place his wares on sale in a large number of stores in each territory.

Consumer Insistence

The third stage in which the demand for branded articles manifests itself is consumer insistence. When the consumer approaches the purchase of an article in this attitude of mind, he accepts no substitute unless it is an emergency. This attitude of consumer insistence holds commonly in the purchase of specialty goods. To warrant undertaking to develop this attitude, the product must be so individualized in quality, in its special features, or in the service rendered by the manufacturer or retailer as to differentiate it distinctly from competing articles and to induce consumers to put forth special effort to secure that brand. The manufacturer of an electrical washing machine, for example, undertakes to present his sales arguments in such a way as to lead the consumer to insist upon the purchase of his particular make. Through advertising, the manufacturer of such a machine seeks to convince the consumer that his is the machine which should be purchased and that a store carrying this brand should be sought out.

The difference between no standing at all in the mind of the consumer, consumer recognition, consumer preference, and consumer insistence is one of the degrees to which the selling process has been carried with the consumer before he visits a retail store to make his purchase. If the consumer has no familiarity whatsoever with the brand of product to be purchased, the entire sales burden rests on the salesman in the store visited. If the consumer recognizes the brand, the manufacturer of that brand has taken the initial step in consummating the sale to the consumer. If the manufacturer has established consumer preference, the sale has proceeded one step further. If the consumer has the attitude of insistence, it remains merely for the retail salesman to close the sale.

An Experiment in Distribution: The Winchester-Simmons Company[2]

John E. Otterson

We are welding together a manufacturing business, a jobbing business, and several thousand separately owned retail stores into a national organization with a common purpose. We aim to lower the cost of distribution as it affects the merchandise we manufacture and job.

In the first place, we had no quarrel with the established methods of distribution. They served us (The Winchester Repeating Arms Company) very well up to the time of the war. With the war we were, of course, thrown headlong into producing munitions: principally U.S. rifles, U.S. cartridges, and Browning machine guns. When the Armistice shut us down, we had 21,000 employees and several times the plant capacity of pre-war days. Incidentally, we had been the first plant to make deliveries to the Government, on each of the articles we were making. That is a record we are proud of.

Essentially, we are highly skilled forgers; almost every metal part of a fire-arm is forged. So we had been planning, in the few spare moments that the war had left us, that on the coming of peace we should turn our excess plant capacity to forge products. That was about as far as we had gone with the plan by November of 1918.

The Armistice brought us face to face with the whole problem. We had to design and get quantity production on a whole new line of products. We had to get distribution for our output. And we had to accomplish both of these results in record-breaking time.

[2] Adapted from John E. Otterson, "An Experiment in Distribution," in *System*, vol. XLIV, no. 5 Nov., 1923, pp. 567ff; reprinted in F.E. Clark, *Readings in Marketing*, New York: Macmillan, 1923, pp. 328–35.

When it came to deciding on the products we should make, we considered carefully the whole hardware field. Obviously, we could not make the whole line; what part of it, then, should we select as our own?

Specialization on Articles of Personal Use

Considering our long history and good name as makers of firearms, we saw that we could build most quickly and surely on articles toward which we could divert our reputation. That meant articles of persona! use.

If you carry a pocket-knife, you probably know who made it. You selected it largely because you considered it of good make. We saw that, to a man who owned a Winchester rifle, a pocket-knife of the same make would be a preferred brand. If he used a hammer, be would be favorably inclined toward a Winchester hammer. If he took his winter recreation on the ice, he would feel sure Winchester skates would be of high quality. To anyone who knew our reputation in our pre-war field—and nearly everyone did—we could sell articles of personal use with comparative ease.

It would be harder if we went into what I may call impersonal lines. Unless you are closely connected with the specialized field, you care little about who made the hinges and nails in your home, or the castors on your wife's dressing table. Neither does the man who built your home or made your furniture, so long as they serve their purposes. Brand preference, which means easier selling, is much more significant in the articles of personal use.

How we designed the different articles, and then got into production, is a story aside from this one. We had competent factory engineers, and they drove hard to the work. After their plans were completed and put into effect, the production side of the business ran comparatively smoothly.

Distribution Problems

The real problem was that of distribution. How could we go about selling, at a profit, the new hardware and sporting goods lines which we were getting ready to make? Obviously, the existing jobbers could not be expected to push our new line; it would have taken a tremendous amount of selling and advertising energy to build up a consumer demand that would have drawn our large output out of our factories and through the existing channels. We needed something that did not exist.

The Dealer Organization

So we set out to create it for ourselves. We decided to build a dealer organization, and serve it direct. Long before we had any of the new products ready to sell, we had signed up more than 1,000 of the best retail hardware dealers of the country to be our agents, to conduct the local "Winchester Store."

That these dealers were among the best in the country is no idle assertion, based purely on pride. With the utmost care we listed the best hardware dealer in each community. We considered, in making these selections, the general reputation of each store; its financial strength; its stock; its location; and several other facts of similar importance.

It was no simple job to compile this list. But we had arms and ammunition salesmen who had been calling on the retail trade for years. We had a good many executives of wide personal experience in the field. After weeks of painstaking work, involving the whole time of a number of people and the part time of everyone in the sales and executive organization, we had our national list of best dealers.

That is the list upon which our "contract salesmen" called—with instructions to exert every effort to sign up the best dealer.

Dealer Relations

What we offered the dealer, as an inducement to become the local Winchester agent, was essentially what we offer him today. In the first place, he becomes the exclusive local agent for the new Winchester line. He may designate his store "The Winchester Store" in connection with his established name. He becomes a member of the district or state club of Winchester agents, and a subscriber to the company's dealer service.

In return, the dealer agrees that he "shall at all times use his best efforts and facilities to establish, maintain, and increase the sales of Winchester products at the location hereby assigned to him; shall always keep on hand a stock of Winchester products sufficient to supply the demand therefor in his place or places of business; shall constantly bring such products to the attention of the public, and shall always sell them when called for and when opportunity offers. The retailer shall at all times give the products of the company first preference, in display, advertising, and sale." Also, the agent purchases—on the open market, not from the company treasury—at least three $100 shares of 7 per cent preferred stock. The agreement is terminable on 30 days' notice by the dealer, or "by the company, provided the Executive Committee of the Winchester Club of the district in which the dealer is located shall, by a majority vote, recommend such termination, and provided further that the company shall give 30 days' written notice to the retailer, of such termination."

To serve our national organization of dealers, we installed district warehouses. We were, you see, setting out to function as jobbers of our own products. As I have said, this was not because we had any quarrel with the regular jobbers. It was because we had to have a quick and complete distribution that would keep our plants working. The existing jobbers could not, obviously, distribute our new lines exclusively to our agents.

Opposition to the Plan

But if we had no quarrel with the jobbers, some of the jobbers quickly saw a quarrel with us. To some of them it looked as though we were attempting to upset the apple-cart, to do away with jobbers. They rallied to the attack—and soon the trade was hearing dismal predictions of the utter failure of our plan.

It is almost always that way with innovations; the people who are well established under the existing order of things tend to oppose anything new, because it offers the possibility of disturbing the *status quo*.

Strangely enough, we found the general attack good advertising. The dealers who had joined our organization resented the slurs on their judgment. Many who had not signed up decided that if our plan was as good as it must he to arouse such opposition, then they had better look into it. The rumpus brought more dealers to us than it frightened off.

By June of 1920, when we held our first convention of dealers at New Haven, we had over 2,000 agents.

Then the slump caught us amidships. Sales fell off as our dealers liquidated their stocks, and while we went ahead developing new lines and signing up new agents, our volume was badly hit. If we had had the plan two years further along when the slump came, I doubt whether we should have felt it nearly as much. As it was, the chief effect was to delay by almost a year our completing the distribution structure we had begun to build.

The Winchester Clubs

One of the important parts of our plan has been only casually mentioned—the district clubs of our agents. As soon as the agents had been signed up in a state, we helped them to organize a state "Winchester Club." Each club is organized with officers and an executive committee elected from the membership.

Since the very beginning, the clubs have formed one of the strongest parts of our organization. Their meetings have served to build up a spirit of loyalty, of enthusiasm, of whole-hearted cooperation in the ranks of the dealers. And it is no easy task, as a great many businessmen can testify, to enlist any more than desultory interest throughout a large body of retail distributors.

The clubs have given us this extra enthusiasm, this willingness, even eagerness, of every dealer to get behind us with every last ounce of energetic push that he could muster. Without the club organization, I doubt whether we could have succeeded.

Every Winchester dealer is a member of his district club, which in most instances is bounded by the state lines. Each club meets annually for a two-day session. It functions under its own officers, with what assistance they may require from the national secretary, a man at company headquarters who gives his full time to the clubs.

The club meetings are scheduled so that a group of company representatives, usually from New Haven, can meet with several districts in one trip. Usually some of the higher officials of the company go to these meetings.

Through these personal meetings with the corporate officers, the dealers quickly develop a feeling of personal interest in and intimate contact with what otherwise would to them be "only a soulless corporation" hundreds or thousands of miles away. Since each dealer is also a stockholder, he has the proprietary feeling which makes anyone give his best efforts to an enterprise. It is hard to estimate, in dollars, the tremendous value this all has to our plan.

While the jobbers had been fighting the plan tooth and toenail, we had been making steady progress, so that by June of 1922 we had 4,000 dealers. It was plain that our plan was on the way to success.

Combination with the Simmons Hardware Company

In the spring of 1922 it was suggested that The Winchester Company and the Simmons Hardware Company combine. The Winchester Company had excellent manufacturing facilities and an enthusiastic dealer organization. The company had organized several warehouses as necessary channels for regional distribution.

The Simmons Hardware Company operated a few smaller factories, and had a complete organization for the distribution of hardware lines—the largest organization of its kind in this country.

The suggestion for the merger grew out of this combination of circumstances. Here was an opportunity to eliminate duplication of effort with resulting economies and at the same time to develop more complete and efficient manufacturing and distribution facilities.

You see what the whole plan now accomplishes: It has built up an identity of interest among the manufacturer, the distributor, and the dealers.

As manufacturers we are bound to produce the best merchandise we can at the lowest price; so that our distributing organization and our dealer-stockholders can resell it easily and profitably. We sell our new lines exclusively through local Winchester agencies. Our jobbing houses also buy hardware from other manufacturers.

The Winchester agents purchase, through our jobbing houses, all of our new lines of hardware and sporting goods. They buy their general lines of hardware through whichever jobbers they please. Of course, other things being equal, they give the preference to our houses, of which they are part owners by reason of their stock-holdings.

We have been able to reduce operating expenses materially. The savings have been considerable through centralizing sales, buying, finance and general management at New Haven. And savings fully as large have come about through the increased volume per salesman.

The combined companies had salesmen, duplicating effort in a large proportion of the country. That has been done away with.

Where previously a Winchester salesman could make only one sale per town (except in the large cities where we have a number of agents) and where a Simmons salesman could sell the local Winchester store nothing in the lines Winchester offered, the combination salesman can now sell his general line to all the stores in town, and can expect almost all of the business of the Winchester store.

As one of our agents expressed it to us last year, "Every time we have a new line of Winchester goods that we can show in our store, we know that people cannot go outside and get 10 per cent or 15 per cent off on the same make. They can't get the same make, except from us." That is a powerful inducement to the dealer who faces price-cutting competition.

We are approaching—not closely, to be sure, but still approaching—the saturation point on dealers. We have 5,600 today, and have on our prospect map about 2,000 that we desire. When we have attained the desired total of 7,000 or 8,000, our dealer organization can expand only as new trading communities develop. And that will not be as fast as we desire our agency business to grow.

So it behooves us to have as agents dealers who will increase their volume of business steadily. In the aggregate, they will thus keep our sales and production growing.

Service for Dealers

We have a whole department of store service for the purpose of furthering the success of our agents. Each agent pays a monthly subscription to our dealer service. It costs us a great deal more than the subscription price but the subscription money enables us to give a more complete service than we might otherwise feel we could afford to give.

In the first place, we offer a service in store layout. A dealer may have an answer to any problem of store layout which he propounds.

Then there is the *Winchester Herald*, the monthly "Official organ of the National Association of Winchester Clubs." This is not just a casual house-organ; it is a 48-page magazine, more pleasing in appearance than any trade paper I know of.

There is in it always a monthly letter from me to the agents, in which I sum up the latest developments of our plan and keep the retail organization in touch with what the management is thinking. And there is usually at least one article from the head of a department—the manager of the fishing tackle factory tells how his products are made and how they may be used to increase a store's volume; or the chief store engineer gives an idea of some of the principal considerations in layout that makes customers buy more freely; or perhaps the advertising manager outlines our plans for a national campaign, and points out how dealers may "merchandise" this advertising to build up sales.

Each issue urges the pushing of seasonable lines, and usually has an article from or about a merchant who does an unusually good business in the class of merchandise under discussion. Sometimes these articles are coupled with others by factory experts on how to sell these lines most successfully.

Descriptions of plans and methods which have made profits for some of our dealers are given in detail so that the other agents can adopt and adapt them to increase earnings in their own stores. Window-trims are reproduced, mail campaigns described, and everything of the sort is told so that it may be "lifted" with profit.

Besides serving as a clearing-house for the best ideas that have been developed in our whole organization, the magazine develops enthusiasm. When a noted big-game hunter sails, or returns from a trip, we show photographs of him with his favorite guns. We ran a prize contest for the most interesting stories of old Winchester rifles still in existence, and published the best half-dozen or so. When one of our professional trap-shooters wins a championship, we have a feature story about him.

Again, we find this our best way to announce new lines—something we have to do every month or so, nowadays. With a page or two of display advertising on the new goods, plus an editorial article describing them, we can be sure of several hundred orders by return mail.

Our New York City store, at Forty-second Street and Madison Avenue, is one of the most valuable assets in our whole dealer service. Never a day passes but half a dozen or more of our out-of-town agents drop in there, inspect the store, talk with the manager—and go out determined to display sporting goods better and sell more of them when they get back home. That is a service which pays—and, at the same time, is more than self-supporting.

* * * * * *

What are the facts of greatest significance to other business men, as they have been developed through our new method in distribution? Those facts are, I think, to be summarized in four general principles, by no means all new:

1. So long as the respective distributive functions of the manufacturer, the jobber and the retailer are kept clearly in mind, there is no inherent reason why all three of the functions may not be smoothly combined under one management, without giving up the profitable business with others outside the concern.
2. By concentrating on his dealer organization the best available merchandising assistance, a manufacturer can upgrade the whole industry with profit to every one concerned.
3. An established good will for one class of products can be broadened to include a greatly increased line of merchandise if the new lines are well chosen and of equally high standard.
4. "Dealer disloyalty" is absolutely unnecessary. Give a dealer half a chance to get enthusiastic, with some guarantee that he will he free from cut-throat competition, then be will push a line just as hard as does the man who makes it.

The Science of Distribution An Authoritative Survey of the Devious Channels that Lead from Producer and Consumer[3]

When our grandfathers wore homespun clothes, raised most of the food they ate and chopped the wood for their home fires, the cost of distributing the essential commodities was practically nil. But:

"Cities grow and became the marketplaces of agriculture. Inventive genius perfected machines to relieve more and more hand labor and to produce goods in greater volume. Working days became shorter and time and opportunity for recreation became greater. Education and travel created a desire for comfort convenience and refinements not dreamed of in earlier generations. Invention after invention revolutionized habits and customs. Electricity added to the length of the day by lighting cities and providing means of rapid, comfortable locomotion. Telephone and telegraph extended communication and nationalized industry, commerce and finance.

"Refrigeration revolutionized the transportation and storage of food products and changed the living habits of the Nation. Fruits, vegetables and fresh meats were transported to distant markets, the production of the whole country was made available to the large consuming centers and crops of seasonal production were offered to consumers throughout the greater portion of the year. The consumer came to accept unusual service and convenience as a matter of course and finally to demand more. Each new service and convenience drew additional people into the activities of distribution. Time-saving, convenience, comfort and satisfaction became the determining factors in the excellency of service. More and more facilities

[3] From *Scientific American*, vol. 129, 1923, pp. 404ff.

were created, more and more people were engaged, with a constant upbuilding of expense, until we now have reached a point where it costs more to distribute and serve than it costs to produce."

The above is not the work of an imaginative writer, but is quoted from the report of a Congressional Commission. This "Joint Commission on Agricultural Inquiry" has just completed the most remarkable document of the kind ever compiled. Congress in the role of scientific investigator is at least something of a novelty. But this report assumes the dignity of Science; nothing less.

For the first time it lays before us accurate figures and facts on the cost of producing and distributing a great many of the commodities we have come to regard as essential, For the first time we are given a basis for sound judgment on such mooted questions as "the high cost of living" and "profiteering," and, as might be expected, the average conceptions on these questions are far from anything warranted by the facts. For the first time we are given definite conclusions on how conditions may be bettered—conclusions arrived at by the same methods used by the bridge builder for determining the structure of a truss or the size of the foundation.

This knowledge has been gained with the most painstaking care. When the committee was appointed, with Representative Sidney Anderson of Minnesota as chairman, if was instructed to investigate "the present condition of agriculture, the cause of the difference between the prices of agricultural products to the producer and the ultimate cost to the consumer, the comparative conditions of other industries and the prices of other products, and the marketing and transportation facilities of the country." Similar investigations have been ordered before; they have come rather to be expected as a graceful gesture on the part of Congress, even though they mean little or nothing. But this commission was nothing if not thorough.

The first difficulty encountered was the rather startling discovery that "there were practically no fundamental data of a government or public character with respect to marketing and distribution, and it was therefore necessary for the Commission to undertake a pioneering effort to secure from original sources the basic facts upon which a consideration of the problems of distribution might be predicated."

With a view of securing technical assistance and to secure the cooperation of the trades affected the Commission set up in each trade or industry a committee whose function it was to assist the Commission in securing and correlating the information desired from the trades. For instance, the Commission set up retail grocers' committee, a food manufacturers' committee and similar committees in the trades dealing in dry goods. clothing, shoes, hardware, meats, etc.

With the assistance of these committees, questionnaires were worked out, designing to reflect, over a period of years beginning with 1913 and ending with 1921, the actual price ranges of representative commodities distributed by these trades. These, as far as possible, reflected the portion of the consumer's dollar taken by each distributor, manufacturer or producer. In this way it was possible to check the figures submitted in the questionnaires of a given trade with the figures submitted by other factors in a chain of distribution and to obtain substantial accuracy in the figures obtained through the questionnaires. Fifteen thousand questionnaires were sent out and returned, covering a total of more than 200 commodities.

A single instance will illustrate the effort that went into the report. The committee on department stores, at its own expense, rented two floors of a New York skyscraper and installed there a large force of accountants and assistants who worked steadily for some months assembling and condensing the facts about department stores. The final result was a table of figures, occupies just one *page* of the voluminous report. And yet that table contains facts which never before were available, which were invaluable in reaching a final conclusion.

And what of the facts as finally adduced? Are they worth all of this trouble? Is there really anything wrong with our system of distribution? If so, what is it, and is there a remedy?

The facts show unquestionably what we have only surmised before: that in many details our system of distributing the common commodities of life is wrong. For instance, of each dollar spent for bread in the United States in 1921, only about fifty cents represents the actual cost of the bread, baked ready for your table. The other half of the ultimate cost represents what was spent on service, transportation and selling costs in getting the loaf from the bakery to your table.

Of each dollar you spent for rolled oats in 1921 only 30 cents went to the maker for his completed, boxed product. It took 70 cents to transport and sell the oats to you. A dollar's worth of oranges cost only 41 cents to produce and harvest ready for market. Of each dollar you spent. for clothes, 31 cents went for the cost of distribution—the cost of selling the clothing to you. Of every dollar spent for shoes, 28 cents went for distribution.

The freight bill on a carload of cabbage shipped from Texas to the big Northern markets was about six times as much as the original value of the cabbage in Texas. Most of the fruits and vegetables from California, consumed in the East in such large quantities, incur freight bills as great as or greater than their first value. An investigation of 9476 representative carloads of fruits and vegetables sold at wholesale in Boston, Chicago, New York, Philadelphia, Pittsburgh and other large cities showed that about 60 per cent of the wholesale price was paid by the shipper for the commodity, that about 32 per cent went for freight charges, about 2 per cent for miscellaneous handling charges and about 2 per cent for profit.

Incidentally, the profiteering bugaboo which has been raised in the last few years has been roughly handled. In nearly every line examined there is a definite trend toward smaller and smaller profits. Indeed, during the period of highest prices, when the cry of profiteer was loudest, many industries sustained a loss. In 1913 the profit to the manufacturer on canned milk was about 12 per cent. In 1918 the profit was a fraction of 1 per cent; in 1920 the industry showed a loss of 3.15 per cent and the profits in 1921 were about 4 per cent. Most other commodities followed the same trend. Undoubtedly, in many cases, the charge of profiteering was well based, but as affecting whole industries, the opposite was the rule.

One striking observation about profits, as shown by the Commission's figures, is that, generally speaking, they follow the trend of the price of raw materials in an inverse ratio. When the farmer gets high prices for his corn, the profit of the corn flakes manufacturer is low; when the farmer sells cheaply, profits to the manufacturer of finished products increases. This appears to be so because such items as cost of manufacture, selling, transportation, overhead, taxes and the like, which enter in the final selling price of an article are pretty well fixed. These costs have shown a steady upward trend (especially taxes, transportation and the cost of manufacture), and to a certain extent are beyond control. The great army of men and women engaged in the business of manufacture, distribution and selling are assured a fairly constant return for effort invested, while the farmer, who contributes most of the real value of the product, engages in a desperate sort of gamble in values, in which he is often loser.

The fact is, we have outgrown our whole system. We are still doing business by the methods of our grandfathers—the system of barter. This worked fairly well when dealings were between individuals, but I today these methods are wasteful and extravagant.

In many instances, also, the machinery for handling agricultural products is woe fully inadequate. The Commission found, for instance, that the wholesale district in Chicago was crowded into one narrow street and located without any regard to railroad and shipping terminals. It frequently happened that goods were laboriously carted to this wholesale market from a railroad terminal sold and then carted buck over the same route and reshipped on the same line. Of course, the consumer paid for this. Happily, this district is now being abolished.

In New York, however, is a situation is hardly any better, and with little or no hope for immediate improvement. Few railroads have terminal facilities in the actual city and most of the farm produce which comes in is brought to the docks by lighter are sold at auction on the docks. Out of this have grown some strange practices, which to the layman seem almost inexplainable. For instance, boxed apples, to reach the most favorable market, must have New York Central delivery, while barreled apples must come in by the Erie. One result is that if a buyer wishes both boxed and barreled apples he has to buy at two docks some distance apart and pay two delivery charges.

Such a condition of affairs, it would appear, is not exceptional the country over. A few large cities have taken steps to modernize their marketing and distribution facilities, but outgrown methods still add millions to our bill for necessities.

Another evil which the Commission finds of great importance is the growing tendency on the part of manufacturers of food and other products to extend the scope of their activities beyond the field of manufacture and to engage in distribution. A few years ago the manufacturer dealt only with the wholesaler, who attended to the distribution of his products. Today the manufacturer deals directly with the public, with the result that economy in distribution is forgotten. The aim is rather to secure as *large* a distribution as possible.

The famous orchards of the East, which once furnished most of our fruit, have been neglected and have fallen into disuse, because Western fruit growers have been more energetic in creating a market for their product. Western apples are preferred in New Jersey to the home product, although Jersey apples are far superior in flavor. California prunes are sold in Oregon, where better prunes are grown, because of well advertised excellencies; and Oregon prunes are sold in California for the same reason. It is one of the strange phenomena. of this age of advertising that products which have been carted halfway around the world are often preferred to better ones which may be had right at hand.

We might go on almost indefinitely pointing out specifically just what is wrong with our system of distribution. The truth is that many things are wrong. Some of them are so obviously wrong that they will undoubtedly be corrected. But the whole picture presented by this report is that of a mad scramble for materials and markets in which many groups, some of which have opposite interests, are engaged. It is a case of every man for himself and charge it to the consumer.

Plainly, some directing influence is needed, but it is also quite plain that the whole system is in such a state of experimentation that it would be difficult to say just what ought or ought not be done. Many of our newest institutions for distribution, although they have achieved great financial success, apparently are chiefly valuable as experiments. Department stores, chain stores, city markets, cooperative markets and like institutions each have points of merit, but their effect on the problem of efficient distribution as a whole is doubtful.

Department stores, for instance. undoubtedly effect great economy by the grouping of many stores under one roof and one management. But the very size of the institution makes it necessary to draw its custom from a wide territory. The expense of advertising to draw this widely scattered trade, and the expense of serving these customers pretty nearly balance the advantage gained.

The chain store has gone to the other extreme and is scattered a number of individual stores throughout the territory served and has cut out all but the most essential services. It is found that no really great economy in operation of the individual stores is obtained, excepting at the expense of service. An interesting development in the chain store idea, however, is the growing tendency on the part of the operators of such stores to assume the roles of manufacturer, wholesaler and jobber. More and more they are engaging in the manufacture of their own goods, selling under their own trademark. If this idea is carried to its logical conclusion, it may have an important effect.

The chief defect in the retail store, it appears, is that there are too many of them. There is a grocery store in this country for every 72.6 families. This leads to expensive competition between rival stores in the matter of service, furnishings, etc., and is the direct cause of a frightfully large percentage of failures among grocers. The grocery is an extreme example of this evil, but other lines are overcrowded, also. For every 602.7 families there is a men's furnishings store, for every 171.6 families a shoe store, for every 691.5 families a dry goods store, and for every 657.5 families a hardware store.

While it is considered that the larger stores can serve thousands of families, it difficult to see how tine smaller stores can subsist on the patronage left to them. As a matter of fact, thy don't subsist; hundreds of failures annually help to widen the gap between producer and consumer. For the loss occasioned by every failure somebody must pay—and you may be sure it isn't anybody who is able to pass the charge along. The consumer pays, here as always.

The municipal market has been widely heralded as the instrument which would finally bring the producer and consumer together on common ground, eliminating all of the middlemen and allowing both parties to profit by their mutual exchange. From the standpoint of both producer and consumer the city market is a failure. The producer usually does not care to turn retailer, and when he does, he demands a premium over market price for his goods because they are "fresh from the farm." The truth is that in nearly every city where there are municipal market places, the stands are occupied, not by farmers, but by speculators, either openly through some subterfuge. The final argument against the city market is that, even if the idea were practical, and all of the available gardening space within hauling radius of our large cities was intensively cultivated to supply these markets, they could supply only a fraction of the foodstuffs consumed in these cities. New York City is unusually well situated as to the proximity of great areas suitable for gardening, and yet it would be possible to raise only about five per cent of the vegetables used in the city on this land. As a matter of fact, the portion of the city's vegetables and food which comes from this source is a negligible portion of one per cent.

The Commission considers that one of the really promising experiments looking toward the more efficient distribution of essential commodities is the farmers' cooperative movement which is sweeping the country. A whole chapter of the report is devoted to this topic. Statistics compiled by the Bureau of the Census show that in 1919, $721,983, 639 worth of farm products were sold through cooperative organizations of farmers and that 7.9 per cent of all the farms in the country made sales through such organizations. Purchases through the same organizations in 1919 were $84,615,669. No accurate figures are available since that date, but it is safe to say these probably have been more than doubled since then.

The chief hope in these organizations is that they are centralizing, taking over functions of distribution which heretofore have been intrusted to speculators. They sort and grade their products before sending them to market and thus are making long strides toward standardization of farm products. By owning or controlling storage facilities they prevent dumping of large quantities of a product on the market at one time, a practice to be commended because it assures the farmer a fairer price, saves the consumer from extremely high prices by spreading out over the year the process of distribution, and takes away one of the chief assets of the gambler in foods.

The conclusions drawn in the report are general, rather than specific, as we have suggested. The chief value of the document lies, however, not in the conclusions, but in the facts which it presents. It has given us something to think about and, for the first time, a sound basis for action.

VI[4]

Building the Sales Organization

The sales organization must be built to fit the work which is to be done, but the work which is to be done depends upon a number of factors. It depends upon the nature and size of the business which is contemplated or which is already in operation.

Again, the number of buyers and the buying habits of those buyers in reference to the quality of each purchase have to be considered. A company doing millions of dollars' worth of business annually might get along with a very small organization because it dealt with only a few large customers who purchased on a long-demand basis. There are many other companies with much smaller business which have much larger sales organizations because sales have to be made often and the amount of work required to get and handle orders is much larger than in the other case. The wholesaler who has to call upon his customers each week or even oftener must have many more salesmen to do a given amount of business than the steel firm which sells on contract to manufacturers.

In starting a sales organization, it is wise and customary to start in a small way, adding men to the organization as the amount of work to be done increases. But the work may be increased by a change in policy of the company. A company which uses advertising exclusively may require a large advertising organization but a very small force of salesmen. Mail-order catalog houses may have large advertising organizations but few salesmen except those to meet visiting customers. On the other hand, if the firm must personally solicit business every few days, there is no way of avoiding a large sales organization except to shift the burden to wholesalers or other middlemen.

[4] From Harry Tosdal, 'Sales Organization and Operation', in *Manuals of Business Administration*, Chicago, A.W. Shaw, 1924, vol. 3, pp. 31–9.

The factor which often seems most important in the building of an organization is the financial condition of the concern. Many a firm feels that if its financial condition were sufficiently good, it would adopt different policies and change its selling organization accordingly.

There are many concerns which feel that they would try to distribute directly to the retailer if financial conditions permitted them to do so. The very fact that a very much larger organization is required increases the financial burden and makes the financial requirements for running the business much less flexible.

Ultimately, we want a sales organization which will perform selling work with the highest profit and with the lowest continued cost. However, a selling organization may, for a time, secure high profits and yet it may secure those profits by adopting policies which are not sound policies. The high-pressure organization for a time may secure apparently very excellent results and yet in the long run, these may not be the best results for the company.

An instance will make this clear. There is one very large company which hired a certain sales manager, known to have been very successful in increasing the volume of sales for the concerns with which he had been connected, by all the methods which are known as high-pressure selling. He was constantly pressing the salesmen to secure more volume and was successful in making them increase very greatly their sales effort. At the end of two years, the sales organization of this company was on the point of collapse. When he resigned, the organization went to pieces, and the company had to start out and build from the bottom again.

This particular sales manager had never operated in an organization which depended almost entirely upon repeat sales for its business. Successful selling required the loyalty and steady work, month in and month out, of the salesmen. Men working under the high pressure of emotional stress could not keep up the sales effort required.

One of the first qualifications of the ideal organization is adequacy. By adequacy is meant that an organization must be sufficiently large and capable for the work to be done.

A second qualification of a good organization is economy. It means that the organization should use the ability in the organization in the most productive ways and that the organization should be no larger nor more expensive than is absolutely necessary to accomplish the long-run purposes of the sales department.

It is very easy to plan an organization, to make an organization chart without reference to the cold facts. It is a much more difficult thing to meet the pay-roll each month and have something left to show on the profit side of the income sheet at the end of the year.

It is easy to develop a big sales organization but difficult to develop an organization which is closely fitted to the work to be done.

The third qualification of a good organization is that of flexibility—flexibility in meeting the various demands put upon an organization, partly by seasonal fluctuations in business and partly by longer-time fluctuations, such as cyclical fluctuations.

The sales organization is the part of the business enterprise which first feels the result of business depression. If the sales organization were able to continue selling and collecting for goods sold, business depressions would largely disappear.

We must provide in our sales organization, both by organization means and by operating means, to offset, in so far as possible, changes in business, which are disastrous from every point of view.

It will be clear, from the general discussion, what form the adaptation of business in general to the particular business will take. If the financial risks are very small, the kind of organization will be chosen which will probably give the volume of sales with the smallest capital expenditure and the smallest current expenses possible. The concern with limited funds, selling goods which reach consumers through retailers, cannot undertake sales to retailers under such circumstances, if its goods must be distributed over a considerable area. It must choose to sell either through wholesalers or, with even more limited funds, through manufacturers' agents.

In fundamentals, the sales organization does not vary from business to business. Fundamentally, the sales organization for selling bonds is the same as the sales organization for selling commodities. In fact, the developments in the selling organization among prominent bond houses have been those of emulating the successful commodity selling organization and not of increasing the differences.

VII[5]

Developing Sales Policies

The pilot who is attempting to bring a ship to port must have not only a destination but assistance or exact knowledge as to the course which he is to take, together with a rudder which will enable him to take that course. Where the course is narrow, assistance is given him by lights, bell buoys, and channel markers. With these, any pilot can steer a straight course to bring him to his destination.

We may liken sales policies to these channel markers. A sales policy aims to provide guides to action so that between different members of the organization who deal with business problems and between different times there will be uniform steering toward the ultimate destination of profits.

A sales policy implies a definite course of action determined in advance for the purpose of ensuring uniformity of procedure under substantially similar and recurrent circumstances. If the policy of the house is to sell only to jobbers, then whenever orders come from retailers, they are either to be made exceptions to the rule or to be treated according to the rule.

The second purpose of a policy, in addition to securing uniformity of action, is to secure a type of decision upon a business problem which is based upon careful study of ultimate consequences and not carelessly considered on the basis of circumstances of the moment.

To illustrate, a sales manager may be attempting to increase his sales. He gets an order from a price-cutting retailer. He is tempted to accept the order if be has no definite policy. If he has a carefully considered policy of refusing to sell to price-cutters or of refusing to sell to retailers, action can be quickly taken along directions

[5] From Harry Tosdal, 'Sales Organization and Operation', in *Manuals of Business Administration*, Chicago, A.W. Shaw, 1924, vol. 3, pp. 31–9.

which are believed to be in the interest of the whole enterprise. If he has no policy, he may be tempted to accept the order, but the acceptance of such an order may yield effects upon the rest of his business which will cause him to lose much more profit than he would gain from the acceptance of the order from the price-cutter.

It is obvious that when a salesman is sent out to sell a product to dealers, he must know what the price is, whether the price can be varied, what the discounts are; he must know to what classes of purchasers he may sell.

Sales policies may be classified according to whether they are determined by general administrative officers of the concern or by the sales department itself. The directors of a company frequently establish the general policy as to whether a concern is to advertise extensively or not, as to whether sales are to be made directly to the consumer or to the retailer or through jobbers. The directors may determine what products are to be manufactured and sold by the sales department.

It is particularly true that where a policy may vitally affect the welfare of the whole enterprise, it is obvious that all departments of the concern should have some voice in its determination. There are many other matters in which policies may be established as a means of ensuring uniformity of action and promptness of decision.

A sales policy which is merely declared as a policy, but not carried out, is often worse than no policy at all. The company which claims to sell only to wholesalers but which accepts orders from retailers is not living up to its declared policies. A company which claims to have a uniform price but which makes special discounts to particular buyers is acting dishonestly.

Furthermore, the company which changes policies often tends to lose the respect of its customers. It is true that policies must be changed from time to time as conditions which led to the establishment of policies change, but vacillation and weak-kneed submission to requests for exceptions to policies tend to nullify the advantage of having well-thought-out policies.

A policy is a general rule of action to be carried out under given circumstances. It is obvious that, to be effective, a policy must be generally carried out. It is not so obvious that a judicious exception, under circumstances which warrant it, is more effective in building up business than stiff-necked adherence to the rule. There are cases where a policy has to be re-examined in its application to a set of conditions which apparently comes under the policy. Then, either a change may have to be made in the policy or a decision taken that the policy should not be applied to the particular case in question.

In short, sales policies, to be successful, must be adhered to. In order to secure rigid adherence they must be carefully chosen. They must not be changed without good reason, and they must be impartially and judicially applied. Common sense must be used in the application of any policy.

Sales policies may be grouped into several classes: first, there are policies which deal particularly with the product; second, there are policies which deal especially with distribution; third, those which deal with prices and terms of sale; and fourth those which concern relations with customers. Then there are many other types of policies in relation to credit, advertising, and so forth, some of which will be taken up for discussion in later chapters.

Some Notes on Marketing Functions[6]

The teaching of marketing involves three factors (aside from producers and consumers): commodities, middlemen, and functions. In the developing of courses in marketing three methods of approach have been used, each placing particular emphasis upon one of these factors. The commodity approach at first consisted in studying different commodities—wheat, cotton, tobacco, live stock, hardware, groceries, drugs, dry goods, etc.[7] The next development consisted in grouping the commodities into raw and manufactured products.[8] A later development is the classification of commodities according to use, rather than origin, into industrial and consumers goods.[9] The middleman approach consists in studying the operation of various of middlemen, or, as called by some, "market institutions." This method came into use rather early[10] and is still widely used. The functional approach consists in the study of the functions or services performed in the marketing of commodities and in the operations of middlemen.

The first method takes up commodities and considers the methods used, middlemen involved, and services performed in the marketing of each commodity or group of commodities. The second method takes up the various types of middlemen and considers the commodities handled and functions performed by each type. The third method takes the function as the basis of study and considers the functions involved in the marketing of various commodities and the functions performed by the various types of middlemen.

[6] P. D. Converse, *Journal of Political Economy*, vol. 34, 1926, pp. 377–82.

[7] See Grover G. Huebner, *Agricultural Commerce*, 1915.

[8] See C.S. Duncan, *Marketing: Its Methods and Problems*, 1920.

[9] Melvin T. Copeland, *Principles of Merchandising*, 1924.

[10] See first edition of Ralph Starr Butler, *Marketing Methods and Policies*, Alexander Hamilton Institute, 1917.

The purpose of this paper is to discuss the functional approach, and not to discuss the relative merits of the different methods of approach. A function is a service, an act, or an operation. The functional approach to the study of marketing calls attention to the fact that functions must be performed; that different middlemen may perform the same function; that the elimination of a middleman may not eliminate his functions, but merely transfer them to others; and that a function may be performed once or many times in the marketing process. It involves a consideration of who can perform each function to best advantage. It is valuable in a critical analysis of the present marketing system and in making suggestions for improvements.

The teachers of marketing are not entirely in agreement as to what services or operations should be listed as functions. Weld, Cherington, Ivey, and Clark[11] each list the following seven functions: assembling, storing, assumption of risk, financing, rearrangement (standardizing and grading), selling, and transportation. There is a slight difference in nomenclature. What Weld calls rearrangement, Cherington and Ivey call grading and Clark calls standardization. Weld and Clark include under rearrangement (standardization) services which have been listed by other writers as three separate functions—grading, packing, and dividing.

Vanderblue,[12] after reviewing the development of the functional approach to the study of marketing up to 1921, listed ten functions, including, in addition to the seven listed above, buying, dispersing, and assorting. Macklin,[13] writing in the same year, listed eight functions: assembling, grading, packaging, processing, transporting, storing, financing, and distribution. Since he divided distribution into two parts—selling and dividing—he really included nine functions. The writer[14] in 1924 listed nine functions: selling, assembling, dividing, standardizing and grading, packing, transporting, storing, financing, and risk-taking.

[11] L.D.H. Weld, "Marketing Functions and Mercantile Organizations," *American Economic Review,* VII (June, 1917), 306–18; Paul Cherington, *The Elements of Marketing,* 1920; Paul Wesley Ivey, *Principles of Marketing,* 1921; Fred E. Clark, *Principles of Marketing,* 1922.

[12] Homer B. Vanderblue, "Functional Approach to Study of Marketing," *Journal of Political Economy,* XXIX (October, 1921), 676–83.

[13] Theodore Macklin, *Efficient Marketing for Agriculture*, 1921.

[14] Paul D. Converse, *Marketing Methods and Policies*, 1924.

All of these writers include assembling, storing, financing, grading, selling, and transporting. All except Macklin include risk-bearing. There is less agreement as regards the other functions. Macklin alone lists processing. Vanderblue lists buying, dispersing, and assorting. Macklin and the writer are alone in listing dividing as a separate function. Macklin lists packaging as a function, while the writer lists packing. A part of this difference is due to a difference in the concept of the functions performed in the marketing process, and a part is due to a difference in the definitions of terms used. Since there is little difference of opinion concerning financing, risk-bearing, transporting, and storing these are not discussed in this article.

Assembling was defined by Weld as "the seeking out of sources, the making of business connections whereby commodities may he bought, and the study of marketing conditions so that they may be bought at the lowest price possible....It involves all services connected with buying."[15] This definition has apparently been accepted by most of the later writers. Assembling does not include transportation, storing, financing, risk-bearing, or grading. These are listed as separate functions. Should buying be listed as a separate function? The question here arises: is there buying that is not assembling? Is buying a broader term? A purchase at retail is not ordinarily thought of as assembling, but the object of the consumer is to assemble a variety of products for consumption. A factory buys a machine, perhaps only one machine at one time, but the factory is assembling equipment for the operation of the plant. The wholesaler and retailer are assembling goods for resale. But how about a speculative purchase—one speculator buying from another? Or a peddler buying all his goods from one jobber? Can he be said to be performing the assembling function? Is buying, in these last two instances, synonymous with assembling? Apparently not. All assembling is buying, but all buying is not assembling! Should buying then be substituted for assembling on the ground that it is a broader term? The objection to this is that the word "buying" does not suggest to the average person all that is suggested by the word "assembling." To say that the jobber performs a buying function does not convey quite the same meaning as to say that he

[15] Weld, *loc. cit.*

performs an assembling function. Nevertheless, buying should be substituted for assembling if it is a more accurate term. Buying involves the determination by the buyer of his needs, the finding of sources of supply, the negotiation of contracts, and the transfer of title (except where goods are leased, and here a contract for the lease must be made). Buying is thus the converse of selling.

The terms "standardization" and "grading" have been used to denote one and the same function. Perhaps it is more accurate to say that they refer to two aspects of the same function. Standardization refers to the drawing up of rules as to quality, size, etc., while grading refers to the actual work of sorting in accordance with these rules.

Selling is one of the most important and expensive of the marketing functions under the present economic system. There seems, however, to be some difference of opinion as to just what is included in the selling function. Weld[16] says: "Selling involves both creating a demand for the goods and getting the goods into the hands of the purchasers." Getting the goods into the hands of the purchasers would seem to be a transportation function, unless reference is made to get ting them legally into the hands of the buyer—the transfer of title. Clark[17] seems to consider selling purely a matter of demand creation, "the purpose of selling is to find a market." Horner[18] gives the following analysis of selling: (1) advice to buyer as to kind and quality of goods and place where they can be bought; (2) creation of effective desire; (3) determination of price; and (4) determination of the terms on which the sale is to be made.

Selling involves demand creation by personal salesmanship, advertising, or display of goods; the negotiation of the sale—agreement on price and helping the buyer select the specific goods—and the transfer of title, or the legal side of selling. A large part of the time of many salesmen is taken up with non-selling duties. This is especially true of retail salespeople, who devote a large part of their time to dividing and packing (wrapping) goods and filling out sales slips (recording). Credit

[16] *loc. cit.*

[17] *loc. cit.*

[18] 12 John Thurman Horner, *Agricultural Marketing*, 1925.

and delivery services are given as means of increasing sales. They undoubtedly do so, but delivery is transportation, while credit belongs in part to financing and in part to risk-taking.

Dispersing does not seem to the writer to he a separate function unless it means dividing. If the term is used to denote the getting of goods from the central markets into the hands of the ultimate consumers it would seem to be a process made up of several functions—dividing, transporting, storing, selling, financing, and risk-taking. If dispersing is used in this sense then it is a process and not a function. The marketing of many products is made up of two processes—concentrating and dispersing—each of which involves several functions. Concentration means the bringing of goods together in central markets, and involves transportation, buying (assembling), financing, risk-bearing, and oftentimes grading and storing. Dispersion means the getting of the goods from the central markets into the hands of the ultimate consumers and, as just stated, involves dividing, transportation, selling, storing, financing, and risk-bearing.

Assorting is defined by Vanderblue[19] as "the preparation of a variety of goods." It is difficult to see how this can be considered as a marketing function. He lists standardizing separately. If by assorting he refers to the production of goods, then it is not a part of marketing, while if he refers to the purchase of a variety of goods by a middleman, this would seem to be buying (assembling).

Processing is apparently a producing and not a marketing function. It effects a change in form and hence creates form utility. Marketing deals with the creation of place and time utilities and hence does not include processing. The miller, who makes wheat into flour, and the packer, who turns steers into beef, both have important marketing functions to perform, but as processers they are manufacturers and not marketers.

Is packaging a marketing or a production function? Many goods must be packed in order to be marketed. They must be put into boxes, sacks, bales, bolts, barrels, baskets, bottles, etc., in order to be handled in the marketing process. Other goods have their values increased by placing them in cartons. But may not the placing of such products in the cartons be properly classified as a part of production? The producer may conduct a market analysis to

[19] Vanderblue, *loc cit.*

ascertain what to produce, but this does not mean that the actual production is a marketing function. Is it not just as much a part of production to place the goods in the proper containers as it is to produce the proper kind of goods? The public may prefer goods of a certain color, style, or flavor. Such goods are produced. The public may prefer goods in certain sized or shaped packages, or goods with brightly colored, lithographed labels on the containers. The goods are so prepared. Should not this preparation be considered as a producing, rather than a marketing, function?

A distinction may be made, however, between placing goods in such containers and wrapping or crating in order to effect delivery. The retailer must wrap many of his wares after dividing and weighing them. The manufacturer must often crate his goods in order that they may be transported. Dividing and transporting are both considered as marketing functions. It would then seem to be logical to consider packing as a marketing function. This would lead us to draw a distinction between packaging—placing goods in containers in which they are to be sold to the ultimate consumer and packing, the wrapping and crating necessary for delivery. The first would then be considered as a part of production and the latter as a part of marketing.

Some may object to this on the ground that it is drawing too fine a distinction and that packaging and packing should be considered together and as one function. Others may argue that packing should be considered as a part of the transportation function, since goods are packed to facilitate their transportation. In spite of these objections the distinctions made above seem to be logical, and if logical should be accepted.[20]

Dividing is apparently properly listed as a separate function. Dividing, it is true, is often involved in grading, but there is much dividing that is not grading. Many wholesale and retail dealers divide goods and resell in smaller quantities without performing a grading function.

[20] In some instances packaging diminishes the amount of packing necessary farther along in the marketing process. For example, the consumer sometimes accepts packaged goods from the retailer without further wrapping. In such instances it could be argued that packaging by the manufacturer serves the same purpose and takes the place of packing by the retailer. In most cases, however, it appears that goods are packaged by the manufacturer to increase their salability, and riot to lessen packing farther along the line.

The marketing functions, then, are: buying (including assembling), storing, risk-bearing, financing, standardizing and grading, selling, transporting, packing (as distinguished from packaging), and dividing.

We Threw 67% of our Prospects Overboard – and Our Sales Increased 15%[21]

By H. L. Donahower
President, Standard Conveyor Company

We used to have an old carpenter around our place who did his work by the rule-of-method. He did good work trouble about that. His beams where they were put; his joists solid as a rock. The only rub was the uncertainty of his results. The old man could not read a blue-print if he tried. Told to put up a 6-foot by 12-foot tool-house, for example, he would erect a shack with what lumber he had on hand, allow a bit for the lay of the land, and when the structure was completed, the chances are it would measure 7 feet by 21 feet. He was that kind of workman.

The other day it occurred to me that there is a good deal of selling going by precisely the same method. It selling that brings results, all right, but the results are never what you expected them to be.

The rule-of-thumb method does not go in selling, or in sawing wood. With production on its present fine basis, plant schedules cannot be disrupted to take care of a flurry here or a lull there. We must have an exactitude that assures a knowledge of sales to a very close margin. If we do not have it, something is wrong.

I would say that the elementary principle of manufacturing and of salesmanship is to know your market. By that I do not mean to have easy acquaintance with a group of jobbers and retailers. Nor do I mean the compiling of a few charts, showing percentages of products sold in stipulated territories, with comments that present sales in one of these territories equals 10%; therefore, potential future sales in the same territory are the remaining 90% of the population.

[21] From *System*, vol. 50, November 1926, pp. 577–80.

That is a singularly blind policy to follow, yet it is happening every day. To a certain extent, it once happened in our own company. The story have to tell hinges around that how we cleared out the dead-wood around our potential sales, and bared our true sales possibilities.

How much clearing we did is best shown by the fact that we now have approximately 39,000 prospects for our product where once we had a prospect list which ran above 120,000.

Had any one asked us, a year or so ago, how well we knew our market, it is quite possible that we would have pointed to our old prospect list of 129,000 and said that was the whole of it. It was — and then some.

Today, with our list of 39,000, we name as prospects only those companies which are specifically interested in what we, or our competitors, make, and can use our products in their factories.

That is my idea of knowing your market. When you know that — when you know where your goods can be sold — the actual selling of them is a clearly defined problem.

Every business has its individual peculiarities. If it is to be successful, it must have a definite place, and while its activities might enlarge, it cannot get outside that place. Our own business consists of the manufacture and sale of various conveyors which are of no value to some industries, but invaluable to others. The foremost element in deciding this is labor. A 12-man shop in a back room, naturally, would have no use for an elaborate conveyor installation which would keep production moving steadily.

Yet there was a time when we were expending sales effort on prospects which were not prospects at all, because they had not, and never would have, a use for our conveyors.

Our sales promotion manager worked nearly a year to devise a new method of checking our future sales. Taking our old prospect list, he checked it up with Dun and Bradstreet and learned that a certain rating would average a certain number of employed workers. This seldom differentiated. As our product is either useful or of little use, dependent on the number of men employed, right there we had the means of making a list which would consist only of plants that would have a definite need for our products. Not every business can use that measuring stick but almost every one can find some similar way of picking a real prospect.

When we had pared down our list, we checked the total number with the investigations of others and found it a reasonable one — it approximately agreed, for instance, with the industrial coverage of the Shaw publications.

This was narrowing our selling effort to a point where it could be felt. It was a matter of clearing the decks for action. Our action was to compile an industrial census, telling us the whole story about each one of these 39,000 companies. When the census was completed, we had in graphic detail the fact that there are about 30 major industries which we can serve. We had them divided as to industry and territory; if we wanted to know how many automobile manufacturers, for instance, were in a given territory, our industrial census gave us the exact information.

With this information at hand, when it came to selling, instead of sowing our seeds broadcast, we were dropping. them in well-defined rows —what any regulated business should do. I do not care whether it is cheese, or ball bearings, the principle is the same.

Our own selling is done through territorial branch offices, and, through our industrial census, we have set quotas for each salesman. The element of the salesman entered into the setting of these quotas to some extent. His work for the year before was considered. But the main thing was—what should he be able to do?

The details of the plan we are using are not important — I have gone into them only to illustrate more completely the principle. The important thing is to be so completely equipped with facts that you can control your selling effort and your production effort—to make and to sell for your real market. Too many of us "make" to meet our salesmen's needs instead of our customers' needs—or "sell" what the factory makes instead of what the market needs.

Knowing your market, its possibilities and its limitations, does away with all this. And knowing your market is a principle that should be put to use in every corner of business, in those mercantile businesses that buy and sell as well as with us who manufacture what we sell.

I have in mind a small town where there was a general store — one of those typically country institutions that sell everything from soap to automobiles — which had supplied a rich farm territory for years. Jed Perkins, the proprietor, knew all his customers by their front names. He knew their wants — and he supplied them. Naturally, Jed prospered.

The town grew, and it was not long before two city fellows, seeing the opportunities in this field, opened a new store in competition to Jed's. They spent a good deal of money on fixtures and a good deal more on stock — fancy stock that was calculated to make Jed's plain, serviceable merchandise look sick. Ready for business, they announced a "Grand Opening Week," imported a band from the city, served refreshments, and marked all goods at a discount.

Farmers from miles around brought their families to view this newest monument to civic development. They spent a lot of money, too. When "Grand Opening Week" was concluded, the books showed a handsome sales ratio. It seemed to look bad for Jed and his quiet, home-folks store.

But this Jed Perkins was a pretty shrewd business man for, a country-store proprietor. While the band was playing and the crowds flocking to his competitors, Jed sat back with a serene expression on his face, munching a cracker — but thinking. "Let's see," he said to himself, "there's Ephraim Hawley up in Johnson Township; just bought that strip of pasturage south of his place and is talking about putting up a new barn. Maybe Ephraim's going to put in a herd of Holsteins—he was asking about 'em. That barn's going to need equipment, and Ephraim ought to be interested in dairy supplies."

So Jed brought out his farm equipment catalogs, thumbed the pages, found what he figured Ephraim Hawley was going to need, made a note of prices and descriptions and then jumped into his surrey and went for a talk with Ephraim. When he returned he had an order that ran into a good many hundreds of dollars.

There was no fireworks about it. No big splurge. Jed Perkins simply knew his market.

Meanwhile his competitors, though their store was always well filled, began to wonder why they could not sell the nice line of clothing, guaranteed latest New York styles, which they had put in. They never did sell those clothes. They never did sell, either, a fine line of gardening implements which had been a good number in the city, where gardeners confine their activities wholly to window boxes and terrace strips.

The "latest New York styles" became museum pieces. The effete garden implements rusted on the shelves. These, and a quantity more of the store's stock became obsolete and were eventually a total loss, the while Jed Perkins, in his quiet way, listened to the local gossip, talked to his friends, suggested as to their wants — and supplied them.

That was "knowing the market." Jed Perkins knew what kind of merchandise to carry on his shelves because of real contact with his customers.

Now Jed had an advantage on our larger business — although his merchandising problems were identical. We are not, and cannot be, as close to our market as he was. But regardless of our impersonal element, or the number of our customers and potential customers, we who succeed in business today must devise a means of knowing ours and our customers' limitations.

Some companies hold their contact with the market entirely through their commercial travelers. Salesmen are given geographic territories. Armed with a prospect list and such inquiries as have happened into the office, they are sent out on the road. Spurred on by the burning enthusiasm of a go-getter sales manager, they are given such indefinite instructions as to work their territories thoroughly and do their best to increase sales. It is a matter of "hurrah" selling entirely: "Smith sold so much last month," they are told, "now you go out and sell this much more." The men try it — and sometimes succeed, for enthusiasm is indeed a wonderful thing.

Yet this is not constructive salesmanship. It is like blindly shooting at a covey of quail with a shotgun — because they fly close and your gun scatters wide, you may bring down a bird or two.

In this kind of organization an office conference is usually held to determine production. The sales manager brings forth his records. "Business conditions in the Midwest are good," he reports, "and the salesmen are cleaning up. With any luck at all, their sales should be such-and-such. In the West, the men are aver aging so-and-so." And down through the list of territories he goes, adding up such-and-such, and so-and-so, and this-and-that, until he has figured what production should be — based on what salesmen have been selling.

What a slipshod way of doing business! What an unkind way — unkind to every man in the organization. A production figure is set, but it is not a true production figure. The men in the factory are working on the achievements of the men on the road a year ago. Their jobs, their whole lives, depend on it. The men on the road are content to average last year's mark, or perhaps, carried away by the sales manager's gusts of enthusiasm, to do a little better.

How much better it would be to call the salesman aside, and give him a quota of sales. "You can sell this much," you would tell him, "because in your territory there are so many industries which are particularly adapted to the use of our products. Here are their names."

One of our salesmen came in not long ago, complaining about the quota we had set for him. "It's too high," he said. "You've got me down to sell 7,000 feet of gravity conveyor this year, while last year I only sold half that much and was supposed to have had a good year."

I called in our sales manager and together the three of us went over this man's territory, with our industrial census before us. "Look here," I said, pointing to the census, "in your territory there are 46 lumber concerns. Now last year you didn't sell a single lumber company, though every one of them is a potential user of our conveyors. Here are automobile manufacturers — how many feet of conveyor did you sell automobile companies last year?"

In that manner we went down through the list.

"I'm glad I complained, so that I could get set right," he admitted. "It's a matter of directing energies. I was sort of in the dark, and this thing brightens up the way. I believe I can sell more than my quota."

I thought he could, too — and he did. Those goods can be and are sold, all right, because we know the business is there to be gotten. If we have the right kind of salesmen, we will get it To date, we have received no indication that we have not the right kind of salesmen.

That single incident showed us that the obvious way of doing business is to base sales on what the salesmen can and should sell — not on what they think they can sell, nor on what they happened to sell last month or last year. It is easy enough to say "base everything on what can be sold." It is not always easy or fair to the men to put it down into figures. The only way of doing it is to know the market and its potentialities so thoroughly that there can be no difference of opinion between you and the salesmen.

And when the sales end of the business is working in accord, the production end is bound to keep step. There are many factories (it has happened in our own) where the production chart is spasmodic — up one month and down the next.

No shop like that can operate at best efficiency. Production is more costly than it should be; it is hard to guarantee delivery. And this condition will invariably arise in any business that bases production or buying on what salesmen have been selling, without a true knowledge the market.

We expected improvement on the production side as a result of basing selling on real market needs. But the advantages have gone beyond any thing we expected. The benefits of real control are felt in every corner of the factory.

For many of the advantages of scientific management are possible only where there is a well-determined objective — a figure so soundly based that it will not have to be changed casually. We have been able to pay factory workers by piece-rate, for instance. We have a contract price for production, and on time-work the men are paid a bonus on every hour they have in the perfect performance of every job. With the quota before them, these men see exactly how much there is to be done. They know that by speeding up production they are not going to work themselves out of a job. Consequently, to earn their bonus, they are doing their best work constantly, while the stabilized production enables them to do departmental specialization.

One of our best skilled laborers, a man who has been with us a long time, was called into the office of the shop superintendent the other day.

"Look here, Jim," the superintendent pointed out, "your rate-card shows you to be just 93% efficient. What's the trouble?"

"Well," said Jim, "it's like this. In the job I'm making, I used to use whole sheets of galvanized iron, and cut 'em to fit. At the same time, we've got a lot of scrap pieces that still have enough flat surface in 'em to cut and use for this job. I sort of thought it would be a saving in material."

The shop superintendent checked up. He learned that this workman was effecting a material saving on supplies, simply by taking a little time and trouble to find odd pieces of sheet iron, instead of using the whole sheets. He recalculated the man's card, and gave him a new rating of 113% efficient, which carried with it a nice bonus.

One Guess ahead of Your Market[22]

By Ralph Barstow
Vice-President, Charles G. Lyman, Incorporated

Knowing what to make and to sell, and at what price to sell, and when to put the product on the market — those are the questions important for the sales department, and indeed for the whole business. And those are the questions, too, that we seldom find answered systematically or constructively. We read and we talk much about the organization of the making and of the selling; but we look upon the important part — the deciding what to sell, when to sell it, and for how much as more a matter to be settled by spontaneous genius.

Experience, however, seems to indicate that there is a typical "demand curve" through which all new products go; a curve with important points of change fairly definitely designated — points which have unmistakable characteristics and which can be recognized by those who are watching for them. And those points are worth thinking about.

One might say, offhand, that there is no such thing as styles — and, hence, very small "new goods" problem —in the marketing of small tools. Yet it was not five years ago that the idea of the ground-thread tap was timidly put forth and hoot ed. One big man in the industry waved the idea aside with regal indulgence. "All nonsense! A mere fad," said he. Nevertheless, the current catalog of that same firm contains several pages showing that ground-thread taps are now carried in stock, and that the company is prepared to furnish such material promptly.

You can call this current of commerce, fashion, or style, if you want to, or you can call it the unceasing reaching out for better methods, greater efficiency, and more accurate standards.

[22] From *System*, vol. 51, May 1927, pp. 611–13.

Whatever you call it, you come to the same thing. New goods are absolutely vital to the growth of almost all manufacturing businesses.

If you grant this, then you must do something about it. You can, if you like, sit tight on your job and let other people tell you what must be made. You can say, "Let the rash manufacturers do the experimenting. When they get all through making mistakes and the market settles down, we will step in." It seems a feeble way of doing business — and not especially good business.

It is the truth that in your line, the ultimate consumer is dissatisfied in some way or another with what you are supplying. It may be that your goods can be fundamentally bettered. If so, bettering makes them new goods, doesn't it? It may be that some of the functions of your product are susceptible to improvement, and that an appliance here and there will make this improvement possible. That is "new goods" in the sense we are considering it.

If the buying public had no aspirations for better material, the chances are you would not sell even the goods you make at present. It has well been said that every purchase is a symbol of discontent. Contented people are not purchasers. It is aspiration that makes people buy at all, and it is aspiration that constantly spurs them to try, test, select, reject, and continue anew.

Think of the innumerable brands of preparations — paste, powder, and liquid — on the market. Twenty years ago, lots of people (if they brushed their teeth at all) were happy with 10 cents' worth of powdered orris root! Every formula for toothpaste represents some one's conviction that none of the materials already on the market will do what his formula will do.

New goods justify themselves by the stimulation of the volume of sales. If properly presented to the market, they give you the jump on your competitors.

The stimulation of sales produced by new goods is reflected back from the consumer through the clerks in retail stores and through the buyers to the manufacturer. The customary greeting received by the old-time traveling man with his established line is, "What you got new?"

Do you say to yourself:

"That may be all very true for most people, but it doesn't apply to my business"? Alas, it does apply to your business.

Now, how is one to discover what new goods to make and

when to make them? Experience shows that the determination of what new goods to make, and when to release them, and at what price, is very much like the playing of the stock market, because a man who does it successfully is outguessing his public.

The source of all demand is the consumer. Sometimes consumers are articulate. For example, no consumer is really satisfied with his radio receiver. He wants much more from it than it will give him; he wants as much as is implied in the advertising (which is saying a good deal); he wants 10 kilocycle selectivity; he wants at present, 100% DX in the United States — and he is even now getting ready to demand DX on the whole world, although he is lucky if he can tune in the stations 500 miles from him at the present time, and he knows it. And he wants true tone reproduction.

You see, he knows all these things exist in theory, and after he has had a radio for awhile, he is a little hurt, if not vexed, to see the ponderous and intricate mechanism offered to him, so that he can get his local stations. He knows that the simplest of three-tube sets will do this for him these days, thanks to efficient broadcasting.

Radio manufacturers are not left in the slightest doubt by their public as to what is wanted. The sales director of a silk-stocking manufacturer is not so fortunate. His market has been known to turn upside down overnight, and it may do it again any minute! Think of a hosiery manufacturer with an inventory anywhere from $50,000 up to $250,000 objecting to any reasonable expenditure that will keep him forewarned of the style trend!

Inarticulate or not, the public, or that portion of it that influences the buying, must be the original source of ideas about new goods. We know that even the most plaintive yearner after new goods does not give tongue to his desire every little while; and we know, too, that the most effective way to bottle him up is to ask him what he wants. You have to catch him off guard, and you cannot ask him plainly what he wants. You have to read him and judge him from what he does, to determine what he wants.

The consumer most frequently discloses himself and his wants when he is buying, and that makes the retail store the most fruitful place to discover what is wanted. A sales director who has the privilege of going into some store, taking off his hat and actually waiting on the trade is a fortunate man. He is as near the foot of the rainbow as he will ever get.

Ninety-five per cent of everything that goes into the home either is bought directly by women or is influenced by them. Every home that you visit is bristling with hints and suggestions of forth coming demands. It is neither necessary nor desirable that one's observations should be obvious. A hostess is charmed when a guest appreciates some effective bit of decoration, but she would be uneasy if she felt that her home was being subjected to the critical analysis of a searcher after new goods.

Nevertheless, critical analysis is your only way of accomplishing what you are after. You have to say to yourself: "That is effective. Why did she do it? How does she do it? And what does it mean to me?"

Here is a little domestic story to illustrate, In our gate-leg table is a drawer in which I used to keep my pipe cleaners. Every time for a long while, when I opened the drawer I was conscious of a miscellaneous collection of candles in it. Once or twice I sought permission to throw them away and met with a storm of refusal. It made a faint impression on me. One day in the drawer of the serving table I found some more candles — all different colors. Weeks later I discovered a third collection in a cupboard in the kitchen.

Then I asked, "Why all the candles? Why do you have so many around?" I was told that proper table service could only be accomplished by having candles of colors appropriate to the table decorations, and that certain kinds of candles had to be used for certain kinds of dinners — candles quite different from those that were used at a tea. Furthermore, one kind of flower decoration would require different candle settings from another.

This set me pondering. I found that every department store, almost every stationery and gift store, carried a wide selection of candles, and I was told by the salespeople that they sold, and sold, and sold. I talked with three of the big candle manufacturers of the country, and found their tonnage increasing rapidly. All of this said to me that candles require candlesticks; I began to study what the market offered. Glass candlesticks, crystal, and colored pieces, were available. Clear glass, because it was neutral, was suited to almost any kind of candle, but the colored glass frequently did not match the candle color, nor did it harmonize particularly well. I found china candlesticks, but they all came under the head of "odd pieces." So far as I could learn, no manufacturer of dinnerware made candlesticks to match his set.

Perhaps they would not sell. The china people do not even make center bowls in their sets, and of course, other non-matching china pieces are grossly inappropriate. I found wooden candlesticks, most of them in mahogany, but some what depreciated in value by their presence in such large numbers in the 5-and-10-cent stores. There were also brass and silver candlesticks.

Here was a real opportunity to bring out candlesticks that would match the candles or harmonize with them. I had two attractive designs prepared, made up samples and tried out as many as 25 finishes. There are between 20 and 30 colors in which candles are furnished, to say nothing of the decorated candles. It did not seem practical to carry candlesticks in all these colors because it complicated the carrying of stock. By patiently manipulating the colors of our finish, we finally got 4 colors — an orange, a blue, a green, and an old-rose. These 4 colors represent the 4 best selling colors of candles; and with these 4 colors, we can take 18 different colors of candles.

Two of our salesmen were provided with samples, and in less than two weeks sold 10,000 pieces — a pretty good evidence that six months of thinking, planning, designing, and experimenting, were justified. This company will have the important outlets in the. United States stocked, and will be receiving reorders six months before any competitor can get into action. We have marked the goods at very reasonable prices, and yet we have a little excess margin of profit over and above normal. This is our universal practice for very cogent reasons:

We are entitled to a premium for experimental work.

We are entitled to a premium for the pioneer selling.

Novelties on the market sell better when they are new if they command a reasonably good price.

Our competitors, who are sure to copy a success, will in all likelihood base their plans on our present selling prices. They will strive to shade our prices a little, for they will be dubious about making better looking goods for more money. So they will come on the market, all smiles, with a price a little under us. By that time, we will be in the full swing of production; we will have got all of the grief out of the job, and will know just how cheaply we can make our goods; and two or three weeks after they have flung their first kisses to the buyers, we will come out with our normal prices and normal profit, and be comfortably under them in price — thus forcing them to a readjustment of their whole selling scheme, and giving us not only three to six months more as masters of the market, but at the same time strengthening our prestige with the buyers all over the country.

One other little quirk has a considerable bearing on the situation. When we bring out a new line such as this all of our salesmen and jobbers are tipped off to push as hard as possible, and to collect as many orders as they can (even a few more). We deliberately hold back on deliveries, amassing the goods in cartons, and then release them all at once. They fall on the country simultaneously. Everybody sees them every where they go; buyers and salespeople are all talking about them. A visitor to New York will see them in the stores on Fifth Avenue, and when she gets back to her home town, she will discover them in her favorite store. She exclaims, "Oh, you have some of those little candlesticks — just like the ones I saw in Ovington's on Fifth Avenue when I was in New York!"

This pleases the customer because it enables her to tell the home folks that she has been in New York, and furthermore, that she was clever enough to see what was being offered there. The clerks in the home store simper with delight at the cleverness of their buyer who gets things just as quickly as they do on Fifth Avenue. They tell the buyer, the buyer is happy, the clerks are happy, the customers are happy, and the competitors are confounded. What could be sweeter?

A sales executive must, like a reporter, know what is news and what is not. He will make experiments that will not be fruitful. One sales manager was interested to see that the picture-frame market was a most profitable one. Thousands upon thousands of picture-frames are sold every year. 95% of the product is decorated wood. The other 5% is silver and gold. He thought there might be a chance for him to get into this market with metal, and made some experiments. They were failures. Metal is too heavy. You cannot screw easels into metal without considerable expense. When he got through, he found he had made some thing 50% more expensive than wood, 100% heavier, and no more beautiful. That was not news.

Another condition that frequently occurs is that the time is not ripe for an item. Those of us who can remember the flourishing days of the mail-order business of Robert H. Ingersoll and Brother, about 1898, recall that the automatic pencil was cataloged. You pulled a ring at the top of the pencil; if you kept it up long enough, just about the time a gentle perspiration broke out on you the pencil exploded and the lead came out at the other end.

It was not until a manufacturer worked out the idea of rifling the barrel through which the lead projected, that the mechanical pencil became a commercial possibility. Here is a perfect demonstration of the discontent that gnaws at every man's bosom. This manufacturer came out and said, "Here is a new mechanical pencil —honestly, it will work." He sold thousands of dollars' worth.

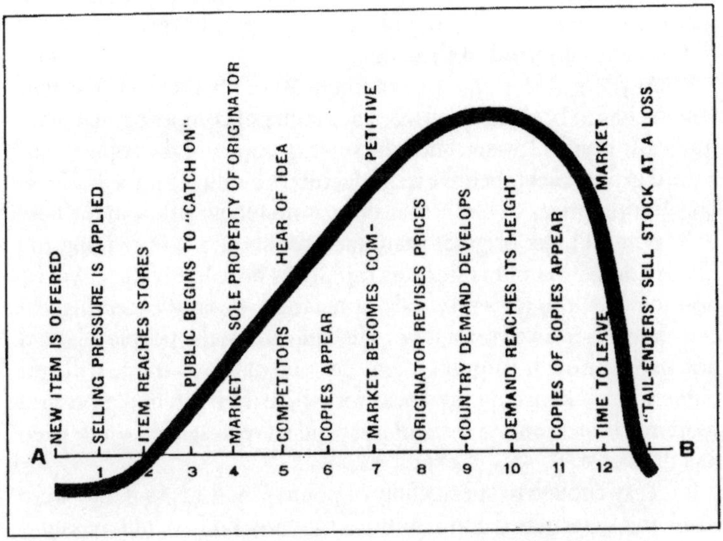

For illumination on the subject of new goods, look at the chart on page 611. The base line of this diagram, A B, represents zero in demand. At point A, some manufacturer conceives the idea of a new item, and works it out to the best of his ability, offering it to the market. Points 1, 2, 3, 4, 5, and so on, are merely convenient divisions of time — weeks, months, or whatever you like. He offers it then to the market. The chances are that the buyers will be skeptical; it is rare that they are anything else. The safe attitude of the buyer is one of constant skepticism; he dare not trust his enthusiasms. Therefore, we will show that demand lies up to Section 1, as below zero.

By force of salesmanship between 1 and 2 we get the demand on the part of the buyers up to the zero line and climbing, which means that the goods are displayed in the stores. Let us assume that the public likes the goods; that they "catch on." Nowadays, the public is given to violent enthusiasms — the more violent the enthusiasm, the quicker it burns itself out; but we will plot our demand line into a healthy two- or three-year curve.

From point 1 to point 7, the market is usually the sole property of the company that brought out the idea.

Alert competitors first hear of the idea at point 5; and by the time the demand has reached point 6, their salesmen are out with copies of the original; and at point 7, the market becomes competitive, so that the originator will probably have to revise his prices in order to hold his command of the trade.

From point 7 to point 11 volume demand is greatest, but that volume has to be divided between a number of competing manufacturers. At point 11 we reached the stage of copies of the copies, with a third group of competitive manufacturers bidding for the business and cutting prices so badly that there is no longer profit in the line.

At point 11 the original manufacturer should quit making the goods and get rid of his stock as rapidly as he can, for there will be nothing but loss for everybody concerned — only excepting the consumer — from this point on. The tail-enders, the people who did not know enough to unload and get out of the market, will still blithely be making copious stocks for which they will find more and more resistance; and in the end they will have to sell at cost or even less than cost.

It is easy enough to speak glibly of points 7 and 11, as if they were fixed and determined combinations that any body could measure. Of course they are not. Point 7, in spite of false alarms, can be determined with a fair degree of accuracy. Buyers will tell your salesmen, "Oh, I can buy that same number for less money." Prior to point 7 buyers have been bluffing. But at point 7 some buyer will produce the evidence, and salesmen should be trained to go behind the returns and see what they mean.

They should buy and send into the home office samples of the competing merchandise, and in some way, learn the prices at which they are offered. This enables the sales executive to reach a decision as to the cut that he wants to make in the price of his own goods, so he can hold the market. At the same time, he can subject the competing prices to severe analysis.

The determination of point 11 is very tricky, indeed. Many manufacturers make the mistake of accepting the decision of New York and Chicago as final. These two markets are the battle-grounds of the United States, it is true, and their influence in the beginning of a fad is considerable.

It cannot be said, however, that they ever wrote "finis" to a boom. Rather should the executive accept resistance in the New York and Chicago markets as a symptom, or warning. Here again we have an analogy to the stock market. It is said — although the truth of the saying has been questioned — that the stock market discounts business conditions by about six months. The New York and Chicago merchandise markets discount the demand situation.

Some salesmen have the faculty of suggesting new goods, and can nose out things that will sell. The sales executive does well carefully to cultivate this faculty in these men, encouraging them in every way possible to report and suggest all they can. Salesmen must understand clearly that all their suggestions cannot be accepted, and they must not be hurt if an idea is rejected. This is, of course, a part of wise and intelligent sales management. In the main this is not work to be delegated. Successes are too profitable, and failures too costly, for the sales executive to allow himself to know less than any one about the matter.

It takes time, extremely intelligent thought, and great awareness of what is going on all over the country.

There is a corollary to this subject of new goods that needs mention. A sales force gets rather stale, selling its old goods. The canvass, little by little, becomes stereotyped, and the only way to keep a sales organization on its toes is to provide it with fresh and interesting sales talk. Some work of this kind can be done by intensive research in the old lines, for new applications or uses can make old goods come pretty close to being the same thing as new goods. Remember, "the prosperity of a joke lies in the ear of the listener."

Selling to the Great "Under-21" Market[23]

By Arthur H. Little

It used to be that far-sighted merchants catered to the youngsters only as a source of future business. Now the younger generation constitutes a huge market in its own right.

These figures from a new coast-to-coast survey of this very market may astonish you; they will certainly make you want to try some of the tested methods — revealed in this same survey and outlined at the close of the article — for tapping this great sales reservoir.

The American boy has grown up. Physically, to be sure, he remains as he always has been; but economically he has put on long pants. And in a deep, bass voice he speaks up for himself and demands the things that used to be considered the prerogatives of the Old Man. He has come to constitute, in his own right, a huge market for goods — that plus a new factor, and a significant one, in old markets.

His ascendancy is something that, of course, has not been entirely invisible. To those of us who have eyes to see and read and ears to hear it has been fairly obvious in very recent years that, among the younger generation, there has been something afoot vastly stirring.

"The other day," a friend of mine related, "I drove my daughter to school. You know, she goes to Northwestern High. As we stopped in front of the building another car parked in front of us — a snappier, better-looking car than mine. From behind the wheel clambered a business-like individual who wore a mustache.

"I asked my daughter, 'What professor is that?'

"'Professor! He isn't any professor,' she said. 'He's a senior.'"

It is all very amusing — the chalk-lettered signs on the rear ends

[23] From *System*, vol. 50, November 1926, pp. 604–5.

of sketchy roadsters, the garterless socks, the dinner coats at high-school dances, the grave, grown-up talk that you hear wherever youngsters gather. But what of it? Of what serious interest is it to, say, a manufacturer? ell, the manufacturer might conduct a canvass — and, very likely, he would be surprised at the things he would learn.

Before me as I write is the report of a survey of the boy market. The report was compiled from information gathered from a total of 562 retailers in cities and towns from coast to coast — retailers dealing in clothing, haberdahery, sporting goods, footwear, radio sets and parts, automobiles, and musical merchandise. These retailers were asked eight questions:

1. How many of your customers are young men from 14 to 20 years of age?
2. How much of your business is with or for young men?
3. How many of these young men make their own selections of merchandise? (a) Apparently without the guidance of their parents? (b) With the guidance of their parents?
4. What influence does the boy exert on the purchase of merchandise used in his own home or by his family, other than that purchased for his own use?
5. Is the boy a leader of fashion?
6. Does he set the buying power or pace?
7. Do you consider the young-man market important?
8. Are you making any effort to win and hold this young-man market? If so, along what lines does the effort run?

To indicate how wide-spread was the canvass, let me name some of the cities and towns it covered: Boston, Lynn, Malden, Swampscott, and Waltham, Massachusetts; White Plains, Mt. Vernon, New Rochelle, and Yonkers, New York; Montclair, Paterson, Salem, and Trenton, New Jersey; Doylestown, Norristown, Philadelphia, and West Chester, Pennsylvania; Wilmington, Delaware; Atlanta, Georgia; Chicago, Elgin, and Evanston, Illinois; Kansas City and St. Louis, Missouri; Omaha, Nebraska; Oklahoma City, Oklahoma; Dallas, Texas; Portland, Oregon; and Los Angeles and San Francisco, California.

The reporting merchants in every line unanimously agreed that the young man does wield a potent influence on the purchase of merchandise other than that bought for his own use. Almost without exception, too, they reported that they considered the young-man market an important source of sales volume, and that they were making special efforts to win this market. The direction taken by these "special efforts" is indicated briefly by the sample replies which are quoted on page 605 at the close of the article.

What Young Men Buy

	Clothing	*Sporting Goods*	*Automobiles*	*Musical Instruments*	*Shoes*	*Radio*
Analysis of the total business showed that —						
Young men customers were	40%	41%	4%	47%	24%	30%
Their volume was..........	45	46	12	51	31	42
Many of the young men did their own selecting						
With or without aid........	89	92	Few	89	96	85
Without parental aid........	62	75	16	81	66	66
Of the reporting merchants these percentages answered "yes" to						
Is the young man a leader of fashion?..........	57	89	62	94	62	94
Does he set the buying power or pace?..........	75	80	43	80	67	53

The merchants' replies to the other questions that were asked — boiled down to the form of a statistical digest — are shown in the table above.

These figures indicate that the young man is decidedly worth catering to — at least in the six lines studied — for the volume for which he is directly responsible. But they also bring out the equally important and less obvious fact that, for the majority of merchants, he is the leader of fashion and actually sets the buying power or pace.

In explanatory remarks accompanying his answer, many a merchant waxed enthusiastic. Here are some typical comments:

"We attach great importance to the young-man market because it is the coming generation."

"If you can get a fellow store while he's young, treat show him every consideration, you make him a steady customer; and when he grows older you'll hold his business."

"The young man's business is the best business. There is no limit to the amount that the young man of the future will buy."

"They grow up overnight."

"They help interest their parents and other adults."

"The young man is the one who makes the old folks like it."

"If you are building for the future, the young man is the whole thing."

"My meal ticket!"

"The boy appeal, in many respects, is the strongest that can be made. It applies to a fresh market, as yet unexploited."

As to methods for winning and holding the young-man market, the merchants' answers revealed a wide range of resource and enterprise — such expedients, for instance, as these:

Special advertising, in newspapers and by mail;

Monthly house organs;

Pocket trinkets, lapel buttons, watch fobs, and so on, for certain purchases;

Location of boys' departments in places easily accessible;

Special window displays;

Free adjustments;

Personal activity among young men;

For athletic goods — promoting the organization of teams; discounts on team equipment;

For radio and automobiles — personal counsel over the counter concerning technical details; distribution of instruction hooks, lubrication charts, and so on, to schools and boys' clubs;

For musical instruments — free playing of records; Saturday afternoon concerts; organizing boys' bands; offering free lessons.

All these, plus something that every merchant, nearly, mentioned separately— something that, in all lines of business and in dealings with customers of all ages, can be depended upon to hold and win friendship and build patronage — something that more than one merchant thought sufficiently important to print in large capital letters thus — SERVICE.

Chapter V
Marketing And Advertising[24]

By L. Urwick

1. Definitions

Distribution is the third of the great groups of activities which are common to all industrial enterprises. It is not sufficient to create goods or services. A further step is immediately necessary, the disposal of those goods or services to the persons who require them. Such persons are described as "Consumers." Their need for the goods or services is called "Demand" ; where they are in a position to satisfy that need by offering value in exchange for such goods or services, their" Demand" is " effective." Where they are definitely related to a producer or distributor by previous or habitual dealing, consumers are called "Customers." If they are not so related, but may be assumed to have an "effective demand" for any product, they are called " Prospects."

Before communication and transport were facilitated by modern inventions, determinate areas and times for inter course between buyers and sellers were a necessity of all classes of trade. Such gatherings were known as "markets." The word is used to-day in all the meanings implicit in the functions of the original market. One of these was price adjustment; to-day, a client who inquires of his broker as to "the state of the market " is inquiring about price levels. To his broker, however, "the Kaffir market" will imply a group of dealers standing ready to buy or sell South African Mining Shares. From the standpoint of the producer, the word "market" implies any group of consumers combining a demand for his product with the ability to offer the values necessary to make that demand effective. Distribution covers

[24] From C.H. Northcott *et al.*, *Factory Organization*, London: Pitman, 1928, pp. 154–88.

the whole of the activities of any enterprise concerned with the discovery and development of markets—that is, with the transfer of the product to the consumer.

The functions of the original market were fourfold. The first thing a producer had to know was where he could find a group of persons who would be willing to purchase his goods or services. Having discovered this market, he would transport his product to it. On arrival, he would display his wares to attract the attention of possible customers. Finally, having gained their interest, he would carry out the actual transaction of sale, centring round the question of price. All the complexities of our modern distributive system are merely new combinations and rearrangements of these four basic processes. They constitute the four main activities carried on under the general heading of distribution.

The first of these is concerned with the discovery and examination of the market. But since most business concerns are already established with a certain definite sale, this activity involves two separate conceptions.

Marketing.

Marketing is "reviewing the established methods of distribution by which goods or services are supplied to the consumer and initiating improvements therein." It is concerned with—

1.The product itself, and changes which may make it better adapted to the market.
2.The character of the demand.
3.The channels through which the product is brought to the market.

Merchandising.

On the other hand, merchandising is "Establishing a method by which future markets for goods or services may be prescribed." It is concerned with—

1.Investigating potential markets.
2.Creating new channels of approach to the consumer.
3.Initiating changes in the form or presentation of the proposition.
4.Devising sales and advertising methods calculated to increase returns.

Advertising.
As a result of marketing and merchandising activities, we get advertising, which is: "The communication to possible consumers by display, by sample, or by written or printed symbols, of ideas about the product of any enterprise, designed to create a demand for that product."

Selling.
Only when these preparatory activities have been carried out does the actual operation of selling take place. Selling is: "Obtaining contact with customers and translating their demand into purchases of the products of any enterprise at a price at which the enterprise is prepared to supply them."

Transport.
Finally, we get transport, which is: "The group of activities concerned with the physical transfer of the product of an enterprise to customers who have placed orders."
Portions of this process may have been carried out prior to, or at the same time as, the processes of advertising and selling. But the actual physical transfer to the consumer is almost invariably the final transaction.
Each of these four activities raises definite problems in the control of an industrial enterprise which call for specific methods and machinery for their solution. We shall, therefore, consider in relation to each in turn, first, the administrative questions which come up for decision; and, secondly, the action to be taken by the management as a result of such decisions.

2. Marketing and Merchandising

The Administrative Problems.
From the definitions already given of marketing and merchandising activities, it is clear that there are certain cardinal questions which must be answered in arranging for their administration. The first of these is: "What are you going to sell?"

In most established businesses, this is, of course, already partially settled by the product, in goods or services, which is already on the market. But in any organization which is alert to commercial opportunities, suggestions are constantly put forward for enlarging the existing range of products or for offering entirely new products which seem to hold out hopes of profit. In fact, the question: "What are you going to sell?" is never completely answered. Any business administrator is forced to keep constantly before his mind the possibility that the demand for the article which he is manufacturing may cease. He must be prepared, if he is to maintain his plant in profitable occupation, to adapt it to such changes.

Apart from changes of fashion, in the purchasing power of the public, and in world activities, technical developments may suddenly destroy the demand for a particular article. A factory builds up a trade in some specific article of motor equipment, such as acetylene headlights. Almost in a season, improved electrical devices supersede acetylene lighting, and its market disappears. The action of competitors calls for incessant watchfulness from this angle; both in quality and price the manufacturer is perpetually open to attack by competing lines. It is probable that a higher proportion of business failures may be attributed to a sense of false security in a comfortably established market than to any other single cause. On the other hand, uncertainty as to policy, a too-ready ear to fresh suggestions, or a straining after novelty may dissipate the distributing energies of a concern. The integration of distributive and productive policies is a vital matter under the stress of modern competition.

Immediately depending on the question: "What are you going to sell?" is the question: "To whom are you going to sell it?"

The administrator requires much information before be can make his decision on this point. He has to *relate his product to the consumer* and to assemble particulars as to the habits and economic position of the people who will buy his goods. A special technique for such inquiries, under the title of "Market Research," is a recent development. It is sufficient to note, at this stage, that he must have a constant supply of facts and figures as to the whole body of consumers. He can no longer afford to solve his problems by guess-work or by general knowledge. Specific inquiries for samples from the general public, reinforced by census figures, and subjected to the most rigorous statistical treatment, are essential tools. It is possible for a man who has typewriters to sell to discover in any given area who are the potential users of typewriters, to ascertain which of his competitors are already well-established in that area, and to weigh up the advantage of quality and price which his machine offers as against others. Lacking such a detailed review and detailed figures on these points, he is not likely to arrive at sound conclusions as to his marketing policy.

Having decided to whom he is going to sell his goods, the administrator must next turn his attention to the presentation of them. There are countless different methods of presenting goods to the consumer, and in each trade there is a method of presentation which is particularly suitable to the goods and to the period. But, as in the case of the goods themselves, fashions in this respect are always changing. Twenty years ago, most chemists' shops in this country presented a series of bottles filled with coloured liquid, and of jars filled with salts. Goods were weighed out into paper bags or bottles as required by each individual customer. To-day, the bulk of the retail trade in chemicals is done in proprietary packages. In trades such as the confectionery and fruit trades it is frequently urged that the display of the actual goods, since they are foodstuffs, arouses the desire of the consumer, and is the surest method of presentation to effect a sale. It is not impossible that a similar argument lies behind the unpleasant spectacle of the English butcher's shop. Nevertheless, in confectionery, groceries, and fruit, the sale of goods in attractive packages made up at the factory is gaining ground. Obviously, prepared packages, usually filled and sealed by machinery, make for less handling and greater cleanliness. There is a great economy of time spent in retail selling. Countless cases can be quoted of men who have failed to sell perfectly sound and genuine articles to the public, only to be succeeded by others who achieve success with the same article merely by dint of presenting it in a more attractive form.

The question of the presentation and appearance of his product is one which is constantly in front of the industrial administrator. Having decided on his article, its presentation and the consumer whom he desires to reach the administrator then turns to the most important question of all from the commercial standpoint, "How much of it is he going to sell?" Upon the decision as to the quantity of goods to be sold depend many issues closely affecting the productive side of the enterprise.

The forecasting of future sales is one of the most difficult and intricate decisions to which the industrial administrator must commit himself. Because of its difficulties, and the liability to error, the responsibility for such decisions is frequently undefined—production being adjusted to the orders received more or less haphazard from week to week, the factory putting up a special effort where orders are unexpectedly large, and contracting its activities if they happen to fall off. This lack of defined responsibility, supplemented by emergency methods of adjustment, takes the place of the definite decision of an administrator. It possesses the doubtful advantage that it is difficult to blame a single person for a miscalculation. But with the growth of scientific thought on business questions, it is coming to be recognized that, however much it may relieve individuals of responsibility for difficult decisions, it leads to haphazard working and excessive costs of production. Increasingly, a deliberate effort is made to supply to the administrator such figures of past sales, the purchasing power of the community, and special factors affecting different parts of his market, as shall enable him to make a definite forecast of his sales over a period varying from months to years ahead.

The complexity of modern methods of distribution presents a further problem to the administrator. The product may pass through many pairs of hands on its way to the consumer. The manufacturer sells to a broker who deals with the wholesale merchant. The merchant supplies a retailer, and so on. There may be fewer or more links in the chain. The matter is obviously of great importance to the manufacturer. He must acquaint himself with the distributive structure of his particular trade. Any change or possibility of change in the channels by which the product is finally marketed must be foreseen and studied. Usually, he will find an established method of handling this question. Every trade is full of conventions and customs as to methods of charging from manufacturer to broker or wholesaler, and from wholesaler to retailer. But in spite of this, there are nearly always possibilities of varying the channels of distribution, particularly if the manufacturer is dealing on a large scale. The outline of our distributive machinery is being modified at an accelerating speed. Broadly speaking, there is an incessant and desperate struggle for control between the various factors in the chain of supply. The manufacturer who wishes to adopt mass production methods is under an increasing necessity to secure a certain market for his large output. The economies open to large scale production "only become fully available if and when the plant is fully operated. The market must be of sufficient extent to absorb all that is produced in the establishment. A large, expensive plant, continuously employed, probably produces more cheaply per unit than a small plant, but if it is not given full scope the cost of production per unit may be far higher than in the latter."[25]

On the other hand, the same economies in administration, skilled direction, and purchasing power, which are an advantage to the producer, operate with equal force in the distributive field. In this country, we have the growth of large general department stores, such as Selfridge's, Harrod's, John Barker's, and others. Retail establishments, which up to 1900 were usually managed as small single units, tend to fall more and more under the unified control of large corporations. In the book trade, Messrs. W. H. Smith & Son; in the chemical trade, Messrs. Boots; in the grocery trade, Messrs. Lipton, The International Stores, and others; in the catering trade, Messrs. Lyons, have all established large chains of retail shops.

These corporations are, obviously, very powerful buyers, and in a position to control a considerable percentage of the market for various classes of goods. Faced with this situation, the manufacturer has attempted various counter measures. Some large companies, feeling that the ordinary channels were insufficient to guarantee their market, have endeavoured by widespread schemes of national advertising to secure a steady demand for their goods from the ultimate consumer. The wholesaler and retailer, however powerful, are thus forced to stock their products. In other cases, manufacturers have actually started retail trading on their own account establishing chains of shops usually confined to the supply of goods of their own manufacture.

From the point of view of the individual manufacturer, two main questions are involved: "Do present channels through which his product is distributed offer him a reasonable security in the control of his markets?" And, if this is not the case, "Can he obtain such security with out too great a risk of incurring the hostility of those upon whom he relies for his existing distribution?" Obviously, a manufacturer who is dependent upon another independent manufacturer, or upon a large wholesale or retail enterprise which absorbs a large proportion of his output,

[25] J.H. Jones, *Economics of Private Enterprise,* p. 110.

is in a very insecure position. He is always open to the possibility that his customer will seek another source of supply, or, more probably, will undertake manufacture himself with a view to obtaining the profits of both production and distribution. At the same time, any attempt to undertake retail distribution himself, or to ignore one of the links in the existing chain, involves great difficulties. He is entering into competition with those who are already established in a branch of trading to which he is unaccustomed—a venture calling for long and careful preparation and large resources in skill and capital.

The whole question of outlet to the market is one of increasing complexity to the manufacturer, the importance of the distributive process being emphasized by the technical requirements of large machine production. The power of the distributor has been much enlarged. It is no longer possible for the manufacturer to rely on a steady business secured through normal and customary channels. He must be constantly alert to the possibility of improving both his connection with the consumer and the actual outlets for his goods.

Turning to our definition of merchandising, we see that it involves the same problems as marketing, but viewed from the creative angle. The administrator is not so much concerned with the existing channels through which the product is brought to the market, as with the possibility. of opening up new markets. These markets may be either vertical or lateral. The manufacturer, by cheapening his product, may create a demand among strata of the population which have not previously been in a position to afford his goods. Or, by making arrangements for advertising and selling in areas where he has not previously traded, he may tap more population on the same economic level as those who buy his goods already.

Viewing the same problem from another angle, he may think that his present consumers will buy more of the goods he has to offer if they are presented to them with greater intensity both as to display and as to selling effort. This will again involve him in the consideration of devices and channels of approach other than those customary in the trade. For instance, we find greengrocers displaying packets of chocolates, or dealers in motor accessories using their shops for the sale of leather coats, and similar articles of clothing. The tobacconists in this country, faced with the necessity of early closing in accordance with the Shops Act, have placed shilling-in-the-slot machines outside their shops for the sale of cigarettes in prohibited hours. The possibility of such methods must be constantly in the mind of the administrator.

Under the heading of merchandising he will consider methods of packing his goods in a different form. Some years ago, a very large trade was built up in a mouth-wash, which was based largely on the fact that it was contained in a flask with an attractively-curved neck. The administrator must have constantly before him the possibility that by some slight change in the form of his product, the way it is packed, or the lines along which it is presented to the public, he may achieve a large increase in his available market.

Or, he may devise an entirely new method of selling and displaying his goods There are many examples of such new methods In the last few years, the practice of circulating catalogues of goods for distribution by parcel post has gained increasingly in popularity. Producers engaged in the sale of expensive commodities such as pianos, furniture, motor-cars, and similar articles, beyond the immediate means of persons with a narrow income, have introduced the instalment method of payment, thus widening their market to an appreciable degree. An increasing variety of goods is offered "on sale or return." The art of advertising is in an active state of evolution, and apart from the more eccentric devices by which traders have sought for publicity, there is constant development in legitimate means of communicating ideas about the product of different enterprises to the public. Competitions, electric signs, sky-writing by aeroplane, the use of the cinematograph, the circulation of books by leading authors,[26] bearing only indirectly on the product supplied, are among recent developments of advertising method. Marketing is colonizing a discovered country: merchandising is pioneering.

The Management Problem.

We must now consider the executive machinery required by the marketing problems and policies of an enterprise. Marketing and merchandising, while constituting a separate and clearly

[26] Professor Oman's book on *Castles*, issued by the Great Western Railway Company.

defined distributive activity, have only been so regarded within the last few years, and in a very small number of businesses. In the majority of cases, there is no separate department set aside for this purpose. We must, therefore, regard the question of organization as in an experimental stage. It is possible, however, to indicate the problems which management has to solve in providing the administration with the necessary basis for its decisions on these issues. A consideration of these problems and of the devices adopted to meet them in certain instances will illuminate the nature of the management work required, while leaving open the position of the marketing activity in the general structure of the business.

In the first place, successful marketing and merchandising must be based on definite research. In the United States, the conduct of market research is frequently carried out not within the business itself, but by the advertising agent. Developments in this direction have now reached the point where advertising agencies with a national reputation will refuse to undertake a campaign in support of any product until they have satisfied themselves both as to the quality and form of presentation of the product and have, by means of detailed market research, satisfied themselves that there is reasonable ground for anticipating successful results There are strong arguments for entrusting market research to an advertising agency. Such agencies possess a number of clients in various trades. They are more closely in touch with the conditions in various markets, and are able to transfer experience gained in one market to another. They are largely free from the personal influences which are bound to affect those actually employed in a productive organization. They have not been responsible for the creation of the goods under consideration, and can, consequently, review them more impartially and, therefore, more scientifically. As advertisers, they are closely in touch with certain sources of statistical information directly required for marketing purposes, such as the circulation of various newspapers. On the other hand, manufacturers argue that they are in closer touch with their own problems, and the provision of material on which the final administrative decisions of the business are based should be in their own hands.

As far as Great Britain is concerned, it seems probable that the development of the work of market research will be threefold.

The exact avenue through which the inquiry is conducted will be determined by the nature and scope of the particular problem under investigation. Certain of the basic information required for a scientific consideration of marketing problems is of such a character that it can be gathered most effectively only by an organization of the largest size, enjoying the support of the government.[27] Other information is of a character requiring specialized knowledge of a number of trades, and in this sphere the advertising agency will render the most effective service. For instance, there is much comparative information as to the public response to various types of package which can be transferred from one trade to another. But there will remain a residue of questions so highly technical or so intimate in their character that they demand the special interest of the individual business concerned, and will be investigated most fruitfully by men trained in and employed by that business.

Wherever the work is done, the manager who is responsible has the definite duty of arranging for market research and for the presentation of the information on which the administrator may base his decisions as to marketing and merchandising policy. This information may be classified in various ways. Usually, it falls into two broad classes, that which is specific to the particular inquiry and that which is wanted for any inquiry on which the men responsible for marketing may be engaged. The first class must deal with such problems as arise when marketing policy has already been translated into definite selling and advertising effort—the situation in all established businesses. It is concerned with questions such as—

1. The existing demand—is new demand being created by the selling and advertising methods at present operated?
2. The product—are orders being received a second time from those customers who have already purchased?
3. The effects of competition and of competitive advertising.
4. The attitude of distributors towards the concern, both as regards its goods and its policy—are they friendly and co-operative ? If not, what are the reasons?

[27] "The recent report of the Balfour Committee was essentially a piece of broad market research. "—Sinclair Wood in *Business Research*, May, 1926.

General information is more complicated and of wider scope. First, it is concerned with the general character of the population. It includes such matters as the social classes into which they are divided, their location and their buying, reading, and general habits of life.

A second group of data is concerned with the analysis of the markets under such headings as the number, location, and attitude of the retailers and wholesalers in various trades in each district, and the marketing channels and procedure and the physical features of each area. A third group deals with facts definitely bearing on the problem of distribution, such as districts which are likely to show a ready response to marketing effort, the details of selling plans in various trades, and notes on the influence of retailers on the body of consumers.

The methods available for obtaining such information are, of course, varied. Broadly speaking, the sources are either bibliographical or personal. Bibliographical sources include libraries, books, periodicals, official or semi-official publications, and statistics. Under the personal head come the staff of the organization concerned, competitors, dealers and retailers in the trade, trade journalists, specialists of various kinds, and the whole body of consumers. Personal information may be collected in conversation, by letter, or by questionnaire. One writer, after four years' experience of research in British markets, says: "I have found the questionnaire sent through the post to be the most expensive method of all. However large the number of informants that have to be seen, provided that the area is not too scattered, the extraction of information by face-to-face conversation is the best method."[28]

The person responsible for gathering this information in an established business will naturally inquire how far he can make use of the information supplied by the existing sales force as the basis of his researches among actual consumers. On this point, there is no general agreement. On the one hand, there are very strong arguments of economy and custom in favour of using the information gathered by the salesmen as the basis of market inquiries. A body of salesmen who do not feel that their views as

[28] Sinclair Wood, "Market Research from the Advertising Point of View," *Business Research*, May, 1926.

to the conditions in the market are an important factor in determining the policies of the enterprise, are apt to lose constructive interest. On the other hand, the very nature of the salesman's task and daily experience is apt to render him unsuitable for work which essentially requires a detached and unprejudiced attitude. He has his own work of selling to do, and is likely to be embarrassed and irritated by frequent requests to compile standardized market data. His reports are more likely to reveal his immediate prejudices than a real attempt to survey his situation objectively.

Second only in importance to the task of arranging for research is the manager's problem involved in sales planning and sales forecasting. In order to supply the figures necessary for the final estimate, he has to arrange for the collation of much of the information already provided for by his research organization, but regarded from a somewhat different angle. He has to determine in advance, not only what the total sales of the enterprise are likely to be, but what individual sales may be anticipated for each article on its price list. He has to show where and how these sales can be secured.

Broadly speaking, the categories of facts available to him on which he may base his estimate are five—

I. Those relating to the general level of purchasing power of the whole body of consumers.

2. Those relating to local conditions modifying the conclusions which would be drawn from a general estimate of purchasing power.

3. Those representing specific past experience, such as the actual figures of sales in the line under consideration or in similar lines.

4. Estimates of the selling possibilities of each particular line drawn from the experience of salesmen or from the material provided by special investigations.

5. Knowledge of the advertising and other assistance which will be available in support of the sales of any particular line.

The general purchasing power of the community is the resultant of many economic forces which require specialized consideration for their correct interpretation. The cyclical rise and fall of general business conditions which was regarded at the end of the last century as an inevitable visitation of nature, is now conceived to be due to a complexity of definite causes which may ultimately be brought under general control. The signs of such movements in bank clearances, credit rates, value of stocks, tonnage carried, wage rates, wholesale prices, cost of living figures, and similar indices, are increasingly the subject of economic study. The task of applying such, general economic knowledge to the problems of a specific business is now sometimes allocated to a trained statistician or economic adviser. Certain universities prepare charts and diagrams showing the general statistical position. The marketing manager should provide from whatever source both a general estimate of purchasing power on any national market, and calculations as to the local causes which will involve fluctuation about the mean of the national average.

The chief factor to be considered by the manager in preparing estimates of forward sales is the detailed figures of past sales of the same or similar lines. A word of caution is, however, necessary. In any market where fashion exercises a considerable influence, or there is a wide choice of alternatives before the consumer, the possibilities of sudden and inexplicable fluctuations are very great. It is his duty to ensure, by maintaining the necessary contact with the officer responsible for statistical work, that these figures are presented in the most illuminating form. He takes into account the possibilities and probabilities. For instance, the figures may reveal that the sale of a particular line per thousand of the population is three times greater in one portion of the market than in another. This is an immediate challenge to special inquiry and a suggestion that past figures do not represent the full possibilities of sales. He should, therefore, reinforce his statistics by a careful analysis of the information supplied by men who are actually in contact with his customers, and of the material obtained by his research organization. Finally, the amount of the resources available for advertising, the character of the advertising, and whether advertising of special products is in view, will all influence the sale of particular lines.

In certain trades, such as the sale of machinery for special purposes, it is possible, by detailed analysis, to arrive at an appreciably accurate estimate of the total number of possible buyers in any given area. Starting with a presumptive .sale to each prospect, it is possible to construct a complete plan of sales based on the individual transaction. In other trades, where the manufacturer is several degrees removed from the consumer by wholesale and retail channels of distribution, or where the article sold is one of general consumption distributed in detail to large numbers of customers, this method of estimating is clearly impossible. The sales plan, to be of practical utility, must generally start with the total estimated sale based on past experience, corrected by the economic position, and work down to the details of individual lines from that initial calculation. The marketing manager should determine exactly which type of calculation is best suited to the conditions, and make his arrangements accordingly.

A second problem arises from the relations between the manager responsible for the sales forecast, if he is an independent person, and the manager responsible for sales. While the manager responsible for the sales forecast can prepare, in broad outline, the estimate of the sales which should be achieved in each predetermined area of the market, there are factors arising from the character of the sales force which may profoundly modify the statistical situation in this respect. It seems doubtful if, in any case, where a large sales force is employed, the marketing manager can be expected to allocate his quota of sales to the individual salesman. The general principle which has been adopted in some businesses for dealing with this problem is to limit the duty of the marketing organization to determining the total sales of the business and of each line on the price list. Beyond that point, the planning of sales is taken over by the sales manager, who, with the assistance of information supplied from other sources, allocates the total estimate to his different sales areas and, sometimes, to individual travellers.

With the greatest care and skill in the preparation of the figures and of the estimates based upon them, it is unlikely, in a business with a large price list, that the marketing manager will invariably forecast the sales of individual lines correctly. He has frequently to make his estimates a year or more in advance if he is to give production and the selling force the guidance which they require. The public is fickle and competitors are active. The marketing machinery must provide not only for the initial estimate, but for rapid adjustment of the sales plan in detail and for the communication of such changes. More over, where the production of particular lines involves the purchase of considerable supplies of ancillary material, such as containers, sudden changes in the level of sales may involve serious loss in accumulated stocks. It is the duty of the marketing manager to watch the progress of sales in comparison with his estimate almost daily, and to take the earliest opportunity of warning those responsible for the purchase of materials should he think it probable that be will have to alter important estimates to any appreciable degree.

In this connection, the placing of new lines upon the market throws a special responsibility upon those who lay the foundations of the estimate. Where a line is already on sale, there is a considerable mass of past experience which is, at all events, some guide in framing calculations as to the probable sale. But where an entirely new product is involved, the problem is a very different one, and the possibility of error is very much increased. In these circumstances, it is becoming usual to sample the market by selling the line over one or more selected areas sufficiently in advance of its introduction to the market as a whole, to enable an estimate to be made on the records of this practical experience before orders for machinery, materials, and so on, are placed. Such experiments are essentially market research, and while they will usually be managed by those in charge of selling, the marketing manager will consider with special interest their results, the opinions expressed by salesmen, and similar material. As a further guide, it is frequently possible to obtain sales figures relating to similar lines. These figures, if presented graphically, can be made to form the basis of a comparison with the initial sales of an experimental kind also expressed in graphic form. It is then frequently clear from the mere trend of the line expressing the sale of the new article, that it is likely to follow a similar course to that of the line with which it is being compared. While there are risks about comparisons of this description, they probably offer the best prospect of an accurate and scientific forecast of the sales of an entirely new product.

In general, in dealing with forward estimates of sales, the manager responsible for marketing will be wise to make the fullest possible use of the graphical presentation of figures, since it is often only when complicated data are satisfactorily charted that immediate tendencies reveal themselves.

The third main duty in the management of marketing activities is the translation into executive action of decisions as to what goods are to be sold, and the form in which they are to be presented. The manager will have to present to the administrator the designs and suggestions on which such decisions are based. Here, again, there is large variety in industrial organization. In many industries, new design is left to the casual suggestion of salesmen or the bright thoughts of those who happen to be engaged on production. But continuous and constructive thought on the problem of new products, the translation of ideas into experimental samples, the testing and costing of such samples, and their adaptation to the conditions of mass production, the artistic work and experiment necessary to the achievement of dignified and economical design, are specialized activities which must, in due course, be separated from the absorbing administrative work of the factory departments, and cannot be achieved as the by-product of a salesman's evening hours.

It is clear that this question of design closely affects both production and distribution. The product itself is the most intimate interest of the production manager. He is responsible for effectiveness and economy in methods of manufacture. On the other hand, where display of the article itself, or of the container, is an important influence in securing sales, the character of such display is an important factor in advertising. In any business where a supply of novel products is an integral factor in commercial vitality, the task of securing suggestions and ideas, of selecting between alternatives, and of making the detailed preparations for launching new products upon the market is a continuous one. In the majority of enterprises, the traditional rights and authority of the production and advertising departments necessitate a cautious development. It is clear, however, that the very overlap of production and advertising considerations involves the necessity for co-ordination. This is probably more effectively secured by the appointment of a third party with powers of decision and constructive responsibilities for maintaining the supply of new products, than by any system of committees or conferences. His intimate contact with the market, and constant research into consumer demand, suggest that this duty is properly allocated to the marketing manager.

The question of the price at which a product shall be placed upon the market must form an integral part of the whole discussion as to marketing policy. Broadly speaking, three main lines of approach have characterized the handling of this question. Many undertakings have determined their prices on the principle of charging all that the existing market would bear. A second and more usual method has been that of charging a standard gross profit on the actual cost of production of the article, or on the selling price. Both these methods have been incessantly modified in practice by the influence of competition. And thus, in some cases, manufacturers have fixed their prices almost solely in relation to the prices charged by their competitors. The question of pricing has, however, been profoundly modified by technical advances. Manufacturers are beginning to appreciate more clearly the full possibilities of economy latent in mass production by machinery, provided that a sufficiently wide market can be secured. At the same time, the influence of price reductions in enlarging the market for a commodity has received closer attention.

Since most enterprises manufacture not one single article, but a range of allied or similar products, the relation between production cost and the quantity produced must be viewed from this angle. Many of the economies possible with mass production are lost if the range of articles manufactured is a wide one. Machines have to be changed over from one process to another Administrative expenses are multiplied by the purchase of a large number of different ingredients, difficulty in tracing various stocks, uncertainty as to the division of costs between the various products, and so on.

Assuming that marketing is a separate function under an independent manager, he will require only a small staff. Someone has to arrange for the collection of the facts and figures involved in market research; if elaborate inquiries are undertaken, outside staff, for the definite work of investigation, will be required. The task of designing and selecting new products involves the employment of a few artists or technical men under the close control of a single person responsible for novelties. The estimation of forward sales is a question of making use of the figures provided by the statistical records of the organization, not of preparing elaborate material specially. In short, the marketing man supplies the link necessary to guide and co-ordinate the executive activities of others. He does not manage a large number of persons himself. He constitutes the transmission system of the industrial machine. This does not, however, detract in the least from the immense importance of his function to the health of the enterprise and the weight of the responsibility which rests upon his shoulders.

3. Advertising

The Administrative Problems.
The administrative problems which arise in connection with advertising inevitably depend, to a large degree, on general marketing policy. The growth in advertising methods and technique which has taken place in the last quarter of a century is one of the most striking features of our business evolution. The power wielded through successful advertisement is undoubtedly enormous, though open to grave abuses. But against the great expense of competitive advertising there is a very big credit account. The attempt to improve the form of modern advertising, both in typography, illustration, and design, has undoubtedly been a factor in improving public taste, spreading a demand for improvement in the form of the goods themselves. The "Truth in Advertising" movement, which has made great headway in the United States, is evidence that those engaged in advertising as a profession appreciate the necessity of high ethical standards, and we may look for a growing professional distaste for the advertising of' goods which are other than they are represented to be.

The first question which the administrator must ask himself in approaching the general problem of advertising, is whether he is going to advertise or not. Advertising of some kind there must be. It is integral to the very process of distribution. It is not possible to conceive of any person entering into a transaction for the purchase of goods unless, in some way or another, his attention has been called to those goods. For instance, the manufacturer's traveller may have shown him samples, or the manufacturer may have sent him a catalogue or circular. Both these activities are forms of advertising; they are concerned not with the actual sale of the goods, but with their *display with a view to sale*. But, while it is doubtful if it is sound business policy, it must be remembered that it is still possible to conduct a prosperous business with very little display of the goods other than that conducted by competent salesmen, the wide distribution and reputation of the particular manufacturer's products being maintained by their high quality and the goodwill of the retailers. In most trades, however, under modern conditions, this is a procedure which will lead straight to disaster. The exigencies of competitive trading demand a wider margin of security than is represented either by the public's memory for high quality, or the trader's goodwill. Expenditure on advertising there must be, and sometimes very heavy expenditure The task before the administrator in determining the policy which should guide such expenditure is fourfold. The first question he must ask himself is to whom will his advertising be directed?

In a trade where the distributive machinery is complicated the wholesaler or the retailer is the immediate customer of the producer. By providing retailers with material for dressing their windows in the form of show-cards and posters, by equipping wholesalers with catalogues, illustrations and other matter descriptive of his products, he may assist these partners to the distributive process in attracting the attention of the consumer. A large annual expenditure is devoted by manufacturers to Press announcements in the trade papers which circulate largely among the wholesalers and retailers in their particular trade. The limitations of the policy of advertising through the wholesaler and retailer have already been indicated. But on the other hand, a larger and more immediate effect can sometimes be obtained in this way, with a smaller expenditure than would be involved in a direct appeal to the consumer. Undoubtedly, the salesman behind the counter has a very large influence in determining the direction of public demand, particularly when there are a large number of alternatives open to the consumer. It is doubtful whether it is possible to create a reliable and persistent demand for a specific brand of jam, pills, boots, or motor cars without enlisting and maintaining the goodwill of the intermediate partners in the chain of distribution. But the administrator is bound, at some stage of his development, to consider the direct appeal to the consumer by means of the Press, posters, and similar channels.

The condition of the public mind, which leads the great body of consumers to ask for a particular brand of an article in general use, and to insist on obtaining that brand, is described by Americans as "brand consciousness." In England, we often say that the name of a particular manufacturer has become a "household word." But, perhaps fortunately for humanity, household words are very easily forgotten. And the instability of public demand, unless maintained and reinforced by persistent advertising, is one of the most interesting features of our modern economic system.

The attempt to forecast and to control this unstable demand is one of the primary tasks of the business administrator. One of his chief resources in obtaining such control is the power wielded by modem methods of advertising. Nevertheless, however great his expenditure on Press advertising, he will certainly find himself in difficulties if he does not pay constant attention to the strong influences wielded by those in direct contact with the purchasing public. That influence is personal—the suggestion conveyed from individual to individual when they are face to face. Certainly, at our present stage of development, and, so far as we can tell, permanently, that influence in its more restricted sphere is always likely to remain a stronger force than the influence exercised by printed symbols.

The second question he must ask himself is: "What is the general object with which I am advertising?" Of course, he is advertising in order to increase his sales and to secure a permanent market. But there are two angles of approach to this general object. A manufacturer may seek either to advertise his goods directly or to advertise his business. The two things are not quite the same. In the first instance, the administrator will think primarily of his current sales; be will relate his advertising to specific articles in his price list to which he wishes to call the attention of the public. He will be inclined to judge the failure or success of his advertising schemes by their effect on the demand for particular products. And if changes of fashion or other causes force him to remove those products from his price list and to substitute others, some part of the effect of his advertising will inevitably be lost. Realizing this, he may determine on the somewhat slower process of advertising the name of his business, with a view, in the long run, to making the public associate that name inevitably with the class of article which he is producing. This form of advertising—commonly known as institutional advertising—can have very far-reaching effects if pursued persistently and carefully over long periods. One leading company in the United States, in the front rank for its particular product, has never mentioned the goods it has for sale over a long period of years marked by colossal advertising expenditure.

The pros and cons of this broad question can hardly be stated theoretically. They differ for every trade and for different stages in the development of a business. Certain classes of goods lend themselves to direct advertisement in the majority of instances, services do not. But even to this rule there are many exceptions. A railway company will often draw the attention of the public to the attractions of a particular watering-place which it serves, or to a special excursion, though the trend of its advertising is to emphasize the general amenities of travel to be enjoyed upon its lines. The problem must be settled empirically in relation to the circumstances of the particular business. But in the case of all great businesses which are strongly influenced by changes in fashion and taste, there comes a stage when the waste involved in the advertising of particular products which can only enjoy a temporary popularity has to be reviewed. The possibility of concentrating advertising expenditure on the institution rather than on any particular lines which it manufactures must be seriously considered.

A review of the actual behaviour of business organizations in this matter reveals that, at the present juncture, no definite principle has been worked out. In women's clothing, the practice of advertising certain branded goods, particularly silk stockings, is largely on the increase; formerly, the particular retailer or department store tended to emphasize the name of the institution. In many trades there is a tendency towards group advertising which emphasizes the uses of the general class of product which the trade produces, rather than the name or the brand of any particular advertiser. The public in England is well-acquainted with the slogan "Eat more fruit." Cement manufacturers publish an extensive journal emphasizing the use of cement in all types of construction. Insurance companies, again, follow both practices, some of their advertising emphasizing the stability of the particular organization, while other publicity is concerned with the merits of particular policies. The chief considerations which are before the administrator on this matter are on the one hand the necessity for current sales, and on the other the fact that expenditure on institutional advertising usually builds a permanent asset.

The third question which the administrator must ask himself is how much he is prepared to spend in order to press the sale of his goods? The amount he must spend when he is appealing to the general public is much larger than that required if he limits his effort to wholesaler or retailer. His policy, if he is seeking to build a permanent goodwill, will be determined by different considerations than those which will weigh with him if he is concerned almost entirely with current sales. In the first case, his line of action may be determined without immediate reference to his trading account for the current year. A vendor of patent medicines, for instance, in placing a new product upon the market, will estimate that a certain initial expenditure is necessary in order to popularize the line and to make the public acquainted with it. This expenditure he will regard in the same light as the money he must lay down for the formation of a public company, and he will not allow his initial advertising to appear in his trading account entirely against the profits of the first year's business.

If, on the other hand, the manufacturer is chiefly considering current sales, the sum which he "appropriates" to advertising will be strictly determined by the amount of the estimated sales which the advertising is calculated to produce. Thus, a manufacturer producing a large range of products will tend to push those products with a high margin of profit by means of advertising, since the margin enables him to expend a considerable sum on publicity and still leaves a reasonable percentage of profit on his turnover. In most old-established businesses, the advertising expenditure must be considered from this angle, that is to say, the amount expended in any year is deter mined by the margin of profit which it will render available. In practice, there are usually previous years' experience on which to base the policy. The manufacturer makes a calculation that additional advertising will yield such and such an addition to his total sales, representing such and such an estimated gross profit. Deducting the cost of advertising as a whole from his estimated gross profit as a whole, he decides whether the additional advertising cost will yield him a larger margin of profit than he obtained in the preceding year.

Having determined with what general object he is going to advertise, to whom he is going to advertise, and what is the total amount of money be is prepared to spend, the administrator has one more main problem to settle. He has to distinguish between the various channels by which advertising can be carried out, and to decide which of those channels he will use.

The manufacturer who wishes to exhibit his goods through retailers may take one of several courses. In the first place, he may decide that, primarily for this purpose, he will own a certain number of retail shops in his own line of trade. The same object may be achieved by the purchase of an interest in retail companies, such an investment being dictated primarily by the desire to obtain a favourable exhibit of his goods in the windows of their shops, rather than by any idea of obtaining complete control of the necessary retail outlets to keep his factory busy. Where this is the case, the risk taken in obtaining financial control of such shops or companies is essentially an advertising risk. More usually, the manufacturer will offer inducements to the retailer to display his particular product. The most obvious inducement is, of course, cash. This frequently takes the form of a discount on goods purchased. Alternatively, he will provide the retailer with special services assisting towards the display of his goods. For instance, on the receipt of an order of a certain size, he will issue material to assist him in dressing his window. Such material ranges from the very humblest showcards costing a few pence each, to elaborate structures designed to fill the whole window, electric light for special effects, counter cases, and similar shop fittings. A gift to the retailer of dummies of the manufacturer's goods, which can be freely displayed in the window without deterioration of the stock, is another favourite device. The more advanced manufacturers maintain a specially-trained staff who undertake the actual dressing of his windows for the retailer. They are taught how to arrange goods attractively so that they catch the attention of the passer-by. They do not necessarily limit themselves to their own company's goods. They are taught that the character of the service which they render to the retailer must be such as to dispose of the whole of his stock and not only of a portion. But the opportunity offered by their entrée into the shop results in additional emphasis on the specific manufacturer's products. In the United States, this "dealer's service," as it is called, has been carried to a great length, manufacturers not only providing advice and assistance in the dressing of the windows, but sending skilled accountants and commercial engineers, who will advise retailers as to their system of business, the training of the salesmen and the like. The Co-operative Wholesale Society has done effective work along similar lines in this country.

Turning from display to samples, these may be distributed either to the retailer or wholesaler, or direct to the consumer. In the first instance, samples will usually be carried by salesmen of the manufacturer concerned, and there is room for much ingenuity and discretion as to the range of such samples, and the form of their presentation and packing. Sampling direct to the general public is a form of advertising which is in an experimental stage. In certain instances, retailers have been asked to undertake the distribution of such samples, but on the whole this has not proved satisfactory, even when the samples were supplied gratis to the retailer. The principle of distribution, house to house, by a special staff employed by the manufacturer, has certain advantages in attracting attention, but is extremely costly. The most usual course employed up to the present has been direct distribution to public by post. This has taken two forms. In the one case, a manufacturer has enclosed a small sample of the new line in each package of another product, already widely distributed. This method ensures that the sample reaches the consumer. But considerations of cost limit its size. There is considerable uncertainty as to its effect. Samples reach many members of the public who are not really interested. In other cases, invitations to write for a free sample are issued in the Press. This enables a larger sample to be offered. It secures that a free supply of the product is sent only to those members of the public sufficiently interested to send a post card.

Sampling, which is an extremely expensive form of advertising, should only be attempted after the most rigorous research and experimental work over specific areas or groups. The experience available suggests that it is of the greatest value in the cases of those products where consumption is a habit, that is to say, the products purchased definitely on personal taste. Such habits of consumption, based on taste, once established are comparatively proof against ordinary competitive effort for the time being; they, therefore, repay heavy initial outlay in sampling. A particular brand of shaving cream or tobacco, once adopted by a consumer, is apt to be retained. On the other hand, this habit effect is weakened where other instincts, such as the parental instinct, are concerned. The very wide sampling in such articles as baby food, which is characteristic of modern advertising, is of doubtful utility to producers. Here, the consumer is not consulting his own taste, but is guided by the day-to-day health of his infant, and is very ready to try a change should the child show signs of sickness.

The main expenditure in modem advertising is directed towards the method of attracting attention, by written or printed symbols. The means of conveying such symbols to the consumers are many. The most important is undoubtedly the public Press in its various forms. A very large amount of modem selling is conducted by means of appeals to social groups of consumers through the post. The catalogue which the manufacturer prepares for the use of his salesmen and customers, whether wholesalers or retailers, is the simplest form of advertising expenditure of this kind. It is the modern equivalent of the notice for sale on a particular date and at a particular place originally announced by the town crier. The method survives to-day in the bills displayed by land and house agents. Such printed bills or posters are directed to those members of the public who are likely to be particularly interested in that specific sale. Corresponding to this we have the appeal to the general body of consumers following the same method. Manufacturers of articles in general demand rely very largely upon attractive displays on the hoardings, often coloured, and devoting a considerable portion of their space to pictorial appeal.

The administrator, in allocating the proportion of his advertising to be given to written and printed symbols, must decide between the varying claims of catalogues, price-lists, leaflets, Press appeals, and posters, directed to the general body of consumers, and special letters or pamphlets, addressed to customers and consumers who are presumed to be particularly interested in the article concerned. Appeals to the general body of consumers absorb a larger proportion of advertising cost. The variety and distribution of the daily, weekly, monthly, and specialized Press, offer great opportunities to the manufacturer who desires to interest the general public in his wares. The art of poster design improves year by year, and constitutes a definite factor in the education of the consuming public. The administrator has to decide, in the first instance, between Press appeals and hoardings as a medium for his written and pictorial appeal. Should he decide upon the Press, he has to distinguish between the various media open to him. A certain amount of space in a daily paper with a large circulation costs a great deal more than an equivalent space in a technical or trade journal published weekly with a small circulation to specialized purchasers. His decision between these channels of distribution will probably depend on the answer to the previous question as to whether he is advertising to the trade or to the general body of consumers. Generally speaking, he will attempt to get some idea of the circulation of the various journals which he is considering as a medium for his publicity. He will consider carefully the type of reader which the particular journal commands, and the position of the space in the make-up of the journal. Probably he will work out a standard cost per inch per person of advertising in the various forms of journal, and will then balance out the advantage of appealing to a wider generalized public at a smaller average cost, as against the advantage of appealing to a smaller specialized public at a higher average cost.

Two special forms of advertising carried out through the Press must be mentioned. The first is competitions. The competition in selecting posters recently conducted by Bovril, Ltd., is a case in point. The second is the offer of prizes in exchange for coupons representing the purchase of a given quantity of goods. This latter method undoubtedly exercises a very direct influence on sales, but it is doubtful if it can properly be regarded as an advertising cost. The expense of the prizes and of organizing their distribution is really a discount on the retail price of the article. In this country, the law as to lotteries distinctly limits the ingenious advertiser who seeks to devise new forms of competition. But both competitions and the premium system are very widespread, particularly in the sale of articles of general consumption. The premium appeals to the desire common to most people to get some thing for nothing. Of course, the something is carried in the price of the goods, but in form the prize appears a free gift and attracts a popularity which it does not really merit. The various competitions make a double appeal both to the emulative impulse and to the love of a chance.

It will be seen that the administrator who has to settle the advertising policy of a business, requires the fullest support from the facts collected by those responsible for market research. The financial question is the root of all advertising policy. The administrator is never at a loss for directions in which it is possible to spend money on advertising. His problem is to ensure that that expenditure pays a dividend. There is no drain in business down which it is easier to pour resources than the advertising appropriation. Opportunities for advertising this or that product present themselves continuously. There is constant pressure for larger sales. He has to balance out all these claims and to make the final decision both as to the maximum sum which the business can afford and as to the methods of spending it which will prove most fruitful. It is essential that these points should be decided in advance and that all proposals for expenditure should be subject to them. It is then possible to present the problem of advertising policy in its true form as a careful weighing of alternatives.

The Management Problem.
The advertising policy settled, it remains for the management to provide the necessary machinery to put it into execution.

Under the heading of display falls the work of preparing the necessary material for use by the retailer. This may take the form of cards, bills, or other announcements, the preparations of special dummies of the goods, and the design and trial of various forms of window display. If a staff of window dressers or advertising inspectors is maintained, these men will have to be trained and equipped. When engaged in their work, they must be supervised, their arrangements planned, and their expenses checked. Containers must be studied and improved from the advertising standpoint. Copy required for the Press, the designing of posters, and the preparation of editorial matter have to be arranged. The cost of all advertising placed with the Press, of billposting, and of similar forms of expenditure, must be carefully recorded, and responsibility assumed for retaining the actual expenditure within the total determined by the policy of the administration. Finally, records will be needed which afford some basis of comparison between the cost of various forms of advertising and the results, Such facts are extremely difficult to reduce to measurement. It is frequently impossible to assess the value, for instance, of window displays, except by means of the reports of special inspectors who ascertain, from the retailers concerned, the amount of increased business they have enjoyed as the result of the display.

How far this particular work is carried out within the organization of the manufacturing enterprise is a matter for administrative decision. Where full use is made of the whole of the services offered by an up-to-date advertising agent, the actual managerial work within the producing enterprise will be small in quantity. It will resolve itself into the maintenance of records, liaison with and check upon the work of the advertising agent, and the necessary co-operation with the marketing and sales management.

In most instances, however, businesses have found it desirable to supplement the work of the advertising agent in one direction or another. Both on the marketing and merchandising side, and in relation to the work which more directly belongs to advertising, the position of the advertising agent in this country has not been fully worked out. The profession attracts men of an energetic and original type of mind, who are inclined to be ahead of the manufacturers in the consideration of advertising and marketing problems. The marketing side of the average British business has been neglected in the more immediate past. In consequence, at the present moment, the advertising agents are in a very strong position. There is, however, no historical precedent for the present ineptitude of the British manufacturer in dealing with market problems. Speaking of the period of our history between 1660 and 1760, a recent writer has said: "In this brilliant era of commercial development, business was for the first time departmentalized broadly along the lines we know to-day. Most of the modern methods of marketing, both here and in the United States, owe their origin to these pioneer traders of the seventeenth century. At that date, marketing problems appear to have been as pressing as those of production. The foundations of commercial supremacy were apparently laid then, because Englishmen knew how to sell better than their neighbours, rather than because of any extraordinary merit in English products."[29]

It seems probable that as the importance of marketing problems becomes, once more, keenly appreciated and studied by the English manufacturer, the tendency to place a large proportion of the executive work in the hands of the advertising agent will be reversed. Manufacturers will establish their own staff of artists, window-dressers and similar craftsmen for the executive side of their advertising work. They will leave to the advertising agent his original function of placing copy with the Press.

[29] Cecil Chisholm, "Marketing and Merchandising," *Modern Business Texts*, Vol. III, p. 13.

Chapter VI[30]
The Marketing Point of View

The question which now faces the industrialised nations is not primarily a question of how to produce their requirements. It is how to organise the distribution of what they have produced and can produce. If the present acute financial crisis is regarded in simple terms—and like all great issues it is simple, and only to be understood if treated simply—it is in effect a colossal failure on an international scale to understand and to arrange for the processes of distribution.

The crisis is called a financial crisis. But what is finance? Men are accustomed to talk about business activities as if they were divisible into three main groups: production, distribution, and finance. But this is a deceptive analysis. It is true that there are three groups, three aspects of business activity which are of first importance. But the third aspect, finance, is totally different in character to the other two. Production and distribution are realities: they are concerned with the fundamental purpose of all economic life, to supply and to deliver the goods and services which men and women require. But finance is not concerned directly with these realities; viewed broadly, it is a secondary, a facilitative activity, concerned with assisting in the other two fundamental processes. No amount of money has ever of itself produced a loaf of bread or conveyed it to a human being who wished to eat it.

The present financial mechanisms by which the world's business is conducted are extremely complex. Every, variety of habit pattern has been built up around them. Half the world's ideas about business are based on them. They are the centre of a whole complex of traditions, organised activity and vested authorities, and these things are hard to change. But unless and

[30] From L.F. Urwick, *Management of Tomorrow*, London, Nisbet, 1932, pp. 80–99.

until men become simpler, unless they are prepared to realise that they have elevated a servant into a master, have made of a facilitative service a major function, they have no prospect of getting out of their difficulties. The function of industry and commerce is to produce and to distribute. That is their major purpose. Until that major purpose is viewed directly, and not through a prism of finance, those who control industry and commerce will not be the men who make and supply goods, but the men who run the financial services, the scorers. And since quite a number of advantages can be secured by exacting a premium on those services—it would perhaps be unduly harsh to say by faking the score—it is hardly surprising if control from this angle some times gets production and distribution into a mess.

A further consideration is that this control of business by its servant could not have taken place had the two partners in the business game understood each other and their respective jobs. And since it is manifestly not the power to produce which is at fault, it follows that the muddle must have occurred either in the processes of distribution or in the correlation of distribution with production.

How has this come about? The explanation is a fairly simple one. A hundred years ago, before power production with all its consequences had come to complicate economic arrangements, the producer and distributor were the same person. The work of distribution was carried out, as it is today, for certain types of agricultural and other produce, by means of markets; a market or fair was simply a fixed place and time where buyers and sellers could meet.

The processes which were carried out by means of the markets of a more primitive period were the same as those cared for by the complex mechanisms of today. In the first place, the producer knew that on the market day at the local market town he would find all the potential customers, all the "prospects" for his particular product. By bringing his products to the market he performed the first half of the total cycle of activities called transportation. In doing this he behaved exactly as a manufacturer of today behaves when he delivers his goods to a retail establishment or agent. That function of the primitive market is adequately cared for by the present economic organisation.

In the second place, arrived at the market, he displayed his goods on a stall or stand where people who might want to buy them could see them readily. If he was a pushful fellow he also made a noise to call attention to himself and his goods. That is to say, he advertised them. Today, with postal facilities, printing, the popular Press, radio (except in Great Britain), window display experts and shopping weeks, there are all sorts of new facilities for taking care of this elemental function of Distribution.

When the early producer had carried his goods to market and had displayed them, there followed the process of sale centring round the question of price. Customers passed by his stall. If they stopped and started to bargain, he became aware immediately of the possibilities of sale within a definite price range. With the exception, however, of this greater flexibility with regard to price adjustments, his action in this respect differed little from that of the travelling salesman of today whose bag of samples or book of quotations is the basis of sale across the retailer's counter or purchasing agent's desk.

But there was one function, one need, which the producer-consumer-tradesman satisfied by attendance at the primitive market which the present practice of distribution at a distance has largely failed to replace. From the talk of customers about his stall, from a glance at the stalls of other vendors, from the gossip which characterised the "ordinary" at the local inn, he learned a vital series of facts. He absorbed almost unconsciously a grasp of all that material which is now called market information. He knew almost precisely the quality and quantity of competitive effort which he would have to meet. Defects in his own products, whether as to design, quality or price, were brought home to him immediately either by indifference or by homely comment. The nature, volume and direction of demand were developing under his nose. Since his production was essentially hand production for immediate needs he returned home to his workshop for another spell as a producer with a very lively and intimate sense of what was required of him. He *knew,* not what a design department thought would be acceptable, but what king customer *was* accepting; not what price his cost accountant told him he should get, but the price which, next week or next month, he *could* get; not how much he would like to make to keep his factory running at capacity, but how much he *would have* to make to satisfy the existing demand. That is to say, his actions as a producer were dominated in their every aspect by this directly absorbed knowledge of the needs of the consumer.

This picture is, of course, over-simplified. But it represents fairly definitely the position at the dawn of the industrial revolution. That sudden and tremendous accretion in productive capacity encountered a world still largely under-supplied, as arc great areas of the world today, with the most elementary necessities of civilisation. As a consequence, there was almost a century of a pronounced sellers' market. There were ups and downs, of course. But by and large the main problems facing business were concerned with the development of the new means of production and of transportation. This development has produced the world as it is today, a world in which on the whole business men have taken to thinking of production first and of distribution afterwards. They have come to regard the main function of distribution as selling what production happens to make. In this connection they have enormously developed the first three functions of the original market, transporting, selling and advertising.

In doing so, they have to a large degree lost sight of the main function of those earlier markets—the informational function. The main job of distribution is not to get rid of what production makes, it is to tell production what it ought to make. It is as the nervous system of economic life that distribution should play its vital and controlling part in the economic order. Fundamentally business is suffering from a serious functional disorder of the nervous system.

It may be argued that that is an exaggerated picture. Salesmen are in touch with retailers or agents; advertising people undertake market research; there are all kinds of statistics bearing on sales; business realises that it has to satisfy its customers and that it would be crazy to manufacture except to satisfy a market. All this is true. But it does not bring prosperity. Retailers and agents are not consumers; they are intermediate distributors. Their knowledge of consumer demand and its laws is frequently twisted by the desire to have something with their name on it, or something that the fellow across the road has not got. Market Research, while of supreme value to the individual manufacturer, is almost always undertaken with a view, not to finding out what the consumer's habits really are, but to selling what some particular manufacturer can make. Statistics of sales, while extremely valuable in analysing the past and directing current distributive effort in detail, reveal nothing whatever about the future. Business pays lip-service to the importance of the consumer. But usually it only knows who its customers have been and what they have done. It has no notion who its potential consumers will be and what they will do.

Not only have the growth of machine production and modern communications destroyed the sensitive and direct relationship between manufacturer and consumer, they have also made the necessity for a more sensitive relationship much greater. This has occurred in three different ways.

In the first place, the technique of machine manufacture has altered the conditions of production. Rarely is manufacturing conducted to meet definite needs expressed in orders. Business manufactures in advance for stock. Moreover, the more can be manufactured of a single article, the more production can bc simplified, the lower are costs. There is, as yet, an imperfect conception of the possibilities in this direction. The majority still look at manufacturing costs first and the market second. Ford's whole success in the motor industry is fundamentally due to a reversal of that process. He asked himself first the question: at what price must I put a car on the market to sell half a million or a million? Then he turned his whole energy to making a car at that price. The success of such firms as Woolworth's or Marks & Spencer is again due to a definite realisation of this simple principle. They have created mass-distribution machinery which enables them to secure the sale of all sorts of articles by the hundred thousand or the million, *provided that the price is right.* They then go to the manufacturer and say: we will give you a firm order for a very large quantity at such and such a price. And when the manufacturer looks at unit costs in the old-fashioned way, and says he cannot do it, they are quite prepared to send a cost accountant into his works to show him how it can be done.

Distribution costs, in the sense of the actual expense which occurs between the factory and the consumer, are undoubtedly too high in many instances. But this is due to the low efficiency of the marginal distributor rather than to any deliberate profiteering on the part of more efficient distributors. The problem of price-cutting in many trades is definitely due to the existence of this wide gap between the most efficient and least efficient distributor. Big reforms are needed in this field. Scientific management must be applied to the whole range of distributive processes, as it has been to productive work. But there is a risk that too great concentration on detailed, costs may conceal the more important issue. Methods of distribution, even where they cost more, which are mass methods and therefore enable machine production to operate to its full efficiency, are the greatest source of economy open to the world today.

In the second place, the higher standard of living which is characteristic of a number of countries since the introduction of machine methods has definitely made the market more uncertain. Where two individuals, A and B, are earning what may be called a subsistence wage, roughly ninety per cent. of their expenditure will be devoted to necessities—shelter, clothing and food. And within any given national group the forms which such expenditure will take are fairly easy to predict and are difficult to change by advertising or other means. It is well known that consumption of bread in the British market is relatively inelastic—that is to say, it varies little in response to a general rise or fall in the retail price of the loaf. It is a staple necessity. Where, however, A and B have a subsistence wage plus fifty per cent. or one hundred per cent., the amount of that wage devoted to subsistence remains roughly constant. But the additional fifty or one hundred per cent is added to the total volume of optional expenditure, expenditure whose direction is determined by the personal choice of the consumer and may be highly erratic. This condition of the larger proportion of total expenditure which is optional is responsible for what is called " the new competition "—that is, the replacement of direct competition between manufacturers making the same article by competition between manufacturers making quite different articles for a larger share of the consumer's pound. It is perhaps the underlying cause of the severity of the present depression in the United States of America.

In the third place, modern methods of communication have made industry and trade in fact, if not in appearance, international.

But the effect of this growing internationalisation has been to expose the markets for commodities and services to all kinds of influences from which the local market for basic necessities was relatively immune. These influences are both economic, that is to say, they are concerned with the actual organisation of business, and extraneous. The extraneous influences are such emotions as national feeling expressing itself in economic imperialism, political considerations leading to legislation designed to please specific interests or classes, or fear leading to uneconomic arrangements designed to facilitate the situation of particular groups in the event of war. The economic influences include group selfishness leading to uneconomic efforts to bolster up particular productive equipment, and particularly the inter-dependence of the world financial system leading to great sensitiveness with regard to credit and the confidence on which it is based. A break in that confidence is, of course, one of the roots of the present troubles.

While the two sets of causes are almost inextricable in any given instance they are clearly distinguishable. Could this world forget for a moment its national feelings, its political or sectional or class prejudices and its fears, could its statesmen sit down quietly to solve the problem of supplying the world as a business problem, it would not prove so complicated or so unamenable to scientific knowledge and method. Incidentally everyone would be more prosperous.

The situation is no one's fault. There are no scapegoats. The tendency observable recently in certain countries to look for scapegoats—America sometimes calls them "alibis "—is the most serious psychological feature of the present situation. The, world has adopted in the last hundred years a totally new technique for meeting, its material requirements. People have shown themselves collectively slow in adapting their economic methods to that technique. That technique has first broken the natural contact between producer and consumer found in the early market. At the same time, it has made the penalties of misjudgment of demand more severe. It has made demand itself more erratic, and by extending the area in which it operates, it has made it more vulnerable to outside influences.

If this analysis is correct, if the long sellers' market, coupled with the development of machine production, have resulted in the growth of an incorrect point of view so that business always thinks about production first and distribution second, the first and most essential thing is to break that habit. Bad habits, incorrect ways of looking at problems, usually express themselves in organisation, and one of the ways of curing them is by changes in organisation. Moreover, if it is true that as a result of that bad habit producers have neglected to supply mechanisms in modern factories to replace the touch with the market of the earlier hand producer, there is an obvious practical need which requires attention.

The majority of business enterprises are organised in three main divisions—production, selling, and finance. Generally speaking, coordination between these divisions is arranged for by conference under the chairmanship of the General Manager or Managing Director. Now, such an arrangement is perfectly adequate if the job of distribution is regarded as selling what production makes. But if the first task of distribution is to indicate to production what it should make, at what price and in what quantity, it leaves the daily responsibility for a large number of decisions of vital importance to the business inadequately defined and sometimes unprovided for altogether.

The first thing to be done is, therefore, the creation in every business of a new and separate main division of responsibilities and duties which may be called the "marketing division". The tasks which should be allocated to such a division are numerous and varied; they may be described broadly as all those questions which arise in securing adequate co-ordination between manufacturing and selling. They include:

(a) Determining what the business shall make and sell, how many different lines and how many different sizes or patterns.

(b) Determining the price at which the business shall sell them. Is it more profitable to sell x units at ten shillings each, or x plus fifty units at eight shillings each? This, of course, includes countless detailed decisions as to price policy.

(c) Determining to whom the business can and should sell them. This, of course, involves market research and the development of new avenues and methods of distribution.

(d) Determining when lines should be added or withdrawn. This includes the study of the demand so as to suggest directions in which the range may be improved, or to give an informed judgment on suggestions from other quarters. It also includes direct responsibility for seeing that the supply of new products is adequate both as regards frequency and design to secure the established market and the winning of new markets. It also includes all the detailed arrangements necessary to ensure that when a new line is launched the efforts of all departments of the business, design, production, advertising and selling, are united behind the new venture, focussed as to time, quantity, and range of effort.

(e) If this duty is to be fulfilled satisfactorily, it involves a constant and systematic study of the products and,. methods of competitors.

(f) Determining the quantities at which the business should aim in the sale of each of its lines. This involves economic study of general business trends, of the specific conditions and trends in the given industry and enterprise, of local variations in general trends, and so on. From such studies should issue the general budget on which sales and production plans are based.

(g) Determination of the standard of quality which the business should seek to maintain.

This marketing division or department should not be placed "over" production and sales. It should be a parallel department with its own clearly defined duties and functions of a planning and co-ordinating type, such as have been indicated. In the event of failure in adjustment, the Managing Director should continue to exercise his function of control as at present. Nor is a very large staff required. Some research workers, a small clerical staff, three or four sub-managers, should meet the requirements of even a large business. But the chief of the department should be the best subordinate manager with the most initiative, imagination, foresight and commercial judgment whom the managing director has available.

It may be urged that all these duties and functions are already being attended to by someone. No business can continue if they are not. But the point is that duties which are attended to by someone as an appendix to other preoccupations are usually carried out anyhow. The question of the composition of the price-list is an example. The man who is primarily interested in production naturally presses for simplicity, if he knows any thing about the economies of machine processing. The man who is primarily responsible for selling naturally and inevitably presses for constant novelty and a wide range of choice. It is easier to sell. All too frequently there is a conflict of these two specialised interests. A busy managing director is called in to make a snap decision if he is a strong man, or to suggest a compromise if he is of a more accommodating character, when what is wanted is continuous and detailed study designed to integrate all the various considerations involved into a progressive and unified policy.

Such unification is a continuous job. It is not a matter of occasional decision. And it can only be carried out effectively and satisfactorily if there are definite organs, live organs, within the organism specialised for that purpose. Imagine a man whose nervous system only functioned intermittently, or whose limbs went about their business without reference to his senses.

This suggestion involves nothing more than providing specialised parts of any business organisation to carry out those functions of the early market, which in the pressure of the industrial revolution have been forgotten. As the sub-division of labour has proceeded, the manufacturing and the transport and the selling activities of the original handicraft producer-distributor have been replaced by complex and highly articulated special departments. The knowledge which he absorbed when he went to market has been overlooked. And if the principle of specialisation on which business has proceeded is right, it cannot fill the gap by tacking this function rather vaguely on to the duties of other specialists. It must provide for it specifically and effectively.

If this course is taken, it meets the main difficulties which have been described. The existence of a strong and effective marketing department in any business will not only provide in practice for more constant study and clearer decisions on those imponderables on which the most vital factors in prosperity are largely based. In addition, it will focus the thought of all concerned afresh. They will be brought to appreciate that before production is undertaken or selling can begin, there is a prior process—the study of the market and the determination of what is to be done. They will redress the balance of their thought and approach distribution questions from the correct angle—an angle which no longer takes the factory for granted, and sees what can be done about it—but goes back of the factory to the consumer, appreciating that no productive effort is justified save as a direct response to existing or potential demand.

It will also do much, as much as can be done, to secure the machine producer against the greatly increased risks of manufacturing in advance. In many markets, especially those concerned with consumer goods, it is difficult, if not impossible, to forecast sales in advance with complete accuracy. In the case of producers' goods it is on the whole easier. Where it is difficult no one is very willing to undertake the job of guessing. It becomes divided up among a number of departments who make *ad hoc* adjustments following the actual trend of sales. This is convenient in the sense that no individual bears the responsibility for the very expensive consequences of guessing wrong. But in effect the guess has been made all the same. After all, the factory has to produce something. It is much better that a specified individual should be charged with this responsibility of making a for ward estimate, and that the higher control should view with a wide elasticity the inevitable cases when that estimate is falsified by events.

Such a marketing department will go as far as lies within the power of the individual concern towards solving the problem created by the increased instability of large areas of demand, due to the fact that they are concerned with that greater proportion of the consumer's income which is available for optional expenditure. The last main difficulty was the greater vulnerability of demand due to the international character of business and its consequent susceptibility to general waves of economic optimism or pessimism and to political influences.

In both these cases the individual manufacturer is dealing with factors partly or largely outside his control. As an individual he can do no more than strive his utmost to keep in touch with the facts and take all possible steps within his own competence to neutralise adverse influences. In connection with general economic movements he can, at least, have the available figures before him. And if he studies them objectively, he will be doing something to secure that his decisions, as far as his business is concerned, are not influenced by that general mass suggestion which does so much to exaggerate the effects of the trade cycle.

In addition the manufacturer can do a great deal in his corporate capacities as a member of his trade and as a citizen of his country. Co-operative advertising and co-operative exploitation of export markets, co-operative research into market factors, and the elimination of overlapping as between the research departments of advertising agencies and other organisations which are trying to throw light on distribution—in all these directions there are opportunities for combined action. They will be considered in a later chapter.

Judging by their published statistics, there is not a single Government in Europe which has yet grasped the elementary fact that business depends on consumption. Measurement of income, of purchasing power, of its distribution by areas, classes and commodities, of the channels of distribution and their relative importance—all these vital facts are lacking. Till the manufacturer has them, he must go on guessing—and inevitably guessing wrong. As trader and as citizen he has a double line of attack on these larger problems.

As citizen he can at least do his utmost to curb the national emotions and political prejudices which cut across economic development. He can demand that every policy be put to the acid test—does it or does it not tend towards a higher standard of living for the people? On the achievement of that higher standard his life as a business man depends.

Size of the Business Unit as a Factor in the Efficiency of Marketing[31]

H. B. Price, Chairman

The general topic of this session is size of the business unit as a factor in the efficiency of marketing. The economies of size of the business unit although fairly well established for manufacturing industries are not so discernable in marketing. The organization for selling introduces problems of efficiency that are different from those of physical supply, and apparently costs of selling respond to the influence of size somewhat differently than the costs of handling and storing products. Price realization also relates to size of the business unit in a distinctive manner. Research in marketing has thus far neither differentiated these various aspects of marketing clearly nor pointed out distinctly the relation of each aspect to size and cost of operation; nor has as much attention been given to the factors affecting the efficiency of marketing as of manufacturing or agricultural production. A considerable body of material bearing on the problem is now available from the various public and private marketing research agencies. The object of this round table is to present some of these materials from representative fields in marketing research.

PAUL L. MILLER.—Any advantage that a relatively large-scale marketing business has over a relatively small-scale one must come from one or both of two factors. Either its unit costs must be lower, or the prices that it is able to secure for the product must be higher, or perhaps it has advantage from both of these factors. With respect to operating costs, we must grant that volume of business is very influential. The principles of large-scale production apply to marketing operations as well as to those of manufacturing.[32] In so

[31] From *American Economic Review*, vol. 23, 1933, supp. 98–107.

[32] Clark and Weld, *Marketing Agricultural Products*, p. 470.

far as the utilization of equipment and plant is concerned the cases are quite the same. Many marketing businesses have mechanical and routine operations that can be organized and performed most efficiently in a relatively large-scale unit. It is true perhaps that buying and selling operations cannot be as minutely specialized and reduced to simple routines as many other types of tasks. But in the case of many farm products that may be sold in quantity to large-scale buyers on definite specifications, selling is much less personal and more amenable to organization than in the case of many other products. It would seem to be largely a matter of training and experience together with administrative ability. If so, large-scale enterprises have a great advantage in their ability to command the highest type of service.

The price advantages afforded by volume of business are no less real if somewhat more elusive than the cost advantages. They obtain in the broad markets of farm products and particularly in the ease of those commodities that are sufficiently standardized to be sold on the basis of description. In such markets sellers best able to make the commodity available in quantity and in accordance with precise quality specifications are able to secure the superior outlets. Ability to supply the commodity on such terms, other conditions remaining the same, is within limits a function of volume.

The price advantages enjoyed by such suppliers must be sharply distinguished from those that may in some instances be forced from the market through some degree of monopoly control. The former price advantages result from a more economical meeting of the demand than is possible on the part of small-scale suppliers, who usually cannot cater to the same class of trade but must depend upon intermediaries for their outlets. The latter price advantage, where it can be realized, is obviously purely exploitive and predatory.

It is in the country end of agricultural marketing where marketing business units appear to be particularly undersized. In the wholesaling of farm products business units are for the most part large-scale enterprises and, generally speaking, margins are narrow and costs are low. But, in the country this is not the case. The exceptions to this are in those commodities and in those districts where farmers have co-operated to market on a larger scale and more efficient basis. Outstanding examples of such developments are the large-scale, co-operative marketing enterprises of the citrus fruit growers of California and of the poultry and egg producers of California, Washington, and Oregon. Other examples might be cited. Nearly every commodity furnishes many instances of significant steps taken by farmers to improve farm marketing. Generally speaking, progress has been greatest in highly specialized producing regions, remote from the principal market centers, and in the ease of commodities that go to consumers without processing.

In the ease of grain and livestock, as well as of other commodities produced widely in a general or mixed type of farming, country marketing generally is on a small and inefficient scale. Most of the farmers' co-operatives are loosely formed, and indifferently supported. For the most part they lead a precarious existence competing with local buyers. The majority of the farmers sell to local buyers, many of whom are small, independent operators. Others are representatives of packers, milling firms, or wholesale marketing agencies. These large buying agencies often buy at many shipping points scattered over a wide territory. As rural transportation and communication have improved, such buyers have extended their country buying systems and taken a larger and larger place in buying directly from farmers. They have had little trouble in either driving out the local independent buyers or making them their representatives.

This might seem to indicate that they have been able to place country buying on a much more efficient basis, and they doubtless are more efficient than the independent dealers;[33] yet the extent to which they can increase the efficiency of country marketing is distinctly limited. The reasons for this are first, that they cannot greatly reduce the expense of buying and handling the commodity at the point of contact with farmers. Farmers are naturally pleased to have as many bids to consider as possible. This seems very advantageous to them, and in a sense it is. Yet it makes farm buying very expensive because of duplication of effort. In numerous grain shipping localities in Iowa there are three or more grain companies represented with operators and

[33] E. G. Nourse, *Recent Economic Changes*, National Bureau of Economic Re search, Vol. II, p. 580.

plants where one set of equipment could handle the grain at much lower cost. Cost studies of local marketing agencies reveal wide ranges of costs and close correlations between costs and volume of business.[34] Yet, in the usual local market situation the business is split up among several handlers so that average marketing costs are much higher than they need to be. This seems to be the price that the farmer has to pay for having buyers carry their competition for his, products down to the farm.

A second reason why the integration of local buying by central market agencies does not go far towards greater efficiency in the marketing of the products of a particular community is that such buying agencies cannot be said to widen the market for the locality. In fact where the local trade passes into the hands of a relatively few central market interests, the product of the community may be less widely distributed than formerly. Add to this possibility, the fact that the farmer in his individual capacity is far from being an expert salesman, and there can be little doubt that these developments in large-scale country buying weaken rather than strengthen his trading position. These cursory observations of the inefficiency of local marketing point to small-scale farm selling as its chief cause. The buyers, large, and small, in the country trade cannot be held responsible for the wasteful methods of marketing evident in most localities. They are, generally speaking, not the cause of these conditions, but rather the effects. Farmers' co-operative agencies, organized in a manner that forces them to compete with local buyers, have been able scarcely to hold their own, and have not increased the efficiency of marketing. The roots of the problem lie too deep to be eradicated by reform methods that only aim to substitute one type of middleman for another. For improvement in conditions the farmers need to combine so as to reorganize farm marketing on a large-scale basis.

Much of the co-operative movement among farmers has missed the main opportunities to increase the efficiency of agricultural marketing, which lie in the handling of the commodity at the farm and at local points and in the development of efficient sales units to administer the selling of the product of a district. The farmers of a given locality need to combine on a sufficient scale to enable

[34] Clark and Weld, *Marketing Agricultural Products*, Chapter XXI.

them to substitute large-scale for small-scale methods in the trade of the locality. Much of co-operative marketing fails to bring together the farmers of a given locality or district in sufficient numbers for most efficient local handling of the commodity. The result is that much of co-operative marketing among farmers has failed to increase the efficiency of marketing in the country trade. These weaknesses of local and regional co-operatives cannot be remedied by combining such enterprises into central or even national units. Such agencies cannot remedy inadequate co-operation among the farmers themselves.

NATHANAEL H. ENGLE.—In attempting to measure statistically the influence of size upon the operating efficiency of a wholesale establishment one of the first problems is the selection of a unit of size. Practically this is not a serious problem since there is little choice. Theoretically, there are a number of alternative criteria of size which should be considered.

One of the more definite of these is a unit of physical volume such as a ton of merchandise. Another method is the use of the individual sales transaction. Other methods of measuring the size of a merchandising establishment are the number of square feet of floor space, the number of employees, or the volume of sales. The last of these is the one which I have selected by a sort of Hobson's choice to measure the effect of size upon the operating efficiency of wholesale merchants dealing in manufactured goods. For most purposes the sales dollar is as good a measure as any of the others.

TABLE 1

TOTAL EXPENSES[c] AS PER CENT OF NET SALES FOR WHOLESALE MERCHANTS IN SELECTED TRADES, BY SIZE OF BUSINESS, UNITED STATES, 1929[a]

Size Groups (net sales in thousands of dollars)	Kind of Business (Trade)							
	Drug (general line)	Dry Goods (specialty)	Electrical Goods	Groceries	Hardware (general line)	Hardware (specialty)	Paints and Varnishes	Radio Sets
Total	13.3	10.3	16.1	9.8	18.5	19.5	21.8	15.9
Under 50	17.8	13.5	21.6	13.8	24.3	27.3	28.2	26.7
50 to 100	14.8	12.8	20.1	8.9	21.5	21.9	24.0	21.1
100 to 200	16.1	10.0	18.9	9.0	20.4	22.9	22.5	20.3
200 to 300	13.7	10.3	17.9	9.6	19.0	20.2	23.8	20.7
300 to 400	12.9	9.4	17.9	8.9	20.1	19.7	22.9	16.3
400 to 500	14.2	*9.0*	17.0	*8.7*	20.4	19.4	20.5	18.4
500 to 1,000	13.6	9.7	16.7	9.5	18.7	21.6	22.0	16.2
1,000 to 2,000	13.3	10.0	15.2	9.7	18.1	18.1	19.3	*14.1*
2,000 to 4,000	13.1	9.8	14.5	9.6	17.9	13.6	*18.0*	—
4,000 to 8,000	*12.8*	11.6	*12.5*	11.8	17.3	*12.3*	—	—
8,000 to 15,000	13.4	12.1	—	14.8	*16.7*	—	—	—
15,000 to 25,000	—	—	—	—	20.8	—	—	—

Certainly for purposes of comparison between different establishments operating in the same year it offers a definite and easily understood size unit.

After the size unit has been selected, a second problem is the determination of the best measure of operating efficiency. If by operating efficiency we mean the degree of economy with which the economic factors of production are used in performing the marketing functions, it is reasonable to assume that the money costs incurred in performing these functions roughly measure the Degree of marketing efficiency. I have acted upon this assumption and have used the operating expense ratios compiled by the Census Bureau.

I have based this study entirely upon statistics which I have helped to compile while with the Bureau of the Census. The facts have been assembled and summarized from a special series of trade studies for eight groups of wholesale merchants, each of which carried a different line of manufactured goods. For the most part these establishments constitute a homogeneous group of merchants operating in much the same way and performing most of the wholesaling functions. In addition, I have made a special study from the schedules of 2,418 general line wholesale merchants in the grocery trade in which I attempt to measure the effect of size upon a number of specific marketing functions as well as the combined total of such functions.

A few conclusions may be drawn from the statistics shown in Table 1 which covers the total expenses for eight trades. Without exception, the very small-scale establishments in all the trades reported relatively high operating expenses. Aside from this one similarity, the different trades were affected variously by size of business. In four trades, electrical goods, hardware specialties, paints and varnishes, and radio sets, the total expenses expressed as percentages o net sales declined with minor variations as the size of. the business increased. A large scale of operations is not always best, however. In two trades, dry goods and groceries, total expenses declined from 18.5 per cent and 13.8 per cent of net sales to 9.0 per cent and 8.7 per cent respectively as size of business increased to $400,000-$500,000. As the size of business increased thereafter expenses increased to 12.1 per cent and 14.8 per cent respectively for the establishments with sales between eight and fifteen million dollars. In the two remaining trades the evidence is less conclusive. However, expenses showed an increase in the largest size group.

TABLE 2

NUMBER OF ESTABLISHMENTS AND NET SALES BY SIZE OF BUSINESS, WHOLESALE MERCHANTS—GENERAL LINE GROCERS, UNITED STATES, 1929[a]

	Size Groups (net sales in thousands of dollars)	Number of Establishments	Net Sales	Per Cent of Total Net Sales
	Total	2,418	$1,708,437,660	100.00
I	100 to 500	1,335	376,274,075	22.02
II	500 to 1,000	671	471,712,411	27.61
III	1,000 to 3,000	351	548,896,540	32.14
IV	3,000 to 8,000	55	242,400,418	14.18
V	8,000 to 25,000	6	69,154,216	4.05

TABLE 3

EFFECT OF SIZE ON EXPENSE AND OPERATING ITEMS, WHOLESALE MERCHANTS—GENERAL LINE GROCERIES, UNITED STATES, 1929[b]

Size Groups	Per Cent of Net Sales							
	Total Expenses[c]	Total Wages[d]	Direct Selling Expense[e]	Interest Paid[f]	Rent Paid[f]	Credit Sales[f]	Returns and Allowances[f]	Inventories
Total	9.83	5.56	2.57	0.49	0.52	85.99	2.12	14.48
I	9.03	4.72	2.49	0.53	0.68	81.75	1.70	14.01
II	9.48	5.29	2.43	0.49	0.54	86.20	1.87	14.62
III	9.50	5.44	2.39	0.49	0.46	86.15	2.82	14.10
IV	11.08	6.55	2.91	0.46	0.41	91.90	1.70	14.70
V	14.83	9.51	3.98	0.43	0.46	85.31	3.05	18.23

[a] *Census of Wholesale Distribution, Trade Series.* The number of establishments for each group constitutes all of those reporting to the census bureau—practically all in the United States.

[b] *Census of Wholesale Distribution*, special tabulation. No establishments from communities of less than 10,000 people and no establishments with sales below $100,000 per year.

[c] Exclusive of net profits.

[d] Includes salaries of hired employees, but excludes salaries of proprietors and firm members.

[e] Includes salaries, commissions, bonuses, and expenses of salesmen for only those establishments reporting salesmen.

[f] Percentage based upon statistics from only those establishments reporting these items.

Few if any generalizations are indicated by the statistics in Table 1. If it were not for the dry goods specialty wholesalers whose costs increased in the larger brackets, a rule for specialty wholesalers might have been suggested to the effect that costs vary inversely with the size of the business, The more reasonable explanation appears to be that sales had not been pushed far enough by the four specialty groups to incur increased costs. The evidence, therefore, as to the influence of size of business upon wholesale mer chants as a group is not conclusive. For a few specific trades, however, such as groceries, it seems clear that large-scale business is not the most efficient.

In order to determine the incidence of size upon specific marketing functions, I prepared a special tabulation for 2,418 grocery wholesalers. (See Tables 2 and 3.) Summarizing the facts brought out in these tables it appears that for wholesale merchants in the grocery business, the total costs of performing the marketing functions vary directly with the size of the business after sales have reached a minimum of $100,000 per year. Expenses incurred for labor also increase as the size of the business increases. Selling efficiency as measured by the costs of performing the selling function decreases as the sales volume becomes larger. On the other hand, efficiency in performing the storage function as measured by rent expenditures varies directly with sales volume and is greatest with sales between $3,000,000 and $8,000,000. In so far as interest payments are a clue to efficiency in performing the function of market finance the large-scale houses seem to have the advantage. The granting of credit, however, which also reflects the finance function, does not indicate any very definite relation to sales volume. The two remaining indexes of marketing efficiency, returns and allowances and inventories, indicate that the very large establishments are least efficient.

In conclusion I believe that the facts brought together in this paper indicate: that a very small scale of operations for wholesalers of manufactured goods is less efficient than a somewhat larger scale, that there is a fairly wide range in which size of business has very little measurable effect upon operating efficiency, that there is a maximum size in some trades and possibly in all beyond which operating efficiency diminishes and, finally, that the incidence of size upon marketing efficiency is not uniform for all of the marketing functions.

W.H.S. STEVENS.—In manufacturing industry based upon the Federal Trade Commission's intensive study of plant cost by size of plant in the bread industry for a period of years, we may conclude, first, that though both price (as indicated by sales realization) and cost per unit decline as the size of plant increases, costs decline more rapidly than sales realization and net profit per unit tends to rise. Second, that if the bread results are typical, multiple plant operation does not reduce the cost of producing and selling for plants of the same size.

In the field of retailing as in the field of manufacturing the effect of size may be examined from the standpoint of size of the retail store or since the growth of large chains, from the standpoint of size measured by units operated.

For the effect of size of establishment, the most comprehensive figures available are those of the Harvard Bureau of Business

Research. This organization has compiled as percentages of sales, the gross margins, operating expenses and net profits of several kinds of business for varying periods of from one to ten years or more.

The most comprehensive of these sets of figures is in the department store field where the figures cover the eleven years, 1921-31. The larger stores average substantially higher gross margin, operating expense, and net profit percentages on sales, the higher net profits, of course, arising from the fact that the gross margins of the larger stores are relatively higher as compared with the operating expenses than is true of the smaller sizes of stores. Retail shoe stores show the same tendency as department stores. Excluding the smallest of the grocery size groups, the larger sizes of stores usually show the highest gross margins, as high or higher operating expenses than the smaller stores, and the largest net profit percentages.

All three of these retail lines, it will be observed, differ from manufacturing in showing higher operating expenses for the larger establishments. In jewelry retailing, however, an entirely different tendency appears and the results more closely resemble those in manufacturing. Here, both gross profits and operating expenses tend to decrease with the size of store, the latter figure somewhat more than the former, with a consequent increase in net profit for the larger establishments. Automobile tire and accessory dealers show the same tendencies as jewelry retailers though the figures in this case cover only the year 1928.

Summarizing the results of the Harvard studies, therefore, it appears possible to conclude: that in groceries, department stores, and shoes, the tendency is for gross margin, operating expense, and net profit percentages of sales to increase with increase in the size of store, a greater increase in the margin than in operating expense accounting for the increased net profit; that in jewelry and automobile accessory retailing, gross margins and operating expenses both tend to fall as the size of the establishment increases, the net profit, however, tending to increase because of a lesser decline in the gross margin than in the operating expense; operating expenses do not therefore tend to decline generally in retailing with increases in the size of unit as in manufacturing but in both, net profit tends to vary directly with the size of the particular manufacturing or retailing establishment.

It is by no means certain how far and to what extent variations of operating expenses with the size of establishment are actually dependent upon the size of the store involved. The reason is that there is a considerable volume of data in both the Harvard Bureau and the census figures indicating that operating expenses tend to vary, to some extent, directly with the size of the city, particularly when comparisons involve very large and very small cities and it appears obvious that at least within certain limits the size of store will vary with the size of the city.

The Harvard Bureau of Business Research has tabulated its department store figures for 1929 in nine size volume groups. In these figures, the variations in the gross and net profits and operating expenses by size of city appear to be appreciably greater than by size of store, thus seeming to lend support to the conclusion that the size of city is of greater importance than the size of store in producing variations in financial results.

Time has been lacking to permit extensive computations from census figures necessary to any generalized statement as to the effect of size of city. I have, however, compared the per cent of operating expense to sales for ten kinds of business in all cities in Pennsylvania of under 10,000 and 10,000 to 80,000 population with those for Allentown (92,000 population), Scranton (148,000), Pittsburgh (669,000), and Philadelphia (practically, 2,000,000). For most of these ten kinds of business, cities of 10,000 to B0,000 population commonly show higher operating expenses (proprietors' salaries being included by the census method of average wage of full-time store employee) than those of under 10,000. The average operating expense percentages for these two smaller sizes of cities in Pennsylvania, moreover, are also usually lower than those for any of the four larger cities mentioned, in each of the ten kinds of business, though exceptions occur particularly in grocery, grocery and meat, and variety. At this point, however, the effect of size of city becomes less apparent. Allentown, though under 100,000, is higher than Philadelphia in six of the ten kinds of business while Scranton is likewise higher for a majority of the groups than either Pittsburgh or Philadelphia. Pittsburgh also shows a higher operating expense ratio than Philadelphia in at least six of the ten kinds of business.

This brings us to a consideration of the difference in the operating results of single and multiple unit (chain) stores.

Census figures of the per cent of operating expenses to sales, for both chains and independents, are available for twelve kinds of business. In every one of these types of business, with the exception of grocery, department stores, and women's shoe stores, the chains show a higher ratio of operating expenses to sales. The figures of gross and net profit, of course, are not shown by the census.

Although multiple unit operation in retailing apparently leads to higher ratios of operating expenses to sales, therefore, as compared with unit operation because of differences in functions, this does not necessarily mean that the gross margins or operating expenses involved in getting goods from the producer to the consumer are higher through the multiple unit operations of the chain. Dr. N.C. Engl., formerly of the Wholesale Division of the Census of Distribution, has furnished me with certain computations in which the census independent, wholesale, and retail figures of operating expenses are combined, for five lines, clothing and furnishings, drugs and drug sundries, groceries and food specialties, meat and meat products, and house furnishings. In all these lines except the last named, the combination wholesaler-retailer operating expense percentages exceed those of the chain. Dr. Schmaltz arrived also at the same conclusion for groceries in an article in the *Harvard Business Review* combining the results of the Harvard Bureau's studies of grocery chains with their combined figures for grocery wholesaling and retailing. Offsetting this to some extent, however, is the greater service of the independents who more generally give credit and delivery to consumers.

One further point in connection with the effect of size in retailing concerns the relation of the number of retail units to operating expenses, gross margins, and net profits. Harvard Bureau figures are available for 1929 for all three of these items in the ease of shoe, drug, and grocery chains though for only three size groups. Because of the small number of groups, the results are not entirely satisfactory. There is some indication of a decrease in gross profit with increases in the number of units in shoes and drugs with a better indication of an increase in this item in groceries. Operating expense in creases with size in groceries but declines in shoes and drugs while net profit increases in groceries and drugs and, with some qualification, in shoes.

The census figures on this point are for operating expenses only. I have used twelve types of business in this comparison. In only three of these, office appliances, variety, and possibly hardware chains, is there any tendency for operating expenses to increase with the number of stores operated. Drugs and shoes are, in my judgment, indeterminate though the tendency, if there is any, seems to be for the expense to decline with increases in the number of stores. Department stores I would also class as indeterminate. The remaining lines, women's apparel, furniture, auto accessories, grocery, combination grocery and meat, and possibly installment jewelry show a down ward trend with increases in stores operated. The figures are open to some question because in drugs and the two grocery groups, warehousing and other overhead is not included for the large chains operating warehouses. This might easily affect the showing for the larger chain groups.

As in the case of unit stores, however, there are certain indications that operating expense variations of chains according to the number of stores operated may be due no more or perhaps even less to the number of stores involved than to their location. Chain operating expenses by size of city are available in the census data for only four kinds of business, grocery, combination grocery and meat, shoes, and drugs. In each case, there is an appreciable increase in operating expense with the size of city which is especially pronounced in shoes and combination grocery and meat.

Drugs present the only case in which the census has to date broken down the figures by size of chain within the size of city and though the figures are only for cities of over 100,000 and under 80,000 population, the rather decided differences between them would tend to confirm the view that size of city is a factor of at least equal importance with the size of establishment.

The fact that the variations of expenses are so great for drug chains of the same size operating in cities of different size combined with the fact that in cities of the same size there are still important variations in expenses for different sizes of these chains points to the conclusion that the effects of either size of store or size of chain upon gross margins, operating expenses, or net profits cannot and will not be thoroughly understood until size volume figures are analyzed according to the population of the cities in which they are operated. The Harvard

Bureau must be given credit for recognizing that the size of city was an important factor in operating results and they have in the past presented a number of analyses of this character along with those by size of establishment. An analysis of their past results for unit stores by size of establishment in cities of varying ranges of population would be extremely valuable. And the same applies to their wholesale figures. Such a composite breakdown is apparently not practicable from the published census figures, though the information necessary for it was obtained. It would seem more than worthwhile in any subsequent census to publish either such a breakdown or the data for making it.

W.J. DONALD.—The merger movement is not over and once financial markets become favorable to security flattens, we may well expect it to return in considerable volume. Meantime, the kinds of mergers that are taking place, for the most part, are the purchase of plant, goodwill, patents, and business of small companies by large companies, and the purchase of the securities of a small company by a large company, often conditional on net profits.

The marketing advantages and economies to be secured from mergers vary widely according to the class of merger or combination of classes of merger. Among those which have been generally assumed are the following: stabilization of price in highly competitive markets, standardization of products in the interests of a lower price and a lower cost of production from large-scale continuous operations, reduction of expense of advertising, reduction of the sales force, reduction of the total number of branch offices and branch office expense, improvement in the quality of marketing staff service available in the marketing of all products in the line, the rounding out of a family of products, reduction of sales administration overhead, reduction of sales traveling expense, reduction of transportation charges through elimination of cross shipments, strengthening of the position of the company in reciprocal selling, strengthening of the position of the merged company in relation to large dealers, especially department stores, chains and syndicates, reduction of the number of drops and the amount of distressed merchandise once the initial stages of the merger are completed, partial elimination of competition from inferior products, advantages of more adequate financing of purchases, especially through an allied installment credit corporation, increased security for trade marks, making possible a stronger policy of selective distribution.

While not all of these marketing advantages of mergers apply to all mergers and while many of the plans that could have been realized have not functioned effectively in many cases, and while the marketing aspect of mergers has been most neglected, nevertheless, it is my opinion that the possibilities are quite as great as have been claimed and that they will yet be realized if sound marketing policies are developed for each individual situation.

Pay-Dirt Fundamentals of World Marketing[35]

It is strange but nevertheless true that in many instances concerns which consistently apply the principles of successful merchandising and selling at home, seem to lose sight of the prime requisites upon entering the foreign market. It is the rule rather than the exception for a concern to initiate its entry into the world market by engaging in all manner of non-productive practices and policies which experience has long since proved are not suited to the satisfactory development of the business for the particular product.

This anomaly of action to experience seems to be induced by an underlying belief that the world market is different in most respects from the home market, requiring radical departure from the proved methods of domestic success in its exploitation. It is further abetted by the advices of the host of foreign specialists engaged in the business of selling services to the world trader and who are not versed in the product—a case, almost, of the blind leading the blind.

In point of fact the principles of successful world market merchandising and selling are identical with those which exist for your product in the domestic market. This condition facilitates your task tremendously, since you are not obliged to learn a complete new set of commercial tricks. Engaging in world trade is a vastly different proposition from entering another line of business, the requirements of which are unknown to you.

True, the extension of your present activities to the foreign field requires the working of new markets, but this is simply the embracement of more territory. For the most part these are markets in which the competitive situation is not so rigorous as at home and which, therefore, will return for the exertion of proportionately intelligent and seasoned effort on your part a

[35] From V. D. Collins, *World Marketing*, Philadelphia: Lippincott, 1935, pp. 107–24.

substantially greater volume of business and profit than is afforded by the domestic mar et. On the other hand while the principles of distribution and selling remain the same in themselves, there are certain inherent differences in their application to the world-markets which must be given consideration if the fullest measure of success is to be enjoyed.

So that before you undertake to formulate marketing policies to promote the sale of your product abroad it is essential that the fundamental principles and objectives be crystallized in your mind. Only by this process will you be able to resist the natural and otherwise irresistible tendency to divergence from them, in the essential deviation of detail under which these principles are to be employed.

And in this connection *the prime objective must necessarily be that your efforts produce constantly the maximum profitable sale for the product* permitted by the limitations inherent to your capital structure and competitive standing. *This basic objective must therefore take precedence in your mind at all times in the determination of any and all policy and action.*

The Fundamentals of Mass-Merchandising

Now there is a vast and general misconception regarding the specific business of selling both at home and abroad. Surprisingly enough this misconception extends beyond the layman, where it is perhaps excusable, into the very ranks of the high-priests who are actually engaged in directing the business of selling. Unfortunately it is further fostered by much of the available literature in exposition of the subject which is misleading in the basic conception of the position which selling occupies, although perhaps accurate enough in the presentation of incidental detail. This misdirection is due, not to willful intent to mislead, but rather to failure to recognize the change in fundamental requirements brought about by the new economy, and to assign to these altered fundamentals the proper relative evaluation of the importance which they present individually to the subject as a whole.

We have since the 19th century undergone a radical change in the fundamentals of most business, appreciation of which is essential to all commercial success today. The individualism of the 19th century, under which all human relationships were conducted, governed the principles of manufacturing and selling. During this period custom methods of manufacture to the individual requirements and customer methods of selling suited to the individual psychology prevailed. It was during this period that the salesman, that shining exponent of individualism, became the glorified emblem of business success, a conception that has largely been carried through into the present by many.

Under the new mass economy of the world we can no longer afford to produce a majority of products for, or to adapt selling methods to, the peculiarities of individual requirements. The product must be adapted to the necessity, utility, or enjoyment of the masses. Consequently production must be arranged on a mass basis, and merchandising and selling effort applied to the fundamentals of mass requirements.

These fundamentals of mass merchandising consist of (1) mass consumer acceptance, (2) mass consumer accessibility, and (8) mass consumer consciousness. In the presentation of the requirements of successful modern business I have stressed first the elementary of profitable sales expectancy as governing all subsequent policy and effort. And this is determined in turn by the collective weight of these three pay-dirt fundamentals of mass merchandising.

The Requirements for Consumer Acceptance

The fundamental of consumer acceptance which formerly depended largely upon individual salesmanship has changed materially under mass methods of merchandising, and while personal salesmanship still performs a very definite and important function in business it no longer dominates as it did formerly. The personal salesmanship of the past was the salesmanship of product. Today personal salesmanship is for the most part confined to its effectiveness in selling to the trade channels of consumer distribution rather than to the consumer directly. Further it is not the salesmanship of product but rather it is the salesmanship of *Profit Opportunity*. True, salesmanship still exists in putting the product over, but it is the mass salesmanship of advertising in the creation of consumer consciousness.

As we have already stated the consumer purchases the product for its necessity, utility, or the pleasure it may afford to the gratification of desire, or for all three of these characteristics combined. These properties which lead to consumer desire constitute what we call the "sales appeal" of the product and it must be obvious that since these properties are inherent to the product itself, sales appeal is also an inherent characteristic of the product.

The properties which constitute sales appeal or *consumer acceptance*, as we prefer to call it, are produced by the creative genius of the manufacturing organization producing the product. They have their origin in the design and engineering laboratories of the manufacturer and the extent of consumer acceptance for the product is determined largely by the extent to which these properties have been built into it.

Thus it is that the product must have literally sold itself to the consumer by virtue of its inherent necessity, utility, or pleasure characteristics before it has left the production line, if it is to provide for the manufacturer the full measure of commercial success and permanency essential to consistent and adequate return on the capital invested in the business. Remember that no amount of sales or advertising effort can impart to the product a single iota of consumer acceptance which is not honestly inherent to it.

Since you are competitive in the domestic market we are justified in assuming that your product has in general the inherent requirements for consumer acceptance essential to successful merchandising in the foreign field. We are at least assured that it possesses these requirements to the same extent as does the product of your American competition, and may therefore be expected to compete in the foreign market with the American product.

The Requirements for Consumer Accessibility

Let us then direct our attention to *foreign consumer accessibility*, the second of the pay-dirt fundamentals for achieving the maximum profitable sale of your product abroad. In a subsequent chapter we shall formulate the requirements of the third fundamental, namely *consumer consciousness*. The principal requirements to maximum consumer accessibility may be epitomized as follows:

(a) That the specific market which you are working must be adequately provided with the distribution facilities through which the product is to be made accessible to the maximum number of *potential* customers. This requires

(b) that no trade channel of distribution may monopolize more of the territory than its capital and organization facilities permit it to handle adequately, and further

(c) that each trade channel must be active in developing the maximum *profitable* possibilities for the product in the territory it serves. In order to do this it is necessary

(d) that each trade channel shall be content to operate at a reasonable and normal profit, and that your policies shall be such as to provide such a profit. And finally

(e) that there is no success without consistency and constancy of effort and the closer this attains to permanency the greater the degree of success.

Adequacy of Distribution Facilities

Merchandise markets are of necessity made up of consumers, as has been purposely emphasized previously in this text. Further we have defined the consumer as the individual with the purchasing power to buy the product. This qualification, however, only entitles him to be rated as a potential consumer. He does not become an active consumer until he buys. And he does not and will not buy until desire is created for the product by its inherent properties of consumer acceptance and the appeal consciousness which your merchandising methods must impress. *But neither consumer acceptance nor consumer consciousness can or will make him a real consumer if the essential of consumer accessibility is lacking.*

It is elementary to the business that the consumer will not seek out the product; the product must therefore seek the consumer out. For this reason consumer accessibility be comes the most important of the three pay-dirt fundamentals of mass merchandising. Now merchandise markets are not made up of wholesalers, retailers, selling agents, or trade channels of whatever character. These are merely the vehicles which provide consumer accessibility by conveying the merchandise from the manufacturer's production line into the consumer's hands. Moreover, with every link in the distribution chain through which the merchandise passes after it leaves the manufacturer's hands in its consumer objective, its inherent price is increasingly augmented. Further the higher the price of the merchandise the more difficult it becomes for the consumer to acquire it and the more limited becomes the consumer market for it in consequence. And as we have seen any artificial barrier which stands between the maximum of production and the widest possibility of distribution cannot, unless it is indispensable to the economy of the whole, survive.

All intermediary distribution channels are therefore but the accessory before the fact, and a necessary evil to be countenanced only so long as they perform indispensable service to the requirement of maximum profitable consumer accessibility. It is upon failure to understand this premise that so many a promising commercial venture has been wrecked. And it is as a consequence of this irrefutable and irremedial condition that all distribution policy must be de signed primarily to facilitate the accessibility of the product to the consumer. *Again we repeat, trade channels are only of service and other than a positive detriment to business to the extent that they fulfill the primary requirement of consumer accessibility.*

This essential of accessibility may be achieved through two methods only. The first is for the manufacturer himself to make the product directly available to the consumer. The second is for the manufacturer to make the product available through the intermediary trade channels which act as the vehicle of consumer supply.

In the first category the manufacturer may provide the direct to consumer accessibility by (a) mail-order (b) direct consumer solicitation by his salesmen, or (c), through the establishment of owned points of retail accessibility. These methods are all used in the domestic market with varying degree of success. In practice it has been found however that the cost of conveying the merchandise from manufacturer direct to consumer is substantially as great, if not greater, than the augmentation in price required by the normal trade channels, as a result of the complexity of organization functions and capital requirements and risks thereto which the manufacturer is obliged to assume and provide for in his consumer selling price.

These methods are employed to much less extent and with still less success in the foreign field. Here the almost in surmountable obstacles presented by the inherent lack of detailed market knowledge, and the necessity for capital investment on the part of the manufacturer not normally essential to the conduct of the business, all contribute to make selling on this basis difficult, hazardous, and more often than not unprofitable. Accordingly direct consumer selling is only justified where the nature of the product is such that it cannot be handled through intermediary trade channels.

In the second category the use of the normal intermediary trade channels of distribution provides the more commonly accepted and successful method of making the product of mass requirement accessible to the consumer. In its intermediary transfer the merchandise may pass from the hands of the manufacturer to a super-jobber, who in turn sells to the foreign wholesale trade which supplies the retail points essential to foreign consumer accessibility of the product.

Previously we have referred to a "primary source of supply", by which is meant the export source of supply of the product. In the distribution chain indicated above since the manufacturer himself does not export the product, the super-jobber represents the primary source of supply for the foreign market.

Now by accessibility or availability of the product is meant theoretically that every potential consumer located within the territory shall be able to inspect and purchase the product conveniently. As a practical matter this does not mean that the consumer living in sparsely inhabited areas shall find a retail outlet stocking a complete line of the product right around the next bend in the mountain trail. Nor does it mean that consumer accessibility is to be provided in regions where the potential consumer does not exist. The 11 million blacks in the Congo are not potential consumers for a majority of products.

It does require two things however. First that every potential consumer trading center shall provide a point at which samples at least of the product may be viewed and the order placed. And second, with the practical limitations to distribution arrangements to be discussed later, that collective centers of population which present a sufficiently large potential market for the product shall provide as many consumer display, purchasing, and supply points as can be supported with reasonable deference and consideration for the profit motive essential to all retail operations.

While the actual accomplishment of consumer accessibility lies in the hands of the intermediary trade channels, the responsibility for seeing that it is adequately provided lies directly with the primary source of supply, be it manufacturer or super-jobber. Further it must be evident that the further removed by intermediary trade channels the manufacturer is from the physical function of establishing the retail points of consumer accessibility, the less control he has over the essential of adequacy of distribution, and over the essentials which are next to be expounded. Consequently the more important becomes your initial investigation and subsequent check upon the adequacy and character of the distribution facilities which are being placed at your disposal and maintained by the trade channels to whom you have entrusted the handling of your product and the future of your profits in the foreign market.

Limitation of Territory to Trade-Coverage Facilities

Unfortunately it is human nature to want anything that can be had for nothing, even though its utility, and particularly its disadvantages, are not readily apparent at the moment. So it is only natural for the foreign trade channel, be it super-jobber, wholesaler, or retailer to endeavor to get you to assign all of the territory possible on an exclusive basis.

A rare avis indeed is he who has the intelligence to limit his aspirations, territorial or otherwise, to no more than he can handle and digest successfully. It is quite customary for a retailer, and usually one far removed from a first class operation at that, located in some such commercially forgotten and extinct city as Durazzo to solicit your representation not only at retail for Durazzo, or even at wholesale for the whole of Albania, but as a super-jobber for all of Europe, the Near East, and North Africa as well.

Obviously the ability of any trade channel to achieve maximum distribution and sale for your product within a territory is limited by the same considerations which limit the volume possibilities of your own enterprise at home, namely working capital and the organization facilities which only capital can provide. Based upon your conservative estimate of sales expectancy for a given market, it will be evident that a certain minimum working capital will be required on the part of whatever trade channel is to work the territory, and further that this capital must be devoted *exclusively* to the working of your line in order to achieve the minimum volume which the conditions indicate is readily possible.

The requirement as to capital is of first importance in securing a suitable outlet to handle your product, since capital is the master-tool with which the enterprise provides all of the other essentials to a successful selling job. These consist of adequate stocks of your merchandise with which to assure the supply of demand at least to the minimum set by your estimate of expectancy, travelling and selling expense in providing adequate retail points of consumer accessibility and proper supervision thereafter in their maintenance, and finally the financing of the credit requirements which are normal and inherent to the product. If the capital of the trade outlet is inadequate, or is spread so thinly over a number of lines that the minimum required to work your line is not available, then the arrangement can be neither satisfactory to you nor permanent.

The essential task therefore of the primary source of supply is to determine first what are the strategic points at which wholesale and retail facilities are essential, and second to direct all energy toward the provision of these facilities, limiting the territory to be served by each and every one to that which it is equipped to handle with satisfaction. In this connection experience has proved conclusively that a foreign outlet whose principal organization and facilities are located in one market, cannot adequately serve contiguous territories. In each country, therefore, it is essential to provide wholesale and retail channels whose operations are limited to serving the local territory in which they are located.

While the establishment of wholesale coverage lies in the hands of the primary source of supply to be shaped as desired, the provision of suitable and adequate retail points of consumer accessibility lies in the hands of the wholesaler in each of the markets. This vital function of the wholesale trade necessitates the most careful scrutiny on your part, for the retail points of consumer accessibility are the hinge upon which success or failure turns in the merchandising of your line. *Accordingly the establishment of retail facilities by the wholesaler should at all times receive your best attention, and when required your direct supervision and assistance.*

Necessity for Active Distribution Channels

In the selection of intermediary trade channels great importance also attaches to the character of the outlet as pertains to ability, experience, and initiative in achieving maximum distribution and sales. On the score of ability the outlet must possess qualifications which assure soundness of commercial judgment and management methods. On the score of experience it is desirable that the outlet should be qualified to handle your product as a result of previous successful activity with competitive merchandise in the same or similar category. Past performance is, of course, the best guide to ability and character.

And on the score of initiative the outlet must be of that active and energetic disposition which forever strives with the best that is in him to secure for the merchandise handled the maximum profitable sale under the existing conditions. This latter qualification is perhaps the most intangible and consequently the most difficult of all to assure in the selection of an outlet. In these days of limited business within local markets there are few organizations which can exist on the profits to be derived, from handling a single line of merchandise. The average local enterprise requires a large number of lines which are widely divergent in character and demand in order to make ends meet, and maintain the organization necessary to the sale of any of the individual products handled.

This diversity of sales effort leads to division of working capital, and more often than not of interest and attention, which is not conducive to the consistent devotion of the required effort essential to the promotion of each and every item handled. As a consequence there is an ever present tendency on the part of management to be satisfied when the over-all business of the enterprise is exhibiting a satisfactory return, even though some of the lines are not doing so well. Further when the reverse obtains there is a tendency to slacken effort on the items which are providing a satisfactory return in favor of those which are not, in other words to bolster up one at the expense of the other. And even under conditions which the trade considers entirely satisfactory, sales statistics may indicate to you that you are not realizing the reasonable share of the available business for your product which greater initiative and activity would make possible.

It requires exceptional initiative and energy on the part of multi-itemed enterprise to insure to your specific product at all times the effort and attention which it requires. The further the trade outlet is from the consumer in the distribution chain the greater is the importance of this consideration to the manufacturer or primary source of supply of the product. *In practice the only way to assure adequate handling of your product is through constant, consistent, and skillful supervision on your part.*

Normalcy of Profit Requirements

Here we have a very important requirement to the success of your merchandising venture through intermediary channels, namely the necessity for adhering to a reasonable and normal profit basis. Beyond the requirement that the merchandise itself be placed within reasonable physical reach of the consumer, *consumer accessibility requires further that the price of the merchandise be within reach of the maximum possible number of consumers.*

As we have pointed out in the forepart of this chapter every channel through which the merchandise passes in creases the inherent price of the product to the consumer. The higher the price becomes the more limited in size the potential market for the product becomes. At best the consumer selling price of merchandise in the world market which is handled through trade channels must be approximately 4 to 5 times the actual manufacturing cost, in order to provide the necessary manufacturers and trade spread and to pay for transportation and duty. *So that restriction of profit to that minimum which provides a reasonable and normal working margin under proper conditions of operation is essential to maximum consumer accessibility.*

Of course the price level for the similar product of the competition must determine largely what the consumer selling price must be, and the manufacturer's selling price to the trade determines what spread or margin of profit is available between this and the consumer selling price. There is however a natural tendency on the part of the trade to endeavor to monopolize the margin thus afforded beyond the point of reasonable and normal profit requirements. Where the distribution chain includes two or more intermediaries, such endeavor to monopolize profit margins on the part, for instance, of the super-jobber will result in removing the profit incentive essential to the wholesaler's ability to handle the product properly.

Where the wholesaler endeavors to secure more than a reasonable and normal profit, the profit incentive essential to the success of the retail channels is removed. If, in turn, the retailer endeavors to secure a larger spread than is normal, or to make up for the wholesaler's monopolization of spread, by increasing the price to the consumer, price accessibility of the product is decreased, market potentialities vanish, and business is forced into the hands of your competitors.

But there is still another profit requirement, and this one depends entirely upon you; and that is that *the trade must find the working of your product reasonably profitable under normal and proper conditions of operation.* This involves far more than the mere responsibility on your part to see that your manufacturer's selling price to the trade is in line with that of the competition. It involves that you are directly responsible to see that each of the intermediate trade channels is afforded a reasonable profit margin by its source of supply. It further involves responsibility on your part to see at all times that the product is maintained to the standards of quality set by the competition, in other words that consumer acceptability is maintained to the competitive level at least. Also that consumer consciousness is created for the product to at least the same extent as it is for the product of the competition.

And finally it requires that your general policies and methods of dealing with the trade shall be fair and reasonable. You must realize that the trade is in a position to treat the consumer no better than it is treated by the manufacturer of source of supply. So that the matter of fair and reasonable policies on your part as to price and in fact all other matters is directly reflected in the consumer satisfaction and acceptance enjoyed by your product. Upon this depends to a large extent your merchandising success.

From a commercial standpoint the closer in the distribution chain the trade outlet is to the primary source of supply, the more essential it is that it present the requirements which make for permanency of effort in the handling of the product. Thus if you entrust your export distribution to a super-jobber who fails commercially, or for any other reason drops your line, you are at one blow left entirely without organized distribution and sales facilities in the entire world-market. However if one of the many foreign wholesalers who handle your product in the world-markets should "fold up" on the line be may be replaced more easily and in the interim the loss of a single link in the chain does not paralyze the entire market for the product. Likewise the loss of a dealer or retailer may be remedied with proportionately little loss of business for the product.

Nevertheless, changes in representation are not generally in the best interests of the business and consistently maximum distribution. Aside from the loss of business which they involve through disorganization of distribution and sales facilities, if they become frequent, the product is justly apt to earn a bad reputation with the trade for whom permanency of representation is just as essential as it is to the manufacturer. Under these conditions it will be found increasingly difficult to secure first class representation.

In your search for permanency in your trade relations predetermination of all of the factors requisite to maximum distribution is essential before entering into distribution arrangements. For otherwise you face the possibility that the outlets which you have selected will not be able to consistently do justice to the product, and the arrangement will not endure.

Chapter VII[36]
The Business of Selling Abroad

While the methods under which distribution is to be secured abroad, which we have just discussed, must be given first place in the world trader's plans to embrace the world market, once he has decided upon the type of distribution set up best suited to the individual market it then becomes incumbent that he direct his attention to the practical business of selling to the intermediary trade channels. And the basis under which the selling arrangement is to be carried out must also be pre-determined before the mill of distribution can begin to grind out sales and profits for you.

Now there are two main considerations to entering into a distribution and sales arrangement and these are *first that it shall provide for maximum profitable distribution and sales for you and second, that it shall afford a profitable working basis for the trade channel.* In connection with these considerations there are a variety of methods under which a suitable and equitable working basis may be arranged for. Basically these arrangements have to do with the manufacturer's endeavor to assure that proper attention will be given by the trade channel, be it super-jobber, wholesaler, or retailer, to the sale of the product.

Primarily these efforts at assurance are concerned with the limitation of sales effort, by mutual agreement, to that which the capital and organization facilities of the trade channel can effectively perform, and to the reasonable sales expectancy for the product. Accordingly practical restrictions both as to the territory to be covered and the competitive products to be handled by the trade channel may be imposed.

[36] From V.D. Collins, *World Marketing*, Philadelphia: Lippincott, 1935, pp. 145–70.

About Exclusivity of Territorial Arrangements
As we have previously determined restriction of territory to no more than can be adequately handled is essential to maximum distribution and sales effort. This restriction is determined as a practical matter by the minimum sales expectancy for the territory and the requirements as to capital and organization on the part of the trade channel essential to assure the realization of this minimum volume of business.

In order to achieve the minimum volume which your sales expectancy for the territory indicates is reasonably available for the product, the trade channel must possess capital adequate to provide the sales organization required to cover the territory and secure the essential retail points of consumer accessibility in every potential consumer trading center. Sometimes it is possible to find a single concern which is equipped to satisfactorily perform the essentials of distribution in an entire country. But more often than not you will find that however excellent the prospect is, his. capital and facilities are not adequate to do a satisfactory job in the entire territory.

In this event you will be obliged to limit the area to be covered to that which can be adequately worked, and to provide further trade channels to take care of the balance of the territory, to the end that your sales expectancy for the entire market may be realized in full. Accordingly it is to be assumed that the trade channel which you have selected to handle your product in a given area, which may be either an entire country or some smaller portion of it, is adequately equipped to cover it.

Under these conditions it must be obvious that unless you restrict the sale of the product exclusively to the selected channel, and refrain from selling to others, either directly within his area or to those outside who may find it possible to sell within the proscribed area, the volume of business the selected channel will be able to secure will be something less than the expectancy for the territory. It must further be apparent that the maximum volume of business available will be split by however many channels are selling your product in the territory, on a competitive basis in accordance with the individual ability of each to compete with the others.

Moreover the total volume which each is able to achieve under these conditions may not be sufficient to provide the necessary profit incentive to continue handling the product. As a result the competing channels will either drop the product entirely or else they will be forced into unprofitable practices of price cutting in an endeavor to secure the volume essential to continued operation. In either event the effect upon the business will be demoralizing.

Accordingly it is sound practice, insofar as is practicable, to permit the trade channel selected for the territory to handle the sale of the product upon an exclusive basis within his bailiwick, so long as the results secured provide a satisfactory volume of business for you. For this reason foreign distribution arrangements usually contemplate exclusivity of product within the assigned territory.

There are, however, conditions under which exclusivity of territory becomes impracticable and a detriment to the securing of the maximum volume of business. Unless the distribution and sales facilities of the trade channel have been ascertained to be beyond reproach by personal investigation on the ground, the only sure gauge of the satisfaction which it may be able to afford is a reasonable period of working experience. Should the experience so gained prove unsatisfactory it may then become desirable and necessary to supplement the existing activities by the addition of further channels operating in the same area.

In arranging for additional channels to bolster up unsatisfactory distribution areas, here again it is not possible to definitely ascertain the abilities of the contemplated new outlet unless personal investigation on the ground has been possible, or until a reasonable period of working experience with it has been bad. The new channel may prove under actual working conditions to be no better, or in fact not so good as the old outlet. So that it would not be good business to discontinue the old channel entirely, particularly if the results obtained have not been too poor, and operate on an exclusive basis with the new outlet until experience has proved the wisdom of such a course.

On the other hand *non-exclusive territorial operation should be engaged in only during a trial period of experience with new accounts,* such as you will be obliged to deal with when establishing distribution facilities in new territories, or when the failure of an old account to deliver up a satisfactory volume of business makes corrective action essential. Under these conditions non-exclusive territorial operation is justified. Nevertheless, it presents at all times the inherent vices indicated above and is not conducive to continued and orderly development of your business. Non-exclusivity of territorial arrangements should, therefore, be of temporary character only, with a view toward the ultimate extension of exclusivity to one or the other of the elements involved based upon the performance record of each during a trial period of operation of say six months.

It is highly essential that your distribution arrangements be kept as clear cut as possible in order to assure orderly and satisfactory development of the business. To this end it is desirable that they be held as closely as possible to exclusivity within defined territories, while at the same time affording flexibility and latitude of action should circumstances subsequently make change in this basis essential.

In order to accomplish this *it is suggested that these arrangements be entered into on a non-exclusive basis, with the understanding that you will not undertake the addition of further trade channels so long as the representation afforded is satisfactory to you.* Under such an arrangement the trade channel enjoys all of the benefits deriving from the actual and practical exclusivity of territory accruing to him so long as he does a satisfactory job, and at the same time the way is opened to you to add additional channels when ever the volume received fails to conform to your reasonable sales expectancy. Should you enter into such an arrangement you will, of course, be morally obligated to ascertain definitely in advance that sales made by you to export channels elsewhere will not be shipped into the territories in which you have provided for virtual exclusivity of established trade channels.

About Exclusivity of Product

In the endeavor to limit the activities of the trade channels to no more than they can perform with satisfaction there is a further limitation, beyond that of territory which enters into distribution arrangements. And that is the restriction of the activity of trade channels in handling competitive products. It is common practice for the foreign trade channel to endeavor to secure representation for as many identical and competing products as possible, to the end that competition from others may be prevented.

Usually this results in the complete throttling of business within the territory for all except one of the competing products, which by virtue of greater profit margin afforded, or for other reason, the channel may prefer to concentrate his activities upon. Further even though such an ulterior motive does not exist, and usually it does, when competitive products are handled there is no definite incentive for the channel to actively push your particular product. In any event the energies of the outlet will have to be divided among the various competing products handled instead of being concentrated upon yours, and in all probability you will fail to achieve your sales expectancy.

Of course, there are instances in which the nature of the product is such that the necessity for exclusivity of handling does not exist, and in fact would be decidedly impractical. Such products are usually those of expendable and highly essential character. In connection with many products of this character the handling of competing items by the trade channel becomes an essential to his existence. As far as the consumer is concerned if he cannot secure his favorite tooth paste in the corner drug store it will lose his patronage entirely. Moreover the retailer himself finds a practical advantage in limiting the number of wholesale sources with whom he must deal. So that the wholesaler is obliged in connection with such items of mass demand to handle competitive products.

Unless your product falls in the above category you are justified in expecting that the trade channels to whom you have entrusted your sales and profit opportunities will concentrate on your product, which means that they will handle it exclusively and will refrain from handling competing lines. And particularly if you limit your distribution exclusively to a single channel within a territory you are entitled to receive assurance on his part of concentration of effort on your product.

Arrangements to Guarantee Sales Performance

In the endeavor to assure a satisfactory volume of business the distribution arrangement may also exact a guarantee from the trade channel as to the achievement of a specified minimum of purchases within a given period. In other words if the manufacturer has arrived at a reasonable sales expectancy for his product of $10,000 for a given territory, before entrusting his distribution to the wholesaler he may require some form of guarantee that this minimum will be achieved in whatever period the estimate of sales expectancy covers.

Such an arrangement may be extended, beyond the wholesaler's mere statement that be believes be can accomplish this volume, to provide under formal contract that he will accept, for example, shipments amounting to $2500 every 90 days. The agreement may even go further and provide for a penalty to be paid by the wholesaler in the event of failure to meet the conditions, and in the guarantee of this penalty he may be required to deposit in trust an amount sufficient to cover the penalty.

Now all of the above sounds like a sure-fire way of making a success of the business but in practice it does not work out that way. First of all the manufacturer will find that it is impossible to get the wholesaler to bind himself to what has been calculated as a reasonable sales expectancy. And if the manufacturer consents to the always lower figure set by the trade channel, he then binds himself legally to consider this as satisfactory, whereas, in point of fact, subsequent sales statistics may conclusively prove it to be extremely unsatisfactory. Further, assuming that the manufacturer does unwisely agree to accept an arbitrarily reduced expectancy as a basis for the agreement, the trade channel will be quite within his rights in insisting that the agreement provide for outright exclusivity and that compliance with this figure shall automatically entitle him to the extension of the agreement on this basis for another prolonged period. Thus the manufacturer may easily be come married to a liability instead of an asset to his business.

Now as to the enforceability of such a contract. Whether there has been a penalty provided for or not, attempt to enforce the contract will always lead to counter-charges on the part of the trade channel to the effect that the manufacturer did not cooperate in a reasonable manner, that the conditions within the territory were such that it was impossible to fulfill the agreement, that the merchandise was not suitable and up to the standard of the competition, and so on ad nauseum. And then the manufacturer has the alter native of suing the trade channel, or if he is wise of dropping the matter with the least possible loss of money and prestige.

If he is still wiser he will not enter into such agreements which are apt to involve unpleasant consequences and often expensive litigation which has to be carried out in an alien country. Rather he will endeavor to *avoid all specific agreements which define the relationship as other than that of non-exclusivity for a specified area, under which the manufacturer agrees to refrain from selling to others so long as the relations with the channel are satisfactory to him.* A simple exchange of letters regarding this matter and in the form and substance indicated above is all that is necessary.

Methods of Selling Abroad

Having established the essentials of satisfactory distribution policy let us now investigate the basis under which the product may be sold in the foreign field to the elements involved in the distribution set-up. There are three methods under which you may handle the product with the intermediate channels of distribution through which the ultimate sale to the consumer is effected. These are (1) on consignment (2) on commission, and (3) on outright purchase. A clear knowledge of these methods and what they involve is essential to the determination of sales policy.

Above all a clear concept of the fundamentals under which successful business must operate as it pertains to this phase of merchandising is essential. *The fundamental of all selling requires that the product be sold to provide as prompt a cash return and as little risk as is consistent with the requirements of the business.* And these requirements consist of what is customary practice with the trade in the sale of the specific product and is therefore required in order to meet the competition, what your capital structure and mar gin of profit will permit in the getting of the business, and finally what the requirements are for securing maximum *profitable* distribution.

Consignment Placements

Consignment signifies that you entrust the merchandise to the intermediary channel of distribution for sale by him for your account and risk. During the time that the merchandise remains unsold in the consignee's hands the title to it remains with the consignor. Not until the consignee has sold the merchandise, at whatever price he has been instructed to by the consignor, does the consignor receive payment, from which the consignee receives an agreed upon commission on the transaction.

Now like all things in life this method of obtaining distribution has its inherent advantages and also its insurmountable drawbacks. So we must weigh the one against the other and if we find that the bad features exceed the good points we will not be justified in employing it.

Among the advantages are that, since the title remains with you and the consignee acts for your account in effecting the sale, you are at entire liberty to dictate what selling prices shall be employed and how, where, when, and to whom the merchandise shall be sold. Thus you have complete control over the merchandise from the time it leaves your hands until it is sold. If the consignee is a wholesaler this control lasts only until he has sold it to the retailer. If the consignee is a retailer the control permits you to dictate what price the consumer must pay for the product, a right by the way which no other method of selling through the intermediate trade channels provides. This is a decided advantage where the product is of such character that uniform and consistent price is essential to the maintenance of trade and consumer confidence and goodwill. It also serves to prevent the sale of the product at lower prices at the sacrifice of such distribution and merchandising effort as your policies may require.

In some instances products are inherently slow in their movement and consequently of such character and uncertain demand that the normal trade channels of distribution could not profitably stock them, and assume the capital investment which outright purchase would require in view of the risk attached to their sale. Irrespective of this fact the product may be of such character that unless it is stocked and readily accessible to demand, the sales possibilities will be diminished considerably and perhaps lost entirely. Under these conditions consignment placement may become advantageous.

As against these factors however we have serious and almost insurmountable obstacles to the employment of consignment in foreign distribution. Obviously the consignment transaction requires on your part the closest supervision. You are the party who is holding the bag and you must be in a position to see that the merchandise is sold with reasonable dispatch and that you receive your money promptly when it is. This necessitates that you be constantly on the ground to push and check which obviously is not practicable in most instances in the foreign field.

In addition the merchandise is held and sold by the consignee for your risk. As far as the selling goes this means that if the account to whom it is shipped, perhaps on credit, fails to pay the loss and the headache of trying to repossess the merchandise is yours. This however can be overcome by having the consignee guarantee payment on all sales transactions. The risk incurred however before the merchandise is sold is quite another matter. While you may be able to arrange with the consignee to insure the merchandise at his own expense against physical damage from the elements, or loss by theft or pilferage, you cannot insure against the commercial and none the less actual loss which will arise if the merchandise becomes unsaleable. And many products are of such character as to rapidly become unsaleable through seasonal or obsolescence qualities or through inherent vices which cause physical deterioration as a result of shelf-life. These are therefore your greatest risks against which you have no protection.

Accordingly consignment placements are to be entered into abroad only as a last resort, and then only where the character of the merchandise is such that consignment presents the sole method for securing consumer accessibility. Even then you are justified in entering into consignment arrangements only where investigation has proved that the commercial, financial, and moral reputation of the consignee is in all respects beyond reproach, where you have established facilities for constantly checking and pushing the consignee, and where the product itself is not likely to depreciate unduly before sale

Commission Basis of Selling

In its application to foreign sales the commission basis of effecting sales follows second after consignments in undesirability. Essentially this method of selling is confined to effort on the part of a commission agent to secure orders for the product which he does not stock, either from samples or from the catalogue description or manufacturers descriptive literature. The order is then forwarded to the primary source of supply to be sold and shipped direct to the customer, the financial responsibility for collection lying with the source of supply rather than with the com mission agent. Such a transaction is known as an *indent.* When payment is received by the vendor an agreed upon commission is paid to the commission or sales agent for his services in securing the order.

There are, of course, many variations under which a commission arrangement may be carried out. The hurdle of financial responsibility for collections may, as in the case of consignments, be satisfied by the commission agent agreeing to guarantee the acceptance of, and payment for, the merchandise by the customer. Basically, however, commission arrangements do not fulfill the requirements of sound distribution. As the commission agent does not carry stocks his financial responsibility in the development of the business is academic. Because of the absence of specific financial responsibility in the product, he is not subject to the normal limitations of capital in the diversification of his interests and therefore is in a position without danger to his capital to take on a larger number of products for sale on this basis than he can do justice to. Summed up the philosophy of the commission agent is "Any commission is velvet".

Moreover the failure of this type of arrangement to pro vide and assure reasonable stocks of the merchandise being locally available on the ground with which to satisfy demand is not in keeping with the principles of successful merchandising. *Commission channels are not therefore conducive to the maximum development of the business.* They are to be employed only where the more satisfactory methods to be described next cannot be taken advantage of owing to the nature of the product.

Outright Sale

Of all of the methods of selling and securing maximum distribution of the merchandise that of outright sale to the intermediate trade channels is by far the most satisfactory for the following reasons. First, it provides you with maximum safety to your capital investment in the merchandise. Second, it affords prompt return of both capital and profit on sales, thus greatly extending the productive capacity of your working capital. And third and perhaps most important to the requirement of securing maximum sales effort from the intermediate channels in the distribution of the product, the capital investment made by the trade channel in the outright purchase of your merchandise forces him to assume an active, definite, and positive interest in seeing that it reaches the consumer's hands. Since, insofar as the manufacturer is concerned, the product is not sold until the consumer actually buys it, this last consideration is of the greatest importance.

Further this same financial interest on the part of the trade channel provides an inherent limitation to the diversification of his activities to such items only as his financial capacity is able to digest profitably, thus affording to some extent assurance of maximum sales effort and consequently the satisfaction and permanency of the arrangement. So wherever the product and the conditions will permit *your energies should therefore be devoted to building up distribution facilities which purchase and stock the product out-right for their own account and subsequent financial risk.*

Credit Requirements of Foreign Business

In effecting sales through the intermediate channels of foreign distribution the *extension of credit on a reasonable basis in keeping with the nature of the business and the normal requirements of the trade is essential to the development of maximum sales possibilities for the product.* For the manufacturer, or for any of the subsequent intermediary channels of distribution, to fail in this important function is for him to restrict to a large extent the real and profitable opportunities which exist at the present time.

On the other hand today, as never before, the extension of credit is loaded with dynamite and must be conducted with wisdom and full knowledge of the existing conditions. Failure to understand the fundamentals governing this important phase of the business can result only in unhappy consequences, and in no phase of the business do these consequences follow with swifter rapidity and with such disastrous results as through the unwarranted extension of credit.

Let us then formulate the fundamentals governing the extension of credit so that these may be impressed upon our minds and constantly before us in our consideration of the further details concerning the matter. These fundamentals are:

(a) That the credit you extend is a part of your working capital, accordingly,

(b) by its extension you are reducing by that much the working effectiveness and profit opportunity of your own business. Unless—

(c) the recipient employ the capital loan, extended by you in the form of merchandise, to further the sale of your product on a sound basis. This means

(d) your capital must receive in the recipient's usage of it the same safeguards which you would apply yourself, and

(e) that you must be assured of the safe and prompt re turn of your capital upon the expiration of the loan period.

When you ship merchandise to an account and agree to accept payment some 30, 60, or 90 days thereafter you are in effect making a loan of capital in the amount of the cost of the merchandise to you, and insofar as the recipient is concerned in the amount of the billing price of the merchandise to him. To this extent you are reducing the amount of your working capital and hence your profit opportunities. So that the only means by which you can expect to receive an adequate return for the accommodation is through the use of the loan by the recipient to further promote the sale of your product.

Now this means that he shall utilize this loan to finance the credit requirements of his own trade beyond the point which his own capital facilities will permit, or to finance increased merchandising and sales effort *for your product*. The profit on the additional volume of business which you may receive under these conditions represents your recompense for making the loan. And if the recipient makes any other use of your loan it is an abuse of your credit extension which will not then become productive for you. Which is simply another way of saying that an account is entitled to credit only so long as it provides a satisfactory volume of business.

In actual practice the function of credit has been abused for so long that few today realize its true significance and proper basis of operation. It has long been employed as an added trade inducement by the competition in an endeavor to chisel a larger share of the business than the competitive working conditions permit, with the result that it has de generated into the largest of the organized rackets with which business must contend.

It is demanded as their inalienable right by concerns without adequate working capital of their own, in order to enable them to secure the profit returns on your line, working on your capital. This is the situation that must be met by you. The true function of credit has been cited here to the end that you may endeavor to confine its extension to the reasonable and profitable purposes for which it was designed.

In the extension of credit your capital must necessarily receive in the recipient's usage the exercise of the same sound business judgment and safeguards as you would apply in its employment yourself. Otherwise it will be lost with resultant unpleasantness to the recipient's business and possibly to your own.

And finally you must be assured of the return of your capital upon the expiration of the loan period. In order for the recipient to accomplish this he must so order the employment of your capital loan to him that it will be available in liquid form with which to pay his credit obligations when they fall due. If you do not receive your capital back promptly when it is due it is indicative of an abuse of your credit facilities, arising in most instances out of unsound business management and practices on the part of the recipient.

With these fundamentals in mind we are ready to proceed with the practical business of extending credits. *The extension of credits may be justified only when the financial condition of the applicant for credit indicates the business is adequately financed, soundly conducted, and under the management and ownership of responsible and honest people with a reputation for meeting their obligations promptly and faithfully.* This can only be ascertained through examination of the financial statement of the applicant, by careful investigation of the commercial references of other concerns with whom he has had dealings, and through the reports of the banks to whom the reputation and financial standing of the applicant is known.

Unless your investigation of the applicant reveals all of these virtues, you will under no circumstances be justified in extending credit. Remember, it is easy to extend credit but often very difficult to get your money back. Also that it is easier to refuse credit in the beginning than to try to withdraw without a loss when at some later date you find that the account is going sour.

Aside from satisfactory credit standing on the part of the applicant to assure the prompt and safe return of your loan when due, the new conditions of world turmoil impose another restriction to the extension of credits abroad. *Credits may not be extended in countries which have rigid exchange-control restrictions and in which dollar exchange releases require a prohibitive length of time to materialize.* Otherwise as we have seen in Chapter V the recipient will deposit local currency with the bank in satisfaction of your loan but you will not receive your capital back until the exchange control board releases the corresponding dollar exchange, and in the meantime you may suffer an exchange loss that will wipe out any profits to be otherwise gained.

Moreover care must be exercised not to extend long-term credits in countries whose financial condition is not good, and which may therefore be forced into exchange control, or even into moratoria on private debts. Further, caution is essential in the extension of credit in countries where the political and social situation is insecure, and where a sudden change of government may result in radically changed monetary policies.

Just a word now about the length of credit terms employed in the foreign field. In general it will be found that the terms granted to foreign trade channels are patterned closely upon those current in the trade for similar lines at home. This is justly proper because your capital should be entitled to earn as much abroad as at home, in fact more because of the greater risk which it assumes when it leaves the country. Accordingly it is recommended that your credit extensions be limited to at least what obtains in the domestic trade in your line.

The super-jobber should pay on whatever terms are nor mal to the domestic jobbing trade; usually 2% off for cash in 10 days, or 30 days net. The foreign wholesaler may be extended terms ranging from 30 to 120 days, depending upon the product, his standing, and the conditions existing in his country. Remember, whatever terms you extend usually mean considerably more in export before you actually receive your money back, as to them must be added the time of shipment required for the merchandise to reach the foreign country and the time required for the money to reach home after payment.

Means of Securing Foreign Distribution and Sales

You are now ready to look into the means for contacting the intermediate trade channels of foreign distribution and effecting the sale of the product. There are an infinite variety of methods under which this may be accomplished. There are however two elementary processes by which con tact with distribution and sales channels may be had, and these may be classified as indirect means and direct means. Under both processes the names of concerns likely to be qualified to handle your product are secured through various channels and correspondence or personal solicitation entered into with the following ends in view. First, to interest them in your line, second, to ascertain whether their qualifications appear to be satisfactory and in the affirmative, third, to enter into a sales arrangement with them.

Sources and Methods of Contacting Foreign Trade Channels

The indirect sources of these leads are varied. Foreign trade-papers are constantly receiving inquiries from, and have in their files the names of thousands of foreign concerns in every line of endeavor to which their domestic advertisers have access. In addition publications of this nature are in a position to furnish financial and credit in formation regarding the commercial standing of these concerns at a nominal charge, or this information may be secured from some of the commercial credit rating companies direct, such as Dun & Bradstreet's.

A further source of such leads are the domestic trade journals pertaining to the product most of which have a wide foreign circulation and also constantly receive inquiries from abroad from concerns desiring to represent American manufacturers. The Department of Commerce is also in a position, for a nominal charge, to provide you with the names, addresses, and financial standing of concerns in each territory of suitable calibre to handle your distribution.

In the initial contact with these leads care must be taken to discriminate between those of true wholesale calibre and those who are retailers pure and simple. As we have seen there is often apt to be an overlap and consequently confusion regarding this distinction even in the mind of the trade channel himself. Indiscriminate distribution of catalogues and export price lists showing lowest trade prices should be avoided until you have definite knowledge as to whether you are dealing with a wholesaler or retailer. Even further, quotations to houses abroad should not be sent until you have ascertained whether the parties desiring this in formation are legitimate and desirable trade channels. Otherwise this information is frequently used by unscrupulous concerns handling the competition to embarrass the legitimate outlet with whom you may effect an arrangement.

Under direct means there are also varied channels through which direct inquiries from concerns interested in handling your specific product may be received. These means are the most promising of all, and undoubtedly the most fruitful, as you already have the importer's interest. Otherwise he would not take the trouble to communicate with you.

The first means for securing these direct inquiries is by advertising in the domestic trade papers having foreign circulation, and in the export journals proper, indicating that you are interested in securing representation abroad. Such advertising will result in a veritable deluge of inquiries, to be run down by you with care and diligence. A still further means is the judicious placing of advertisements in the local foreign newspapers of the key cities of the countries in which you desire representation, soliciting correspondence from qualified concerns.

There is an additional channel lying closer to home than any of the above and that is the local purchasing agents and foreign commission houses handling purchases in this country for many foreign importers. The local purchasing agents for foreign sugar mills, plantations, etc. often provide a lucrative source of business as the foreign organizations for whom they act, as we have seen, are not generally permitted to effect purchases through any other channel.

Last of all, and *best of all, is the distribution and selling arrangements which your own travelling representative can effect for you on the ground.* This requires the outlay of the most money initially in securing distribution, but long experience has conclusively proved that it is the most fruitful and satisfactory of all, and the least expensive in proportion to the rich return it provides. Correspondence methods of securing distribution must of course be resorted to initially to some extent in the building of world distribution, and in many instances where the sales expectancy for the individual territory does not indicate a sufficiently profitable volume to pay for the expense of personal coverage.

But for the building of a satisfactory and lasting distribution in the major territories personal coverage by your travelling representative is imperative. And I do not mean by special commission arrangement with travelling representatives who make a business of covering certain territories for any and all representation they can get. Sales representation of this category does not know your line nor does it know effectively how to work it, however thorough its knowledge of the territory may be. What is required is your own travelling representative, working exclusively on the business of your product, and thoroughly versed in the line and the methods of working it. He will soon enough learn the ropes of the territory.

How to Interest the Trade Channel in Your Line

Whether your contact with the foreign trade channel is indirect or direct does not in the least alter the fundamental under which your efforts to interest him in your line must be conducted. And this, in essence, is that he is primarily in business to earn a profit. Accordingly, *there is only one basis under which you can induce him to handle your line and that is the profit opportunity which it holds out to him. His interest in your product, in your concern, and in your policies, is purely academic and incidental to his prime objective of earning a profit on his investment.* This is elementary to your efforts to "sell" the trade channel, be it super-jobber, wholesaler, or retailer, and yet it is an obvious fundamental entirely overlooked by many concerns in their efforts to sell in the foreign market.

Reams of letters are written to the trade prospect on the qualities and merits of the product, bushels of expensive literature printed on vellum in gold describing the product are sent to him, but withal not one concise, intelligent, and concentrated effort is made to develop for him the actual profit opportunity, translated into terms of dollars, which the product holds. It is the old, antiquated, and obsolete conception of salesmanship of merchandise to the individual, or consumer channel, rather than to the trade channel.

Now the total U. S. sales expectancy which you have estimated for the product in the specific territory as described in Chapter V provides the Big Bertha for your attack upon the trade channels profit motive and incentive to handle a product of the general character which yours presents. It shows him that there is a very definite and concrete market in his territory for such an item which is actually being enjoyed at the moment by his competition. But this is not enough. It does not clearly demonstrate for him the possibilities which exist for your specific product.

In order to do this you must carry him through the steps of the reasoning process by which you have arrived at the reasonable sales expectancy for your specific product, and which represents the actual volume of business he may expect to enjoy under normal and proper methods of operation. You should emphasize to him that first and foremost among these proper methods are the provision of adequate points of consumer accessibility on his part, so that there may be no doubt in his mind that your policies require, and his success depends, upon this pay-dirt fundamental. Assuming that your selling prospectus to the trade channel has reached this stage you have accomplished the main objective; namely that of interesting him in the investment of his capital, facilities, and energy in the handling of your product.

Preliminary Pre-Determination of Trade Qualifications
Once the trade channel is interested in handling your product he will be more inclined to cooperate with you in your endeavors to ascertain just what qualifications he possesses to insure the satisfactory handling of your line, and what specific territory he is adequately equipped to cover. You will find that it is extremely difficult to secure this in formation before reaching this point, because until the trade channel is definitely interested he is naturally averse to disclosing the intimate details of his business which are essential to you.

If the contact has been carried out by correspondence, always a long drawn out and exasperating process, you will be obliged to take the statements made regarding these matters at face value to a large extent. Remember, many apply, but few qualify. That is why personal solicitation of accounts, with the opportunity afforded for investigation on the ground, presents the most satisfactory method for developing the business.

However there are certain preliminary qualifications which you can ascertain with reasonable certainty, and which will go a long way toward assuring that you are on the right track. The first of these is a *signed* statement of financial condition. This will serve to show whether the channel is properly financed, and in good financial condition. It will indicate whether his working capital is adequate to maintain the supplies of your product essential to the distribution requirements of the territory, and unless this is the case he will not be able to secure for you a satisfactory volume of business.

Second, you will require a statement of the lines of merchandise at present handled by him, and the suppliers of these lines. This information will serve a dual purpose. It will afford an indication of whether the capital structure is adequate to do justice to all of the lines handled, and at the same time to your line if added. And it will enable you to communicate with the various other suppliers to ascertain what satisfaction the channel has afforded in the distribution of the other lines, and what the character and financial responsibility of the channel has been determined to be as a result of actual working experience with the other suppliers. Unless the concern is doing a satisfactory job for a majority of the suppliers it represents you will not be justified in entrusting to it your own business destiny in the territory.

Third, you should secure a statement of the organization, distribution, and sales facilities which the channel has at present available to place at the disposal of your product, indicating specifically the points in which consumer accessibility is to be provided and the character and general qualifications of the retail points involved.

If the preliminary response to these natural and essential inquiries on your part is made freely and with reasonable degree of satisfaction of your requirements, you are then justified in endeavoring to close with the prospect. Otherwise you will waste no further time and energy on him.

How to Close with the Trade Prospect

The closing of a distribution or sales arrangement then becomes merely a matter of bringing to bear upon the prospect the weight of the incidental, though essential, reasons for the assured profit opportunity which your product presents. These incidental reasons consist of an exposition of the *consumer acceptability* of the product which you have built into it at a definite and competitive trade price affording assured *consumer price accessibility.* You will also outline to what extent you propose to create, maintain, and constantly increase *consumer consciousness* for the product, and by what methods. Last, but by no means least you will emphasize the satisfactory character of your policies, and the justly earned reputation for equitable and honorable dealing which these policies have earned your concern with those with whom it deals.

On the part of the trade channel the closing requires expression of willingness to cooperate in the satisfactory carrying out of your policies as to distribution and sales, particularly as to the carrying at all times of adequate stocks of merchandise to enable the existing demand to be supplied, to the end that you may achieve your reasonable sales expectancy for the territory. And the first essential in this connection is the placing of an order for a reasonable trial quantity of merchandise with which to judge its merits under practical operating conditions.

Just remember that unless you follow this procedure for selling to the trade channels you are in effect depending upon the ability of the trade to "sell itself" on your proposition. For the most part the trade has neither the facilities to gather the specific facts, nor the time, nor the inclination. So it becomes strictly your job to do the initial "selling". No one else can or will do it for you.

Chapter XI[37]
Solving World Marketing Problems

The preceding chapters have been devoted to the merchandising and sales fundamentals involved in launching your product to a profitable and permanent career in the world market. Insofar as possible the presentation has been arranged and ordered so as to afford as little distraction from the elementary requisites as the material would permit. Accordingly while the major problems of world marketing have been covered in detail, there are others with which the world trader will have to cope, in whatever market and with whatever product, which must at this time receive consideration.

As might be expected these secondary problems are concerned with one or all of the three pay-dirt fundamentals of world marketing. And they are directly concerned for this reason with the prime objective of all enterprise; that of producing a profitable return on the capital invested. It is essential therefore that these problems receive your close attention and study. Accordingly we shall outline the fundamentals which they involve and the means of their solution, to the end that application to the specific phases which they present to you shall become merely a matter of simple substitution of existing known factors.

Adapting The Product To The Market

The first of these problems which invariably confronts the world trader is the problem of consumer acceptance of the product. In theory it requires provision of the product in the form which incorporates the maximum degree of those elements which constitute consumer acceptability at the price level which affords maximum consumer accessibility. In practice it consists of the

[37] From V.D. Collins, *World Marketing*, Philadelphia: Lippincott, 1935, pp. 239–65.

practical compromise which must always be made throughout your marketing endeavors between the ideal and the prime objective of profit return on the capital investment.

The ideal is, of course, the ideal as judged by consumer standards and requirements. And the practical is the extent to which this ideal may be incorporated in the product without destroying either profit opportunity or consumer price accessibility. Which is simply another way of saying that product adaptability to individual market requirements may be provided only where the potentiality of the existing market will return sufficient profit to pay for any changes in the standard product of domestic sale that may be required.

To whatever extent your product has competitive consumer acceptance in the domestic market it will, in general, enjoy proportionate competitive acceptance in the world market. Changes in the product will not, therefore, be required in a majority of the world markets, except when changes in the product of the competition make such action on your part imperative, or where the special requirements of the market itself cannot be met in any other way, such for instance as by price inducement. In adapting the product to the market the required changes may assume two forms, namely (a) major changes and (b) minor changes.

For example radio manufacturers found early in their endeavor to develop the Latin-American market that the relative paucity of local broadcast facilities then existing in that territory made the supply of a receiver capable of picking up the American broadcasts essential to consumer acceptance. They further found that the standard product embodying a high degree of consumer acceptance in the United States did not serve in Latin-America due to the fact that satisfactory reception of programs on the standard wave-lengths employed here is not possible in distant regions lying in and below the static belt which exists to the south of us.

However, it was known that short-wave transmission and reception was inherently capable of covering much greater distances than was the standard wave propagation, and in addition was comparatively free from static disturbance. So in order to adapt the product to the Latin-American market the short-wave receiver, previously used for commercial work only, was developed and short-wave broadcast transmission encouraged by American manufacturers. This required changes of major character in the product and in the manufacturing methods, but the market was adjudged to be of sufficient potentiality to warrant the expense involved.

Now the subsequent development of this effort to adapt the product to the market requirements is most interesting indeed. Little by little local broadcast facilities, employing our standard domestic wave propagation, were made available in Latin-America. And the demand which had formerly been for short-wave receivers only changed and required the supply of combined short and standard-wave receivers, or all-wave receivers as they are called. Again American manufacturers found it necessary to provide a product which would meet the new requirements for consumer acceptance.

In the interim, the great depression had materially reduced the market potentialities at home, and as a matter of fact the public generally had lost a great deal of its enthusiasm for radio. In its apathy, however, it was getting quite a kick out of hearing European broadcast stations on short-wave. It was at this moment that the all-wave receiver of foreign demand was perfected, and the home market found in it a new toy embodying new features of consumer acceptance which the standard product did not possess. Revived public interest in radio resulted and consumer acceptance in the domestic market turned from the standard product to the special product of foreign demand. And thus the barely profitable product of limited foreign demand became a highly profitable product by virtue of the tremendous added volume of domestic demand which it had acquired.

Now this does not always happen The example is cited, however, to illustrate that change of the product, to embody the sometimes special requirements of foreign consumer acceptance, may often permit it to embrace an increased portion of the domestic market. Where this happy condition exists the cost of changing the product will be distributed over the larger production and hence will be proportionately less. So that in considering the adaptation of the product to meet special foreign requirements it is essential that you investigate the possibilities which may result from increased consumer acceptance and greater volume in the home market.

There are, moreover, many changes in the product in adapting it to the special requirements of the individual foreign market which do not require a major and expensive change in manufacturing methods. Thus the manufacturer of cotton goods may find that certain color combinations or pattern designs are required in Mexico, while the manufacturer of men's hats may discover that whereas lavender colored felt is not popular at home, it is decidedly high in consumer acceptance in Bolivia. Or he may find that the mere substitution of brightly colored hatbands for the more somber preferences of the home market is requisite to consumer acceptance in some markets.

Or the manufacturer of a proprietary medicine may find that the inexpensive addition of a descriptive pamphlet printed in Spanish, French, and German is essential to consumer acceptance in the world market. The cost involved in meeting consumer preferences and requisites of this nature is small, and well worth the world trader's while, if he is to secure the widest profitable distribution of the product abroad. In their pre-war exploitation of the Latin-American market the German traders were past masters in the lucrative art of adapting the product to the consumer preferences of the market. Your trade channels will be quick to advise you whenever change in the product is necessary to meet the competition, or to materially increase market possibilities.

In effecting any change in the standard product, whether major or minor in character, it should be appreciated that in addition to the increased cost of the product which the change involves there will be an increase in the organization expense required for the extra attention and handling which must be afforded to the special merchandise. This must, of course, also be taken into consideration in determining whether the change can profitably be made. *But the factor which must in the last analysis determine to what extent the product may profitably be adapted to special market requirements must always be the increased sales expectancy which will accrue to it.*

Upon this increase over the normal sales expectancy for the standard product depends the *profit volume* out of which the cost of the product change must come. Where the anticipated increase in profit volume is not adequate to meet the cost of the change and still provide a reasonable and normal working profit, or where the cost of the change requires an increase of consumer price beyond the limits of reasonable accessibility, you cannot afford to adapt the product to the market. Otherwise you will, in effect, be lowering your profit margin on both the product of special and standard requirements, in other words on your entire sales volume.

In this latter event, unless the volume increase is sufficient to make profitable the lowering of profit margin, the market as a whole for your product will be more attractive at the reduced volume afforded by the product of standard production. *In fact it has been our endeavor throughout to stress the futility of endeavoring to do business where the difficulties prevent the return of a reasonable and sure profit. Out of the total of 125 world-markets there are too many which do not present such difficulties and which are as yet comparatively undeveloped to warrant or make necessary the risk of capital in the others.*

Identifying the Product to the Consumer

This is the second of the important problems of everyday concern to the world trader. By product identification is meant the use of trade-name or trade-mark as a consumer means of identifying the specific product. Now there are two methods under which you may sell your product. The first is to provide for the essential elements of consumer acceptance and consumer accessibility, and to omit the third requisite of consumer consciousness. By so doing you will be able to offer the product to the consumer at a lower price than the product of the competition which creates consumer consciousness through advertising expenditure. And to some extent the consumer price inducement and larger market potentiality thus afforded will serve to compensate for the lack of positive consumer consciousness.

Further there are some types of merchandise which lend themselves particularly well to this basis of merchandising. Such products are confined for the most part to the most elementary of the essential consumer staples. Here the urgent necessity of the consumer for the merchandise makes it imperative that he buy without discrimination, and the price inducement ranks high. Merchandise of this character rates lowest in the requirements of selling as the element of extreme and urgent need in its acquisition by the consumer removes the necessity for selling it to him.

But the minute the product is divorced from the elementary requisites of urgent necessity it becomes for a large portion of its potential market a luxury product, and as one to be bought with discrimination as to its qualities, Under these conditions the creation of consumer consciousness becomes highly necessary and profitable, since without it neither consumer acceptability nor consumer accessibility may achieve their maximum reward. Here the product must be *sold* to the consumer, inasmuch as in the absence elementary necessity he may forego purchase entirely. And *in order to create consumer consciousness for the product must be positively and consistently identified through advertising so that the symbol thus afforded may become synonymous in the consumer consciousness with the product itself.*

It is only under this stimulus that the consumer may be brought to the decision that your specific product has be come essential to him, and to the positive and profitable action of seeking your product out from amongst the competition. But even assuming that the consumer considers the product essential, and has made up his mind to purchase it, in the absence of positive identifying advertising there is no good reason why be should not buy the product of the competition.

Accordingly positive identification of the product is essential to the realization of the maximum market potentialities, which are reduced in most instances to the minimum where hit-and-miss methods of merchandising prevail which do not create consumer consciousness. Now this requires that the product itself or its consumer container or package be positively marked, labeled, or branded so that the consumer may readily be able to identify it in the store.

The positive identification required may be provided either through the use of your trade-name or trade-mark. Obviously when trade-name or trade-mark, or both, have been used to create expensive consumer consciousness they become valuable from a trade standpoint. One prominent manufacturer in the United States values his trade-mark at 14 million dollars. If these trade assets which you have built up and maintained by the expenditure of your money are not properly protected they may be appropriated by others who may thus trade upon the definite selling value which they present, to the detriment of your own sales.

Protecting the Product from the Trade-Pirates

By product protection is meant the protection to the manufacturer's stock-in-trade afforded by the trade-mark and patent laws of the foreign countries comprising the world market. Trade-mark protection is provided for in the laws of every civilized country in the world today. In a majority of countries these laws are based upon the English law, under which it is the *priority of actual trade usage* which confers ownership and the right to exclusive possession and usage of the trade-name or trade-mark. In addition these countries have entered into international agreement which makes the establishment of priority of usage in any country of the group effective in the others. In still other countries which do not pattern after the English law, the right of ownership and exclusive usage is extended to the first person to register the trade-name or trade-mark in accordance with the local requirements.

On the former basis the fact that we are entitled to ownership of a trade-mark by virtue of priority of usage in the United States, and the fact that we enter a market, advertise our trade-name and trade-marks, and sell therein our product bearing these means of identification, affords legal protection against attempt to pirate these valuable trade-adjuncts to the purposes of other channels. In fact so potent are these laws in some countries that the legitimate owner of a trade-mark may embargo a piratically branded product at the point of customs entry to the end that it may be prohibited entirely from entering the country.

It is in those countries where *priority of registration,* rather than of trade-usage, confers legal ownership that the world trader must be careful to protect his interests by complying with the registration requirements *before* introducing his product into the market. In such countries it has long been an established racket for individuals to piratically register the trade-names and trade-marks of the unwary world trader, thus forcing him either to abandon them or buy them back at an exorbitant figure.

Accordingly there are two major requisites toward assuring the safety and permanence of your trade-name and trade-marks in the world market, and consequently the vital of consumer consciousness for your product. First, consult a reliable attorney on international trade-mark law and as certain in which countries legal copyright is essential to ownership, and arrange to so protect yourself in any of your major markets where this requirement exists. Second, keep an accurate and complete record of the following essential information namely (a) the first instance in which your trade-name or trade-marks were disclosed, and to whom, in the foreign country, and (b) the documentary evidence as represented by your commercial invoices and steamship bill-of-lading covering the first shipment of the trade-marked product made by you. This evidence is essential to the establishment of priority of usage.

Now as to protection of the product itself against piracy. A majority of products embody original elements of design or construction, or of manufacturing methods which are inherent to the consumer acceptance which they present. For the protection of these vital merchandising elements the laws provide for patent protection through registration. Here again, by international agreement, a majority of countries refuse to issue patent rights, to an applicant for such exclusive ownership, where the improvement claimed has already been patented in other countries, and is not therefore truly original.

The granting of a patent, however, in any country does not in itself afford protection to the holder against infringement. It establishes rather the legal right of the holder to court proceedings against an infringer in determination of his rights. Accordingly there are two considerations which the world trader should investigate before launching his product in any of the important world markets. He should endeavor to reasonably ascertain that it does not infringe upon local patent rights already granted. Otherwise he may find himself with a suit upon his hands and damages to sustain. And if the product is patented in this country it is desirable to extend the rights to the principal markets to be worked, in order that your local legal standing and possibilities for enforcement of your rights in the prosecution of infringement by others may not be impaired.

It sometimes happens that your local trade channels, in protection of your product against unscrupulous trade practices, may request you to temporarily assign to them your local trade-mark or patent rights. *This is never to be done under any circumstances.* Trade relations are only too frequently impermanent, and besides the transfer of these rights may weaken your standing and ability to enforce them after they have been returned to you.

Maintenance of Trade and Consumer Good-Will for the Product

I have previously stressed the importance of a satisfied consumer to the creation of favorable consumer consciousness and increased sales and profits for the product. And by the same token it is just as essential that your policies maintain the good-will of the trade channels handling it to the end that they will consistently extend themselves in its sale. These requirements involve, therefore, your relations with the trade and your consumer policies which must be carried out by the trade on your behalf in their direct con-tact with the consumer.

It is inherent to the conduct of business where the principals are separated by time and distance that misunderstandings should creep into it, and things go awry in general which would not happen under normal conditions. It is not necessary here to enter into a detailed discussion of the various difficulties which can and do frequently arise to disturb the otherwise placid tenor of relations between the supplier and his customers. I do, however, wish to stress the fact that when such instances arise they call for tactful and sympathetic handling on your part in order to compensate for, rather than to aggravate, the difficulties inherent to conducting your business abroad Here again, the intermittent visits of your personal representative are invaluable to arbitrate and equitably adjust such differences and claims as may arise from time to time.

In any event be sure that your analysis of these problems includes all of the vital factors, i.e. those affecting the profit opportunity of the trade channel as well as your own, and that your adjustment is equitable to both. *Remember that it does not pay to be unfair or picayune with your trade channels.* A minor adjustment in which both parties share in the expense involved will often return large dividends in the form of increased incentive on the part of the trade channel to push the line more intensively. Even further the trade channel who feels that his complaints are equitably and fairly adjusted by you will be inclined to extend this policy of fair-dealing to the consumer, to the everlasting benefit of the business.

Aside from these general problems requiring intelligent adjustment to assure the maintenance of good-will on the part of the trade and the consumer, there are certain types of product of technical character for which provision must be made in the manufacturer's *policies and prices* to assure to the consumer expert services in maintaining the product at satisfactory consumer acceptance level. Products of this character are, for instance, automobiles, radios, and all of the mechanical and electrical products used by the consumer individually and by industry generally. These products re quire that provision be made by the manufacturer in each territory for supplies of repair and replacement parts, at reasonable points of consumer accessibility, and for expert services in order that the consumer acceptance qualities originally built into the product may be maintained throughout its reasonable life.

Now all of this sounds like a task of tremendous difficulty, but actually it involves two things only. First, that the trade channels selected by you shall be adequately equipped as to organization and experience in the handling of similar products to undertake to handle the work on a satisfactory basis. Second, that you establish a policy of trade cooperation and consumer service which will insure the maintenance of good-will for the product on the part of the consumer, and will not unduly reduce the profit incentive of the trade in the handling of the product.

The first essential in this connection is that the consumer shall be protected for a reasonable length of time against *defects* in the product which may result from such manufacturing causes as faulty material or workmanship. It is generally assumed that manufacturing defects will appear within 90 days from date of purchase of the product from the retail channel serving it to him. And second the consumer must be assured of service both as to the supply of parts and installation beyond this period throughout the normal life of the product, in order that it may be maintained in service as operating conditions and normal wear and tear cause it to deteriorate.

Accordingly it is customary to guarantee the product to the foreign consumer against all defects of material or workmanship during the 90 day period subsequent to its purchase. Your policy with the trade in carrying out this guarantee will require that it replace, *absolutely free of charge to the consumer*, any parts failing during this period by virtue of manufacturing defect. Beyond the 90 day period it is good policy to arrange to have the trade replace free of charge, insofar as material only is concerned, any part failing in the succeeding 90 day period, but making a reasonable charge for labor. And beyond this six months period the consumer should be obliged to pay for both parts and labor on a *fair and reasonable basis* in connection with any service required, since it may be fairly assumed that the necessity for such service is due to the normal wear and tear of the product under the usage to which it is put.

Insofar as the trade is concerned the manufacturer's policy must enable it to carry out the above consumer policies on an equitable basis. Accordingly the manufacturer should guarantee the product to the trade against all defects of manufacture for one year from date of invoice covering the shipment from the factory. This affords to the trade channel a reasonable period of six months to cover the time of transportation to him and the time it remains in stock before being sold to the consumer.

Inasmuch, however, as the trade channel should be just as interested in maintaining consumer good-will for the product as is the manufacturer, it is only reasonable that he should assume some portion of the expense of such service as be may be required to render under the above policy during the first six months of its operation. It should be appreciated that the manufacturer exercises every reasonable precaution to see that the product is perfect before shipment abroad. Further it is frequently extremely difficult to ascertain positively whether failure of the product after it has reached the consumer's hands is due to manufacturing defect, or to damage which may have been incurred during transportation, or to the perils of usage and abusage to which it may have been put.

For these reasons the manufacturer limits the extent of his responsibility to the replacement of parts on an F.O.B. Factory basis. To the trade channel attaches the responsibility for paying the shipping and importing expense, and, during the first 90 days after sale to the consumer, the cost of installation. Now obviously the manufacturer must have some means of checking upon claims made by the trade for parts replaced owing to manufacturing defect.

There are two ways in which this may be done. The first is to require that the trade channel return the alleged defective part to the factory for inspection and subsequent determination whether the failure was actually due to defect or to other causes for which the manufacturer is not responsible. This is the method most commonly employed and it is extremely unsatisfactory. First of all the cost of returning the defective part, which must be borne by the trade, is often greater than the actual value of the part itself. Unless the part is of such character that it can be repaired and made serviceable again, which is not usually the case, the expense of return is, therefore, not warranted. And second, the trade channel has already replaced the part for the consumer and if the manufacturer subsequently rejects his claim he is out of pocket not only for the value of the part, but for the cost of returning it as well. In addition the return of parts and inspection at the factory requires a considerable period of time during which the investment made by the trade channel is unproductive.

In order to avoid these drawbacks the following policy has been adopted by some manufacturers with considerable success. The trade channel is required to submit monthly statements covering parts replaced due to alleged defect of manufacture. At the same time he is required to hold the parts covered by each claim aside until the manufacturer has passed on the claim, which should specify for each part replaced the date of original purchase and the manufacturer's invoice covering same, the name or numerical identification of the part, and the apparent cause of failure.

Unless the percentage of failure thus reported is excessive, as determined by the manufacturer's domestic statistics covering this phase of the business, the claim will be allowed and credit will either be issued for the F.O.B. Factory value of the parts or else the manufacturer will make replacing shipment in kind, of course on an F.O.B. Factory basis. Upon receipt of credit or replacing shipment the trade channel may then destroy the parts which he has held pending disposition instructions. In this way the unnecessary expense of return and the invariable delays thereon are eliminated.

If on the other hand the manufacturer feels that the percentage of defect claimed is unreasonable, or if he wishes to have a portion or all of the parts returned for inspection, to the end that the cause of failure may be more accurately determined and avoided in future production, he may request the trade channel to do so. The issuance of credit will then depend upon the expert examination which the factory is able to afford, and in the event that the customer's claim is substantiated by the examination the manufacturer assumes the burden of the return charges, otherwise they are borne by the customer.

Naturally the above procedure regarding service will have to be adapted to the requirements of the individual product, and there are some products where it cannot be made effective at all. In some instances the entire product may have to be returned to the factory where repairs are required of such nature that they may not reasonably be performed on the ground by local facilities. The procedure outlined above finds its best reward in connection with the product of mass consumer demand where trade channels handling it may without undue hardship provide the facilities necessary to consumer service. Nor is it necessary that service facilities be provided at each and every retail point of consumer accessibility within the territory. The requirements will be served if a single service point within the territory be provided, and this may be located as a rule with the distributor serving the retail trade.

Experience has proved the above policies, both as to the consumer and as to the trade, to be generally satisfactory. They warrant, therefore, your consideration in the event that you are marketing a product requiring consumer service. If you are acting as a primary source of export supply and are purchasing such a product from the domestic manufacturer you should arrange for a suitable policy with him under which he will participate in making it effective with your foreign trade.

Solving Foreign Exchange Control Problems

Actually this problem has to do with consumer accessibility and it affects both physical accessibility and price accessibility. If the rigors of exchange control are so strenuous as to entirely prohibit profitable selling in the territory, then there will of necessity have to be one unit of the world market in which you are unable to provide for consumer accessibility of the product. And if they are less strenuous price accessibility of the product will be affected by virtue of the excessive premium your trade channels will have to pay in order to purchase exchange through other than government channels in order to promptly pay your invoices.

Now in almost every territory in which dollar exchange control is in effect the world trader with an attractive product of high profit possibilities can usually locate someone who is in a position to arrange for prompt dollar payments. In the first place exchange is allocated to local merchants by the control board based upon the volume of their individual requirements. An active merchant making a large volume of purchases from abroad will therefore be able to secure more frequent and larger releases of dollar exchange against his requirements than will the smaller and less active merchant. Particularly is this true if the merchant at the same time happens to have political standing.

In general your trade contacts in the dollar exchange control territories should be with the most active houses only. Further you may assist the trade channel in arranging prompt payments by drawing a number of small drafts against him to cover large shipments rather than a large draft. It is easier for him to secure exchange frequently for small amounts than it is to handle a large amount. And by the same token it is better to make small shipments frequently instead of large shipments greater intervals, notwithstanding the fact that handling and shipping expense on this basis is considerably greater.

But aside from this there are numerous and devious means through which the merchant may be able to secure necessary dollar exchange with which to pay for your merchandise promptly. First and foremost of these is the merchant who has export dealings with foreign countries, other than the one whose exchange is under control. Thus a Colombian merchant and importer of goods from the United States may also be a coffee exporter to France. When he makes a shipment of coffee the French importer deposits francs in the bank to pay the Colombian merchant's invoices. Depending upon the strictness of control enforcement, it is sometimes possible for the merchant to convert these foreign deposits to his account into dollar exchange which is subsequently remitted to his suppliers in the United States.

Another method by means of which the local merchant may secure dollar exchange in excess of the amounts allocated by the control board exists where he is willing to pay an excessive premium for the accommodation. In all of the exchange control countries there are numerous delightful and shady gentlemen who make an illegal living by securing dollar exchange from various sources and peddling it at usurious rates to the harassed and needy merchants. Thus in many instances the merchant can secure the required dollar exchange to pay your bills promptly providing the price exacted by the exchange "bootlegger" does not completely destroy the price accessibility of the product or its profit possibilities.

A still more dubious practice under which the local merchant has been known to beat the control game, with the collusion of the exporter, consists of "kiting" the exchange application. Under this illegal procedure the merchant authorizes the supplier in the United States to increase the amount of each invoice covering shipments made, by say 30%. As a result the amount of exchange granted by the control board is always 30% greater than it would otherwise have been, and the exporter receives his money more rapidly. Since this method requires direct participation in an illegal act by the exporter it cannot, of course, be recommended.

And finally the bugaboos of exchange control may be evaded by the process of barter. Under this method the local merchant may purchase with his currency some native product which enjoys a ready market in the United States, and which will be accepted by the exporter here in physical exchange for an equivalent value of merchandise, based upon whatever resale value it realizes in this market. Of all of the above methods this presents the least satisfactory as it puts you to no end of inconvenience, causes you to engage in another line of business with which you are not familiar, and distracts your energies from the business at hand. *Barter should therefore be considered only where there is no other alternative, and only where the market for your product is large enough to make it truly profitable.*

Ameliorating Import and Tariff Restrictions

Import and tariff restrictions present a further problem to consumer accessibility of the product in both the physical and price significance of the phrase. In those countries where import embargoes have been imposed on certain products and where inadequate import quotas have been established for others, both of which affect physical consumer accessibility, or where prohibitive tariffs prevail thus affecting consumer price accessibility, the world trader will be obliged to tax his ingenuity to ameliorate these conditions in so far as possible. Not only must the devices he employs in so doing be possible; they must at the same time be *profitable*.

Where total embargo has been imposed or where quotas are entirely inadequate to the market potentialities there exists for the world trader but one of two alternatives. The first is to stay out of the market entirely or to accept what ever small business may be effected under existing quotas. Unless the market rates high in potentiality for the product, this is the only *profitable* course. However, where an extraordinarily potent market exists for the product there is an alternative, and that embraces either complete or partial manufacture locally.

The alternative of local manufacture may be undertaken by effecting arrangements with some local concern possessing the manufacturing facilities to produce the product, employing the technical assistance afforded by your patent rights, manufacturing methods, and machinery. Where complete manufacture of the product is thus undertaken locally, it is usually carried out on a royalty basis. Or the arrangement with the local manufacturing facilities may provide for the purchase of certain parts or portions of the product—not subject to prohibitive import restrictions— which your production facilities are in a position to provide cheaper or better than they could be manufactured locally, for subsequent completion of the manufacturing processes on the ground.

Or failing in endeavors to work the problem out on this basis you may arrange to establish local manufacturing facilities of your own by which the product may be either completely fabricated from the ground up, or by which the complementary operations necessary to partial assembly may be provided. Although this latter method has been undertaken by a number of American manufacturers in an endeavor to crack the difficult nut of import restrictions, it presents a number of serious drawbacks. In the first place it involves the permanent investment of capital abroad, which is always apt to be dangerous. Second the increased consumer cost of the product resulting from manufacture in limited quantities may reduce normal market potentialities to the point where the justification for local manufacture no longer exists. And further where local exchange control exists it is not possible for the owned foreign manufacturing facilities to readily secure dollar exchange for remittance to the parent organization in the States. As a result many American concerns which have undertaken local manufacture have large sums of "blocked" currency on deposit in foreign countries, the use of which they are not only temporarily deprived of but, still worse, which are subject to all of the vagaries and risks of loss through ex change fluctuation.

Like exchange control, import quotas are assigned to local concerns on a basis which is usually proportionate to the size and scale of their operations. In most instances the allocation of the total import quota made to the individual concern is based upon the relationship that its imports of the product, during a given previous period, bore to those of other importers of the product during the period. So here again it is desirable to deal with concerns who have been large scale operators in the product in the past, in order that the import allocation assigned to them may be the maximum possible.

Let us now see what may be done toward ameliorating the evils of prohibitive tariff restrictions, aside from local manufacture. In order to do this it is necessary that we examine briefly the basis under which tariffs are assigned and import duties subsequently assessed. Broadly speaking tariffs are assigned to the myriad of products imported by the country through classification of these products along. the same general lines as was described in Chapter V for that employed by the Department of Commerce.

Imports of products falling in these divisions of classification are assessed at the varying rates of duty which the tariff schedule calls for. Now the assessment of duty is based upon any one of several different methods or upon a combination of one or more of these methods. These are (1) the ad-valorem value of the product as indicated in the manufacturer's commercial invoice for the merchandise to the foreign importer, (2) the gross, legal, or net weight of the product, either in pounds or kilograms, whichever the standard of measurement in the specific country, and (3) in the case of some products upon the value or the weight, or both, of the various constituent elements which compose it.

From the above it will be seen that the study of tariffs in each of the 125 world-markets would be a task of no mean magnitude, and for the world trader to undertake this task would be to forego entirely, for lack of time, the important business of selling. There are, however, certain elementary procedures for limiting the amount of duty to be assessed under any of the above methods to a minimum. First and foremost of these is the general or basic classification into which the product falls in the tariff schedule. It frequently happens that the product is of such nature that it might be appropriately included under any one of half a dozen different generic headings, each of which carries a different rate of duty. For example an electric motor for a washing-machine may be classified simply as an electric motor, or it may be classified as a washing machine part or accessory, or it may with equal propriety be classified as an accessory for an electrical appliance.

Consequently it is of the greatest importance that your product be afforded position in the tariff schedule which provides classification under the *lowest,* rather than the highest rate of duty assessment. Your local trade channel is best in a position to ascertain what may be done to achieve this end and to carry out the necessary presentation of the matter to his local customs authorities. Thousands of dollars are saved in every territory annually and consumer price accessibility and market potentiality increased in this manner.

When the trade channel has determined the classification of lowest duty assessment under which the product may be legitimately entered, he should advise you of the exact wording of the declaration to be employed for consular purposes, in order that it may conform to the Customs ruling in the matter. As a matter of fact, *so important is this that you should make it a rule never to ship the product to the foreign customer until he has provided you with the correct customs declaration to be employed.* Should the declaration made by you be incorrect, not only will the customer be assessed unnecessary duties, but he may be subject to heavy fines. In either case these will be for your account.

Coming now to those products upon which duties are assessed on an ad-valorem basis, your commercial invoice to the customer should show the lowest possible selling price. It is desirable to show the *net* unit and total price for each item of the merchandise, rather than to show the unit list and total list price of the items subsequently deducting the trade discounts from the total of the invoice. Where this latter procedure is followed duty is liable to be assessed on the list prices rather than on the net prices. Further it is desirable that the net prices shown on your invoices cover the *merchandise value only,* and that all additional charges for packing, cartage, ocean freight, marine insurance, etc., etc., be issued on a separate invoice. Otherwise the customer may be obliged to pay duty on such extraneous charges which are not properly dutiable, where they are included in the merchandise totals or values shown.

Where the *net* weight of the product is the basis of duty assessment your prime concern will be to keep the *weight* of the product itself to the minimum. Often the substitution of lighter materials in the manufacturing process pays large dividends to the manufacturer in the increased consumer price accessibility afforded by lower shipping and duty charges. This however becomes a problem of adapting the product to the market, discussed in the forepart of this chapter, and depends on the market potentiality.

Where the duty is assessed on the Gross, or Legal weight of the product your problem is one of devising the lightest packing consistent with the safe arrival of the merchandise at the foreign destination. The *gross* weight of the merchandise is, of course, the total packed weight for foreign shipment And the *legal* weight of the merchandise is the weight of the product itself, plus any wrapping, or consumer carton, or inner packing such as excelsior, in which it is packed in the outer export case. A more detailed discussion of the science of export packing will be found in the chapter to come. Obviously large savings on duty, and also on transportation, can be made by affording a study to this matter.

Where the duty assessment on the merchandise is based upon a classification according to its various constituent elements, there are sometimes tricks which pay dividends. For example: a manufacturer of electric motors some years ago was obliged to declare the contents of the cases in shipping to a certain country, as consisting of fabricated iron, steel, copper, silk, cotton, and rubber His customer ascertained that if the contents of the case included either fabricated hemp, or wood, as well the motors would fall into an entirely different "partido" or customs classification at a much lower rate of duty. So for years every case of motors shipped contained either a ball of twine, or a small package of wooden toothpicks to comply with the customs regulation permitting the lower duty to be assessed.

And finally, where the product comprises a number of assembled units which may be readily detached at the factory and reassembled by the foreign customer, it may be found that by shipping parts, or assemblies separately they may be individually declared under different customs classifications so as to reduce the duty on the whole. Thus radio manufacturers find in many countries that the receiver when shipped complete with its wooden cabinet is assessed at a high rate of duty, whereas when the radio chassis is shipped and declared separately from the cabinet, the resultant duty is much less.

Careful investigation of the conditions surrounding world marketing problems and the use of a certain degree of ingenuity in shaping events into more favorable channels often makes possible the accomplishment of what appears, at first glance, to be impossible. And this often leads to the opening of markets of considerable potentiality to those who are willing to take the time and the trouble to find out how to beat the game. It often represents the difference between operating at a loss and the earning of a profit, and these are days when the profits go to the thinker of thoughts.

The Quantitative Position of Marketing in the United States[38 39]

Summary

Introduction, 394.— The definition of marketing, 390.— Retailing costs, 398,— Wholesaling costs, 398.— Manufacturer's marketing costs more difficult to estimate, 399.— Total cost of marketing in excess of 24 billion, 1929, 401.— Marketing costs compared with value added by manufacture, 402.— Income from marketing, 403.— Census of distribution facilitates estimate of marketing employment, 404.— Total marketing employment in excess of 8 million, 1929, 406.— Employment in marketing increased rapidly during the last two decades, 407.— Conclusions, 411.— Increasing specialization as a cause of increasing marketing costs, 412.

With the data which are available, two approaches to a measurement of the comparative magnitude or ranking of commodity marketing among the economic activities of the nation appear feasible. The first approach is by means of an estimate of the total cost or total value added by marketing activity, paralleling in Principle the well-known Census estimate of "value added by manufacture." The second approach is through an estimate of the total number of people employed in marketing in comparison with all gainfully employed and with the number employed in other economic activity. This approach permits of some comparison of the increase in importance of marketing activity over recent Census periods. No comparison of the sort is possible so far as marketing costs are concerned since data of their kind have only become available with the first Census of Distribution taken in 1930.

[38] J. K. Galbraith and J. D. Black, *Quarterly Journal of Economics*, vol. 49, May 1935, pp. 394–413.

[39] We are indebted to the Harvard University Committee on Research in the Social Sciences for a grant of money which enabled us to carry on the research embodied in this article.

An effort has been made in this paper to develop both of the foregoing approaches. An estimate has been made for 1930 of the total cost of marketing or total value added by marketing, in comparison with manufacturing. An effort has likewise been made to arrive at the total employment in marketing in that year and the trend in marketing employment over the last twenty years, and then to compare these with parallel estimates for other lines of economic activity. Finally the recent estimates of the National Bureau of Economic Research and the United States Department of Commerce are used in an attempt to formulate a third measure, that of total income produced by marketing. The data for estimates of income, however, fall short of what are needed to establish this comparison with precision. We wish to make it clear at the outset that even a cursory examination of the data upon which estimates such as the present are based may suggest that the term "speculative statistics" is an apt description of the findings. Not only is there uncertainty as to the quality of the Census data which must be used, but there are numerous gaps where information of even a reasonably authentic character is lacking. Finally, of course, there is difficulty in defining marketing itself. For example, do we conceive of marketing as including transportation? On this issue turns the inclusion or exclusion of several million workers and a several billion dollar bill for carriage. Economists have amply demonstrated their ability to disagree over much more certain (if more important) matters. But if this be resolved, the larger problem emerges of the blending of marketing activity with other things, frequently within the same business unit. The manufacturer and the farmer alike combine marketing with production. Against the cost of marketing gasoline must also be charged the incidental services of cleaning windshields, checking tires and perhaps of providing a service station with some aesthetic appeal to a race of discriminating motorists. The undertaker and his business might at first thought be excluded from a tabulation of employment in commodity marketing; on second thought, however, it is recalled that he sells coffins and flowers as well as a dignified departure. Numerous such problems rise up to plague the person who makes estimates of the sort here presented.

On the other hand, since the Census of Distribution has become available, a vastly better appraisal of the place of marketing activity in the national economy can be made than has hitherto been possible. From the standpoint of pedagogy, calculations of the value added by marketing and of the percentage of gainfully employed so engaged give the student a more enlightened and better balanced impression of the importance of marketing than is imparted by merely telling him that it is "very important."

Such information has also an important bearing on some major national issues. The gains in industrial and agricultural efficiency of which we constantly hear are placed in better perspective when the large and apparently increasing importance of our system of distribution is fully appreciated. Is it significant that we hear decidedly little about the increasing efficiency of the latter? The possibility of a changing composition of our increasing urban population is also suggested by information of the type here presented. To mention an issue of current importance in this connection, it may be that a failure to appreciate the present-day importance of trade as compared with industry holds serious possibilities of an overestimation of the extent to which reemployment measures should be planned for time industrial rather than the commercial population. These values of the present estimates remain despite the fact that they involve, as indicated, many arbitrary definitions and assumptions (some of which are likely to be peculiar with the person making the estimates) and a certain number of gaps and guesses.

The Definition of Marketing

For time purpose of the following tabulations commodity marketing has been considered in a relatively narrow sense; namely as something rather intimately a part of or connected with the transfer of ownership of tangible goods. On a business unit basis, this includes the great body of wholesale and retail establishments, together with the sales activity of manufacturers and like producers. It excludes the transportation of goods. It may be effectively argued that the service of transportation in relation to marketing shows no logical differentiation from the service of storage as performed by some types of wholesalers. Dividing lines, even though arbitrary, are necessary, and the service of transportation may be regarded as an entity sufficiently large to be set apart by itself. The inclusion of costs of such services to marketing as banking, insurance, and communication on a separate business unit basis in the tabulations would involve double counting since the costs of these services to marketing are already included in the costs of operation of wholesale and retail business units.

Using the term marketing in the above sense, the concept of marketing cost, or value added by marketing, is the equivalent of the total gross margins of business units engaged wholly (or primarily) in the performance of marketing services. This may be arrived at for a given year by adding to the payrolls, expenses, interest, dividends and entrepreneurial withdrawals any reinvestmnent or corporate or individual savings of such participating units, and subtracting any reduction of surplus or savings. Ideally, for any given year adjustments for inventory change would also be made. To the above must be added such marketing expenditures of business enterprises as those of manufacturers who are not engaged primarily in marketing activity yet in the aggregate spend a large amount on the marketing of their goods. Strictly speaking, to parallel for these the treatment given wholesale and retail units would involve a separation of the gross margin taken by the manufacturer into "value added by manufacture" and "value added by marketing," with imputation of costs of executive talent and other overhead between manufacturing on the one hand and advertising, sales management and other marketing activity on the other. Actually, available data for estimating sales costs of the manufacturer are far too sketchy for so complete an exercise. As in the case of the wholesale and retail units themselves, many refinements must be omitted in the actual estimates.

Costs of retailing, as might be expected, comprise the largest item in the total marketing bill. On total sales of slightly over 49 billion dollars in 1929, the Census estimates a gross retail margin of approximately 28 per cent, or very nearly 14 billion dollars. This total is divided among various items as follows:

Total payroll	$5,190,000,000
Proprietors at full-time salary rate	1,820,000,000
All other expenses, including interest where actually paid	5,180,000,000
Interest and profits (residual)	1,560,000,000
Total	$13,750,000,000

Wholesaling Costs

The Census of Distribution does not provide the basis for an estimate of gross margins in wholesaling; hence Census data must be supplemented by those from other sources. Operating costs in wholesaling which are given by the Census amounted to slightly over 6 billions in 1929 on a total volume of wholesale trade exceeding 69 billions. These include payrolls, general expenses, and interest where actually paid. Estimates of dividends, entrepreneurial withdrawals and net corporate amid individual savings in wholesaling have been prepared by the Bureau of Foreign and Domestic Commerce with the cooperation of the National Bureau of Economic Research.[40] While these estimates cannot be credited with detailed accuracy, they indicate that the items in question totalled in the neighborhood of 850 millions in 1929. This brings the total cost of wholesaling in 1929 to approximately 7 billion dollars, divided as follows:

Salaries and wages	$3,010,000,000
Other expenses (including interest actually paidand rent actually paid)	3,130,000,000
Dividends	200,000,000
Withdrawals of individual entrepreneurs	580,000,000
Corporate savings	20,000,000
Business savings of individuals	50,000,000
Total cost of wholesaling	$6,990,000,000
Combined retailing and wholesaling costs	$20,740,000,000

It has been a general experience in the United States to find the first Census of an industry or other sector of the national life to be unsatisfactory in many details. In view of the magnitude and complexity of the Census of Distribution, there can be little doubt that it shares many of the shortcomings of other first attempts. Estimates based on this source suffer accordingly. None the less the figure of 20.7 billions given above as the total cost of wholesaling and retailing appears to be a fair approximation of the actual costs of performing these functions in commodity distribution in 1929.

The remaining major item, that of manufacturer's costs, is not so readily ascertainable. Some estimates may be made, however, which will at least pad the figure for total marketing costs in the direction in which it should go.

[40] National Income, 1929–32. Senate doc. 124, 73d Congress, 2d Session.

Total sales of manufactured goods in 1929 as reported by the Census amounted to $63,409,000,000, which was distributed among various marketing channels as follows:

To home consumers, 2.5% or	$1,553,000,000
To retailers, 18.6% or	11,777,000,000
To wholesalers, 29.6% or	18,759,000,000
To industrial consumers, 31.3% or	19, 850,000,000
To manufacturers' retail branches, 1.9% or	1,233,000,000
To manufacturers' wholesale branches, 16.1% or	10,237,000,000
Total	$63,409,000,000

On sales to home consumers, the combined costs of retailing and wholesaling can be taken as an index of manufacturers' marketing costs; on sales to retailers, the wholesale cost rate may be applied. These calculations may indeed be far off the mark, but for such commodities as are susceptible to handling through wholesale and retail units, the procedure has considerable to commend it, provided the estimates of wholesale and retail costs are valid. The circumstance, for example, that direct-to-consumer marketing channels exist alongside wholesale-retail channels indicates some equilibrium between the two with no overwhelming advantage on either side. On the basis of wholesale and retail expenses only (i.e., excluding dividends, corporate savings, etc.) this calculation gives a marketing cost of some 490 million dollars for direct-to-consumer marketing and 1,040 million dollars for manufacturer-to-retailer marketing. No ready rule, valid or invalid, appears for fixing the marketing cost on the 61 per cent of the output of manufactured goods which goes to industrial consumers and wholesalers. Such scattered studies as those of the Harvard Bureau of Business Research[41] show a wide variation in such costs, and do not differentiate sharply enough between different channels to be of assistance. Dr. L. D. H. Weld in a review of data on marketing costs[42] has suggested a general rate

[41] Marketing Expenses of Grocery Manufacturers, Bull. 79, Bureau of Business Research, Harvard University, February, 1930.

[42] Printer's Ink Monthly, March, 1932, pp. 22–23, 61–62.

of 4 per cent as sufficient to cover the sales cost of the nation's manufactured output. There is little basis upon which to elaborate an argument. The authors have chosen 5 per cent, giving a somewhat greater weight to such strongly advertised and promoted commodities as soap, cereals, tobacco,[43] as these offset the relatively low cost of marketing such commodities as textile fabrics and most capital goods. This gives a total of roughly 2 billions of dollars as the cost of marketing manufactured goods to wholesale and industrial purchasers.

Where goods are transferred to the manufacturers' own wholesale or retail branches, the item of marketing cost not covered by the Census which is likely to bulk largest for purposes of this computation (since transportation is excluded) is that of advertising. It seems probable that a one or two per cent allowance would cover this item; and if one per cent only is allowed, the resulting addition to the costs of marketing is 110 millions.

Summarizing the above estimates of manufacturers' sales costs, there are the following items:

Cost of sales to retailers and home consumers	$1,530,000,000
Cost of sales to wholesalers and industrial consumers	2,000,000,000
Marketing cost incurred by manufacturer on goods transferred to wholesale and retail branches	110,000,000
Total	$3,640,000,000

Total Costs Of Marketing

The aggregate of the foregoing estimates of retail, wholesale, and manufacturers' marketing costs is between 24 and 25 billion dollars distributed as follows:

	Amount	*Per Cent*
Retailing costs	$13,750,000,000	56
Wholesaling costs	6,990,000,000	29
Manufacturers'Marketing costs	3,640,000,000	15
Total	$24,380,000,000	100

[43] Bureau of Business Research, op. cit., pp. 9 and 14. Costs of marketing soaps and cleansers (including transportation) varied from 16 to 56 per cent for 10 firms; for cereals, from 25 per cent to 27 per cent for 3 firms.

To the above figure might be added the costs of such direct marketing of agricultural products as take place.[44] Also an imaginative person might say that the line between the end of production and the beginning of marketing should be drawn at the farm, and hence estimate the farmer's cost of bringing his products to the stage in the marketing channels Where they are comprehended by time present figures.[45] This latter, however, is not usually a cash cost to the farmer, and even for the individual farm a valid cost figure cannot be imputed. We refrain from carrying statistical metaphysics farther than has already been necessary.

Marketing And Manufacturing Costs Compared

Some care is necessary in drawing comparisons between a figure such as the total of marketing costs just given and similar figures for other economic activity. The purpose of such comparisons can only be to show relative size and importance of the entities compared. Total expenditures are by no means an accurate index of such size and might be fantastically unreal in some cases. This is the case where an expenditure for raw materials may enter in one case and be excluded as a matter of course in another.

The comparison of marketing costs with manufacturing costs which avoids the foregoing difficulties must obviously be a comparison of the figures cited with "value added by manufacture." Given the definition of marketing costs here set up, this comparison is valid in principle. Actually it has certain shortcomings, including the item that manufacturing data do not cover firms with an output worth less than $5,000, while retail establishments of comparably diminutive proportions are included. This particular qualification, it may be said, is not of great importance in comparison with the much larger probable margin of error in estimates of manufacturers' marketing costs. The figures of value added for 1929 are as follows:

Value added by manufacture less estimated manufactures' marketing costs	$28,250,000,000
Marketing costs or *value added by marketing*	24,380,000,000

[44] Also omitted are the relatively minor items of cost of marketing unmanufactured forest, fishery and mineral products by the original producers.

[45] In general this means the country assembling unit or country buyer. See Census of Distribution, Part II, Wholesale Distribution, p. 43.

Thus in 1929 for each dollar which was spent on the manufacture of goods, an outlay of some 85 cents for marketing of All commodities, manufactured or other, is indicated. If these figures are a reasonably close approximation of the true situation, it is apparent that marketing costs counted for but a slightly smaller proportion of the total final costs of the nation's commodities than did the cost of manufacture where such was required.

Income From Marketing

Income *produced*[46] by marketing constitutes but a part of the above total of marketing costs. The remainder is an aggregation of income produced by real estate, communication services, utility services, and other economic functions which serve marketing and are covered by marketing costs. In the case of interest and dividends, an arbitrary decision must be made as to whether these are counted as the income accruing to marketing or whether they are counted (in part) as the income produced by the financial institutions which are financing marketing.[47] The National Bureau follows the practice of attempting to allocate such income to its source, which in this case would be to marketing.

The classification *trade* in the national income estimates of the National Bureau and the Department of Commerce ranks second to manufacturing in the volume of income produced in 1929.[48] For the more important industrial divisions, their estimates are as shown below (page 404).

Item	*Amount*	*Per Cent*
Manufacturing	$19,354,000,000	23.3
Trade	11,353,000,000	13.7
Finance	9,633,000,000	11.6
Service	8,453,000,000	10.2
Agriculture*	7,538,000,000	9.1
Transportation	7,020,000,000	8.5
Government	6,456,000,000	7.8

[46] That is, income including corporate and individual savings as distinct from income paid out. See Simon Kuznets, National Income, 1924–32. Bulletin 49, National Bureau of Economic Research, June 7, 1934, p. 1.

[47] Kuznets, op. cit., p. 2 (note).

[48] Senate doc. 124, op. cit., p.26. it is worthy of note that according to these estimates *trade* dropped to third place in 1932, slightly behind manufacture, which in turn was second to government.

* This estimate is not closely comparable with those of the other divisions, since family supplies obtained directly from the farm, and use of farm dwelling, are included on a much lower basis of valuation than prevails in cities.

Of the total national income of 83,032 millions in 1929, according to these estimates, the income produced by trade would account for nearly 14 per cent. However, the definition of trade as used for these estimates covers only wholesale and retail establishments. Some part of the 3.6 billions of estimated manufacturers' marketing costs represents income produced by marketing activity. In the case of both wholesaling and retailing, the ratio of income produced to gross margin is close to 55 per cent (54.4 for retailing and 55.4 for wholesaling), and if this ratio be applied to manufacturers' marketing costs, then the amount to be added to income from trade for this item would be approximately 2 billions. The following comparison might then be made as between manufacturing and marketing:

	Income Produced 1929	*Per Cent of Total National Income*
Manufacturing	$17,350,000,000	21
Marketing	13,350,000,000	16

It must not be forgotten that the above figures involve a considerable range of possible error. Not only is there a narrow basis indeed for the assumption that income produced by manufacturers' marketing activity will bear the same ratio to total expenditure as in the case of retailing and wholesaling, but the estimate of total manufacturers' marketing cost is subject to error. Any interpretation which goes farther than to conclude that marketing ranked a fairly close second to manufacture in its contribution to the total national income prior to the depression is probably open to question.

Employment In Marketing

The Census of Distribution has markedly improved our basis for estimating the number of people who are given employment by marketing. It is impossible after the most detailed dissection of the occupational tabulations of the Census of Occupations to determine, for example, the proportion of the nation's elevator operators who are employed in marketing establishments. Equally baffling is any determination from this source of the proportion of the country's pre-depression army of four million clerical workers engaged in marketing establishments or activity. The tabulation of gainful workers by industry in the 1930 Census does, indeed, make definite progress toward an answer to the above questions.[49] There remain, none the less, over a million gainful workers not definitely assigned to any industrial group, and certain occupational classes of a border-line character (such as garages, greasing stations and restaurants) are listed apart from trade, and sometimes are combined with items purely extraneous to a tabulation of employment in marketing.

The Census of Distribution tabulation of employees in wholesale and retail establishments avoids a large number of the above difficulties encountered in the Census of Occupations. For 1929, retail and wholesale employment was as follows:

Retail:	
Full-time employees	3,834,000
Part-time employees reduced to a full-time equivalent*	123,000
Proprietor owners	1,511,000
Total retail	5,467,000
Wholesale:	
Number of employees	1,605,000
Number of proprietors**	91,000
Total wholesale	1,696,000
Total, wholesale and retail	7,164,000

* On the basis of U.S. Department of commerce and National Bureau of Economic Research estimates. Senate doc. 124, op cit., p. 113.
** As estimated by the U.S. Department of Commerce and National Bureau of Economic Research. Ibid., p. 113.

[49] In the occupational groupings, a stenographer employed by a manufacturing concern is classified under "clerical." In the industrial groupings she is classed under manufacturing. This difference in classification holds true for all such occupations, which, tho involving similar work, may be given employment by widely varying industries. Only two attempts (1910 and 1930) have been made at an industrial grouping of workers.

Employment in the marketing end of manufacturing presents, like the estimate of manufacturers' marketing costs, tile most difficult part of the problem. Some key to this total is presented, however, by the occupational subclassifications of the Census tabulation of gainful workers by industry. Under manufacturing and mechanical industries, nine occupational subclassifications are of such character that workers therein may be fairly definitely classed as engaged in marketing. Aggregating these for the 82 subdivisions of manufacture gives a total of 365 thousand workers divided as follows:

Salesmen and saleswomen	110,900
Shipping clerks	97,800
Commercial travelers	89,600
Canvassers	24,400
Advertising agents	15,900
Collectors	9,800
Weighers	7,800
Credit men	7,500
Sales agents	1,400
Total	365,100

When the above total of gainful workers in manufacturing establishments (as of April 1, 1930) is added to the total number given employment in retail and wholesale establishments in 1929, as reported by the Census of Distribution, an ascertainable total marketing employment in excess of 7.5 millions is established.[50] In addition to the above occupations are a number which serve both marketing and the ordinary business routine. Aside from executives, there are clerks, stenographers and typists, bookkeepers and cashiers, accountants and auditors, agents, messenger and office boys, and office appliance operators, all of which come in this class. For manufacturing, a total of approximately 1.1 million such workers is listed in 1929.

[50] Theoretically this should also include the workers in selling occupations connected with mineral, quarry, forest, and fishing products by the original producer prior to manufacture or where there is no manufacturing process. Actually the total of these is so small that it can be neglected.

It is obviously impossible to make any accurate estimate of the part of the above group which should be assigned to marketing. Indeed, the duties or responsibilities of many individual workers are a combination of marketing and other functions. It is believed, however, that anyone familiar with the relative volume of clerical work associated with sales activity in a manufacturing plant as compared with that involved in management would agree on the basis of total hours to the allotment of at least half and perhaps more of the above group to marketing activities, if half be arbitrarily settled upon, then the total marketing employment in 1929 was somewhat in excess of 8 millions divided as follows:

Retailing	5,500,000
Wholesaling	1,700,000
Manufacturers' marketing	900,000
Total marketing employment	8,100,000

It seems reasonably certain that the above figure is within from 5 to 10 per cent of the true figure for gainful workers in or commonly occupied in marketing pursuits in 1929-30. This places marketing in the third position in terms of total workers employed, coming next after manufacturing and agriculture. The comparison with manufacturing, agriculture, and transportation and communication is as follows:

	Total	*Per Cent of all Gainful Workers*
Manufacturing and mechanical industries	13,400,000	27.4*
Agriculture	10,500,000	21.4*
Marketing	8,100,000	16.6
Transport and communication	4,400,000	9.1*

* Census of Occupations. Gainful workers by industry and occupation. Manufacturing figures are adjusted for marketing workers removed.

Trends In Marketing Employment

In 1928 Professor Slichter, citing the apparent decrease in factory, railroad and farm employment since the beginning of the decade, suggested that a part of the slack, including the new employables, had been taken up in the distributive trades as well as in the professions, public utilities, building trades and elsewhere.[51] No confirmation of this trend is yet available from the Census of Distribution (or the industrial groupings of the Census of Occupations). But such tabulation as can be made of marketing occupations from the Census of Occupations would support the assumption of a rapid increase in employment in marketing pursuits during the last decade. The total of gainful workers in tile occupations which can be segregated from the various general occupational groups of the last three Censuses and definitely classed as marketing, together with the number of workers in the more important of the marketing occupations, is given below:[52]

Occupation	*1930*	*1920*	*1910*
Salesmen and saleswomen	2,069,000	1,192,000	940,000
Retail dealers	1,704,000	1,328,000	1,195,000
'Clerks' in stores	402,000	414,000	387,000
Waiters	393,000	229,000	188,000
Commercial travelers	224,000	179,000	164,000
Laborers, porters, helpers in stores	209,000	125,000	102,000
Agents, collectors, credit men	196,000	161,000	87,000
Restaurant, cafe and lunchroom keepers	165,000	88,000	61,000
Delivery men*	159,000	160,000	220,000
Other occupations identifiable with marketing**	720,000	542,000	381,000
Total	6,241,000	4,418,000	3,725,000

* Laundry delivery men excluded from 1920 and 1910 tabulations on the basis of their 1930 ratio to all delivery men.
** In order of their importance in 1930, these are shipping clerks; 'Other pursuits in trade'; laborers in coal and lumber yards, warehouses, grain elevators, tcs.; wholesale dealers,

[51] American Economic Review. Supplement, 1929, p. 5.

[52] It should be noted that looseness of terminology and definition in designating occupations and the consequent enumeration of certain types of workers under different occupations at different times or by different enumerators makes the changes within certain categories of conjectural validity. The most important of these vagaries are discussed in the text.

importers and exporters; advertising agents; proprierters, managers, and officials not otherwise specified; newsboys; floorwalkers, foremen, and overseers; commercial brokers and commission men; decorators, drapers and window dressers; inspectors, gaugers and samplers; weighers; and apprentices, wholesale and retail.

While the above totals of workers in occupations which can be identified with marketing fall far short of the actual number so engaged, they do constitute a relatively large sample.[53] There is ample basis for the conclusion that employment in marketing pursuits in general increased rapidly between 1910 and 1930 and especially so between 1920 and 1930. This gain was so rapid that the marketing occupations here tabulated increased their share of the total gainfully employed from approximately 10 per cent in 1910 to nearly 13 per cent in 1930. During the same period, the percentage of gainfully employed in manufacture, while increasing from approximately 29 per cent in 1910 to approximately 31 per cent in 1920, declined to 29 per cent in 1930. The percentage of gain fully employed in agriculture was apparently showing a decline over the entire twenty-year period. It is interesting to note that even in the partial total of marketing employment here tabulated, the increase in percentage of gainful workers between 1920 and 1930 was large enough more than to offset the decline in the proportion engaged in manufacturing. It is also of interest to compare the increase in identifiable marketing employment in 1930 to 168 per cent of the 1910 level with the increase in manufacturing employment to but 132 per cent, and with an apparent slight decline in agricultural employment. The detailed comparisons of numbers, per cent of total and percentage increase of gainful workers in manufacturing, agriculture, and identifiable marketing occupations for the three Census years are as follows:

[53] Of the total marketing employment in 1930, according to the estimates given above, about 77 per cent is accounted for here.

	1930	*1920*	*1910*
Total gainful workers	48,830,000	41,614,000	37,167,000
Gainful workers in manufacturing*	14,111,000	10,666,000	11,388,000
Gainful workers in agriculture**	10,472,000	414,000	387,000
Gainful workers identifiable with marketing	6,241,000	4,418,000	3,725,000

	1930	*1920*	*1910*
Per cent of all gainful workers in manufacturing	28.9	30.8	28.7
Per cent of all gainful workers in agriculture	21.4	25.6	30.6
Per cent of all gainful workers identifiable with marketing	12.8	10.6	10
Workers in manufacturing in per cent of 1910	132	120	100
Workers in agriculture in per cent of 1910	92	94	100
Workers identifiable with marketing in per cent of 1910	168	119	100

* Manufacturing and mechanical industries; based on the Census occupational grouping. This grouping differs from the industrial grouping used in foregoing comparisons.
** Vagaries of Census enumeration have played a significant part in the changes in this group. Part of the decrease from 1910 to 1920, as shown by the Census, is the result of an overenumeration of women and children in 1910 and, to a smaller extent, an underenumeration of agricultural laborers in 1920. The figure given here for 1910 is a million less than that shown by the Census. This adjustment is roughly indicated by the increase in number of women and unpaid workers reported as gainfully employed in 1910 as compared with the increase in other workers. Cf. Research in Farm Labor, Bull. 16 of the Social Science Research Council, pp. 1–3.

Examination of the various occupational groups in marketing reveals that the classification of "salesmen and saleswomen" has shown the greatest increase between 1920 and 1930, with a total gain of nearly 900,000 persons. This, how ever, is not a net increase, for the slight decline in the classification "clerks in stores" is undoubtedly the result of a more general enumeration of retail employees in the first-mentioned group. The increase in retail dealers from 1,328,000 in 1920 to 1,704,000 in 1930 parallels the increase in salesmen and saleswomen and constitutes the second largest item in the total increase. The rapid extension of chain-store merchandising, which would inevitably increase for a time at least the total number of stores, appears to be the most important factor in the increase in number of retail establishments. In the grocery field, where chain expansion was especially great, there was an increase in retail dealers from 239,000 in 1920 to 313,000 in 1930. This was apparently an unstable "bulge" which further competition between the independents and chains (combined with the influence of the depression) has served to remove.[54] Also of probable importance is the increase in automobile service stations and employees and in the many other types of establishments which have sprung up to serve the motorist and tourist. It is likely that smaller purchases or hand-to-mouth buying, together with consumer demand for convenience in retail service, also had an influence.

The restaurant group — considered as marketing with perhaps, some license — also showed a striking expansion between 1920 and 1930; in fact, when waiters and proprietors are combined, the increase in total employment in this category was nearly seven times as great as the increase during the preceding ten years. It is evident that the increased resort to public eating places was one of the important changes in consumers' habits during the last decade, altho here also the need for meeting the needs of increasing motor travel is of importance. Possibly the restaurant business may have been attractive to persons who chose to solve or escape personal unemployment by establishing their own business. This factor may also have been of importance in the increase in retail stores during a period when the conditions were relatively favorable to the launching of individual enterprises.

The probable reason for the decline in tile numbers of "clerks in stores" as shown by the tabulation has already been

[54] It is estimated that the number of retail entrepreneurs declined by about 30 per cent between 1929 and 1932. Senate doe. 124, op. cit., p. 109.

indicated. The other major decline was the reduction by more than 60,000 in the number of delivery men since 1910. While the growth of cash-and-carry business may have played a part in this reduction, there appears to have been a tendency, as use of the motor truck for delivery purposes has become general, to classify an increasing proportion of this group under transportation.

Conclusions

Data such as those here presented, whatever their shortcomings, show unequivocally that the marketing of goods is now occupying a major position in our national life. Prior to the depression we spent, it would appear, about 85 per cent as much on marketing as on manufacturing. It would also appear that marketing contributed to the national income perhaps 75 to 80 per cent as much as was contributed by manufacturing and probably more than was contributed by agriculture. In total employment offered, marketing continued to rank third to manufacturing and agriculture in 1929-30; but the gap remaining was far narrower than the erstwhile student of the Census of Occupations would have been likely to suspect. From this latter source, unsatisfactory tho it has been fur purposes of determining the industrial attachments of the population, there is indication of a steady and even rapid increase in the proportion of all workers in marketing pursuits over the last twenty years.

Nothing more need be said of the part played by consumer demand for conveniences or services or of changes in consumer habits in this large and apparently increasing importance of marketing in the national economy. There is a further condition basic to this importance, however, which is woven closely with the entire pattern of modern industrial organization and progress. Upon this we must comment briefly.

We have long since taken an increasing efficiency in our industrial and agricultural plant as one of the primary facts of our national existence. While no longer do we look with Adam Smith upon increasing specialization or division of labor as the sole or even the primary basis of increasing efficiency, we still agree that increasing specialization is an almost inescapable concomitant of the technological progress which does tend toward new and better methods of production. In the case of the famous pins there was little possibility that any influences would be overlooked which acted to offset the gains from division of labor. Most specialization presents a much less simple problem. When the largely self-sustained community or the largely self-sufficing farm comes to concentrate on one or a few lines of production the accompanying increase in the efficiency with which factors of production are employed is usually apparent to all. Such engineering appraisals, however, make no examination of the way in which the commercial contacts of the community or farm have been multiplied; or of the human energy, capital, and enterprise which is now devoted to the task of selling the product or products of the community and in selling the products of the specialized production of the outside world to it.

The large and apparently growing importance of marketing leads to the question of how much of our gains in industrial and agricultural efficiency have been offset by the additional effort expended in maintaining commercial contacts between the increasingly interdependent parts of the economy. The known increase in our real income refutes the suggestion that the offsetting influence has been complete. Yet we may ask if some considerable part of our economized industrial effort has not merely involved the substitution of increased commercial enterprise.

Clearly, in any case, our future appraisals of gains and losses in economic efficiency must include and emphasize marketing not less than industry, agriculture and like components of the economy. The importance of marketing would alone justify such inclusion and emphasis; the fact that increased marketing or commercial costs may be a direct result of increased industrial efficiency, where this is accompanied by specialization, makes it essential.

The people of the United States may, on the whole, be credited with a fair degree of objectivity in their appraisals of industrial and agricultural efficiency. During a time of general unemployment such as the present, it is perhaps inevitable that there should be prophets who would find the volume of employment that is directly provided the criterion of what is desirable in industrial or agricultural processes. However, our sense of the true purpose of economic activity is sufficiently secure that our accepted goals of economic efficiency still stand.

We seem likely to continue to evaluate our industrial plant in terms of its product in relation to human energy consumed. Such objectivity we have not generally brought to bear upon appraisals of our marketing machinery. When we do, it may well be possible that we will find a more fruitful field for future increases in efficiency in commodity distribution than in commodity production.

Towards an Understanding: Designer and Businessman[55]

By R. Haughton James
Art Director, H. K. McCann Co., Ltd.

The aims of the business man are self-evident. The aims of the artist are often thought to be obscure. When the two try to co-operate they sometimes fail to understand each other. Perhaps this is because the artist is incoherent, perhaps because he finds business ideals unsympathetic. Mr. James here makes an attempt to throw light on the vexed question of their relationship and to explain what the artist is really after.

That I am bound to be contradicted is beyond reasonable doubt. There are almost as many theories of art as there are artists. Nowhere does one hear such vehement altercation as at a studio party. Nevertheless, no two artists are as far apart in their views as any one of them and the average business man.

There are artists even now who would, with a lofty disdain, echo the aphorism of Oscar Wilde, that all art is quite useless. Except as an exercise in the expression of their personal neurosis one must concede that this is true of a large amount of modem artists' work. One may turn, however, more hopefully towards a creed fathered by Leonardo da Vinci, the painter-musician-engineer sage, typified to-day by Norman Bel Geddes; that of the designer to Industry.

I want to explain, if I can, how the designer approaches a job, by what standards his judgments are made, where his real value lies. I want to demonstrate his use as a touchstone, a mouth piece, an interpreter; that he can speak to millions with a clearer voice than you can yourselves. In fact I shall expect you to regard the designer as the most valuable unit of all in your campaign to

[55] From *The Packaging Omnibus*, London: Creative Journals Ltd, 1936, pp. 25–28.

increase sales. It makes no difference at all whether you are selling Bibles or boots, cork mats or cascara; the artist can produce an astonishing love for your product among the indifferent multitude.

You must not expect this miracle from every artist so-called. You can't hire talent for £2 a week or incarcerate genius in a printer's studio. Thousands can learn to make a fair copy of a given subject, to make mannerisms of the subtleties of better men, to confuse a detailed imitation of appearance with significance. Many can state where few can suggest. It isn't every Greek who could build the Parthenon.

Men with great gifts are rare. Our mutual aim is to help every man to produce the best of which he is capable, is it not? It only remains to be discovered what we both mean by "best".

Bad composers employ the same notation as good ones. The same paints can produce a problem picture or a masterpiece. In what then, does greatness lie? Evidently not in the materials.

Have those works of antiquity which have commanded the respect of generations of differently-thinking persons some quality in common? Can any link be found between the Winged Victory and the Moonlight Sonata, between the Taj Mahal and Hogarth's "Shrimp Girl"?

I'm told that if the Moonlight Sonata is played back to front it still makes a comprehensible piece of music. I have noticed myself that a photographic negative will lose nothing in composition when compared with its positive print. Values are now inside out, yet the something is in no way lost.

How elasticare notation, colour sequence and composition, if they lose nothing by an inversion of their values! Has this to do with mathematics? Can we find a *law*?

R. H. Wilenski quotes Socrates: "Straight lines and circles, and the planes or solid figures which are formed out of them by turning lathes and rulers and measurers of angles.....these I affirm to be not only relatively beautiful, but they are eternally and absolutely beautiful.....If arithmetic, measuration and weighing be taken away from any art, that which remains will not be much. The rest will only be conjecture, the slickness of hand which comes by practice, and those qualities which are perfected by attention and pains."

Among this "rest" we can put all those completely unimportant attributes which reflect or raise emotion of any sort. Sentiment has no particular relation to art. A picture is no more beautiful because it is of England rather than of Alsatia, or because it shows the hierarchy of heaven rather than a board of directors. Religious feelings, Patriotic feelings and so forth are completely secondary. *A work of art is elevating because it is essentially a harmony.*

There is absolutely no exception to this rule. Think it out for yourself. In music, sculpture, typography, painting, pottery or postage stamps, harmony of colour and form are everything. Could the artist introduce this same harmony of line and substance within its obvious limits, into a tin of baked beans, then Heinz could stand by Titian, unashamed.

Socrates, wise old man, scoffs at the skill acquired by " pains and attention." Without the leaven of intuition such pains are truly wasted.

By intuition the artist feels one thing is right, feels another is wrong.

The intuition of the artist can make a fortune for anyone who is humble enough to recognise it and let it operate. No one is born with intuition such as this. It grows with his consciousness of the beautiful around him. In his contact with life he appraises everything he sees in the light of its design, its colour, its harmony with its surroundings. His passionate interest in these things makes it natural that he sees clearer than the average man.

Do not think that only the artist can be affected by these harmonies; anyone can by the same constant application train his taste to a high level. This is particularly important, especially as the sense of unity and order upon which the artist insists is the one thing which, being not relatively but absolutely valuable, evokes the same pleasurable response from every human being with a grain of sensibility in his make-up.

It follows, therefore, that in any design which is to attract people's favourable attention, much more important than any likeness to "the real thing", is the achievement of harmonious colour and proportions. Granting that commercial art demands certain concessions to non-aesthetic considerations, who can say that a plum's exterior appearance is its most characteristic feature? Aren't exterior appearances rather boring? We know so well what plums are like; to draw them just like that is really stating the obvious, and as such is neither original nor particularly engaging.

What is also very important is that an artist should pay due respect to the idiosyncrasy of his tools and the nature of his materials. This applies more to designing goods than publicity designs for goods. Few creative artists have interested themselves in designing for the machine; such attempts as have been made have been largely amateurish. Designs for pottery, for instance, were recently solicited by manufacturers from artists eminent in other fields, the designs being turned out without reference to the limitations of the material in which they had to be reproduced. This is only taxing the ingenuity of the factory-worker and debasing him to the level of a copyist. If the manufacturer is not satisfied with the work he can get from his own bench workers, why not commission a limited number of outside artists to produce designs on condition that they fit themselves for the task by say, a two years' apprenticeship in the craft before they set pencil to paper? The artists would have to be paid all that time. The new lines would then be likely to embody the maximum of practicability and some element of absolute beauty as well.

Materials themselves have always dictated form. Where artists have tried to impose forms unexpressive of the materials in which they are working, beauty has invariably suffered. Com pare, for instance, sculpture in stone and wood. Stone has no fibre, it does not grow upwards through the grain of its substance as does wood. Stone lies in the earth, submits readily to incision in any direction, is essentially static. The finest sculptures in stone all reflect this static quality. The famous sculptured figures at Chartres are stone as much as they are sculptures. They are great sculptures largely because "naturalism" has been sacrificed to purely aesthetic considerations. On the other hand, while we stand amazed at the intricacy of detail in the German wood-carving at South Kensington, the squirming exuberance of their form is rather disgusting, denying as it does the smooth flow of the trunks from which they arc fashioned. It is apparent that each material demands a treatment of its own.

Do not be surprised then, if the artist voices a protest if you ask him to apply to an article made of aluminium decoration evolved in terms of plaster. The makers of plastics have evidently had their moments of doubt on this point. Here is a completely new material, with no traditional convention of its own. How to decorate it?

".....straight lines and circles, planes and the solid figures which are formed out of them by turning lathes and rulers and measurers of angles these I affirm to be.....eternally and absolutely beautiful."

The Wise Old Man gives us the golden rule.
How horrid are those attempts to reproduce the grain of walnut in plastics as an attempt to enhance the quality of one material by imposing the appearance of another; how false, how damnably unfair to the plastic itself. If we have to resign ourselves to the fact that the beauty of plastics is limited to flat colours, why not do so now and be done with it? It is quite natural that the early efforts of a machine should approximate to the handicrafts they supersede. We still classify air-planes by horse power; but at best it is for want of a better term.

Conceding his right to full enquiry into the material limitations surrounding his job, the manufacturer may still hesitate to leave the final judgment to the artist. What reason has he to believe that the artist's taste will coincide with the public's? It is the public's reaction to design which constitutes the final proof.

There is the fact of the persistence of certain great works of art in the esteem of generations. Simple truths are elevating. Greek architecture speaks a nobility in which we are proud to claim a part. Whatever we are, we are nothing if we deny our spark of significance as members of a sometime noble race. Professor Troward's theory of metaphysics insists that every cognate being not only has a share in the universal force behind appearances but is that force just as much as a leaf of cabbage is cabbage; and that he is capable of insisting on his one-ness with the highest to which human aspiration has risen. In our recognition of the eternal and absolutely beautiful elements in design, we make that same claim. How else can we be affected not by the meaning of words, but by their sound, not by the subject of a picture, but by the orchestration of its colours and architecture of its forms? There is no man living who is not sensitive, consciously or not, to these things. Here, surely, is a weapon to be used as rooted in human nature as hunger or desire itself.

In our weakness, however, we cry out for syrup. That is why pretty-pretty drawings and sentimental effects get the quickest and easiest response. But it is also the reason why these things can never earn our final respect.

At this point the argument will wax most acrimonious. The manufacturer is willing to play on any weakness to gain his ends—sales. My object here is not to prove him at fault, but to show the artist's judgment to be of such practical value that he can even lend sincerity to an appeal actually false in sentiment. History shows us a succession of vast movements under the surface of life, trends leading to new conceptions of living. They are not easy to see except in the perspective of later years, be cause we are all on the tide and moving along together. We will never discover our real direction, for instance, by reading our contemporary newspapers. It is vital to the business man that he should find some instrument that registers such movements.

The artist, I maintain, so far from being the impractical and absent-minded being of popular fancy, is that very instrument. He is so because his mind centres on realities; not the surface commotions like jingoism or the evanescent fashions in polite living, but the eternal and absolute verities of proportion and harmony. What he feels now will be felt by the multitude inevitably.

The artist must be heard. Civilisation is formed in his mould. Machinery has succeeded in cutting humanity off from the valuable influences of the artist's thought. Machinery can justify itself again by inviting the artist back into his proper place.

This Packaging Age
The Marketing and Psychological Angle[56]

By R. Simmat, M.A.
Author of "Personal Salesmanship," "Market Research," "The Principles and Practice of Marketing," etc.

Recently the more progressive of our British manufacturers have been taking stock of their packages. It is no longer necessary to continue preaching the sales value of the really effective package. Most manufacturers realise this, but, like most other movements that towards the better package has been followed over-enthusiastically by some, while the efforts of others have been well meant but misplaced. Because such new package designs as those for Kappa Rice[57] or Kardomah Tea[58] have increased sales, every manufacturer need not think he merely has to change his package design and his selling problems are automatically solved. We may quote, not so much as a warning, but as an example, the case of Hyde's[59] Bird Seeds. Retailers were enthusiastic about the new package and, on all theoretical bases it should have been an outstanding success but, for some obscure season, possibly connected with the psychology of the people who bought it, the new package was a comparative failure. By way of contrast we have a product such as Guy's[60] Tonic, whose package has not been changed for 50 years and which still has a steady sale.

I believe the manufacturer, in considering the benefits of any possible new design, cannot afford to ignore three important factors. First of all, if the product is one of long-standing, there

[56] From *Packaging Omnibus*, London: Creative Journals Ltd., 1936, pp. 19–23.

[57] *Shelf Appeal*, July 1935.

[58] *Shelf Appeal*, July 1935.

[59] *Shelf Appeal*, April, 1934.

[60] *Shelf Appeal*, April 1934.

may be valuable goodwill attached to the old package design. Secondly, he must remember that the package design can, at best, only influence the consumer to try the product and, if the characteristics of the product, price, quality, quantity, etc., are not what the consumer wants, the best designed package in the world will not persuade him to buy it a second time. Thirdly, merely to change to a new package is not sufficient. The new package must be merchandised, that is, given extensive displays in shop windows and advertisements inserted in the press and other media giving the reasons for the change and explaining its advantages.

The Goodwill of an Old Package Design

Most manufacturers have an exaggerated idea of the amount of goodwill attached to a package design that has been associated with their firm for a long period of years, which perhaps the founder of the firm worked out for himself, and which has had a somewhat successful career through the Victorian and Edwardian periods and even up to the present. As a very old friend we might quote Wright's Coal Tar Soap. Investigation among actual users established that the goodwill attached to the old design was such as to be unimportant.

Messrs. Wright, Layman & Umney were courageous enough to accept the results of the investigation and completely changed their package design. The results have not caused them to lose faith in the principle of basing package changes upon adequate investigation among consumers. On the other hand, we have packages of long standing such as those of several manufacturers of sauces whose designs, judged by the standards of to-day, although perhaps half-a-century old, are still as effective as the most "modern"—perhaps they are even more effective than some out bursts of aspiring jobbing printers with an eye to colour.

Merchandising the Package

Many good packages lose a great deal of their possible effect on sales by not being properly "put across" to the consumer. It is now generally recognised that the new John Cotton package has been one of the best designs produced in this country for a long time, yet this package was not advertised in the press or elsewhere when first distributed. Many old consumers no doubt received a shock when the new package was first handed to them by their tobacconist. Probably many had some doubt as to whether they were buying the John Cotton of the olden days. It was a tribute to the merit of the design that sales survived the unheralded shock of the change. This was a case of an excellent new package with unlimited possibilities simply thrown away by careless merchandising. In contrast, at almost the same time as the new John Cotton package appeared, the new Wright's Coal Tar Soap package was presented to the public. This latter package, though a considerable improvement on the old one, yet cannot be described as anything more than commonplace even by the most tolerant. But the way the new package, coupled with an increase in size of the product, was displayed in shop windows, advertised in the press and on the hoardings provides an example of extremely well-planned and effective merchandising. John Cotton was an outstanding package design badly merchandised. Wright's Coal Tar Soap was a mediocre package efficiently merchandised. Of the two probably it would be safe to say that Wright's reaped the greater benefit; but neither got all they should have out of the change. Some manufacturers have done better. Godfrey Phillips[61] used the story of the novel opening for their Cavanders cigarettes as part of their advertising. Quaker Oats[62] have merchandised the idea of their pouring device with some effect.

Economising on The Cost of the Design

An error into which many manufacturers fall is that of trying to economise on the cost of their initial design.

Though the actual package design may be printed many million times, yet they consider the fee the skilled artist asks for a well executed design as being exorbitant. They may spend thousands of pounds in their annual advertising, they may spend equal amounts on printing costs, but the artist's fee of from twenty-five to at most a hundred guineas is considered as being preposterous. Yet each package is an advertisement for the product that many actual and potential consumers must see and, spread over the probable hundreds of thousands of pack ages produced, the artist's fee is almost infinitesimal per unit. A common procedure is to make

[61] *Shelf Appeal*, May 1935.

[62] *Shelf Appeal*, Aug. 1935.

a selection from the stock of an artist who, working on a mass production basis, produces designs that would be equally adaptable to packages of tooth paste or tomato sauce and so can afford to fix his fee at a more modest figure. Alternatively, the suggestion of the printer is accepted, principally because he is willing to "give away" the design provided he receives the printing order.

While many " stock" designs may be very good, I believe that the result is more effective if the artist builds up his creation about the product and its individuality as Milner Gray did for Culmak, as Dutton[63] has done for the Stevens Bakeries products, as George Switzer did in America for Budge-it,[64] and as the best German designers do.

It must be admitted that one regains some of one's respect for the efforts of printers on finding that a firm with modem ideas like Bob Martin's,[65] after considering—and, I believe, paying for—designs from a number of artists— ultimately decided to use a design that had been worked out by their own advertising department in co-operation with Field's of Bradford, the printers.

The Psychological Factors

The more obvious psychological factors affecting the success of a package such as those relating to care of opening and closing, shape, whether the container can be easily knocked over, etc., have gradually become appreciated by both the designer and the manufacturer. The lament of Mr. James of the McCann Company that the top of his tooth paste tube tends to slip down the drain has been taken to heart by those concerned. The Essolube[66] bottles were designed so that they would not slip out of the band. Manufacturers of sauces are using bottles that will pour more easily. Yardley's have made very definite efforts to make their containers appropriate to the product inside it. The Gresolvent[67] Company have made their container look like what the product is

[63] *Shelf Appeal*, July 1935.

[64] *Shelf Appeal*, May and July 1935.

[65] *Shelf Appeal*, April 1935.

[66] *Shelf Appeal*, July 1933.

[67] *Shelf Appeal*, Feb. 1934.

intended to do-brighten things up. But the more subtle factors affecting the success of a package have yet to be appreciated. Two widely different examples recently have struck me very forcibly as emphasising how less obvious psychological factors may operate to vitiate what may, on the surface, appear to be a packaging development that should achieve wide-reaching benefits. A brand of boot polish—Box-all—is being marketed in extremely large tins for the price of sixpence. Yet many users of this type of product, on being shown a tin and told the price, have said to me that it cannot possibly be of good quality or such a large tin could not be sold for the price. Actually, they have no evidence of the good or bad quality. They simply reason that the standard practice of other manufacturers in the field is to sell a very much smaller quantity for that price and therefore the very size of the tin militates against consumer acceptance of any real quality that Box all polish in all probability actually may possess. The other example is even more interesting. After investigating the packing room of a firm I concluded that much would be gained by substituting Fiberite boxes for the heavy and expensive wooden cases that ha4 hitherto been used. Much resistance to the innovation came from the packers, and for a period the time taken to pack a Fiberite case was greater than that taken to pack a wooden one. As packing costs were an important item, this almost meant the resumption of the old method once more. There was no logical reason apparent for the increased time, since the Fiberite cases were identical in size and shape with the wooden ones. Further investigation showed that it had been customary for the packing room to be slack in winter months and during this period the packers were put on to making wooden cases. They felt that with the introduction of the Fiberite boxes there would be no wooden boxes for them to make during the winter and therefore some of them would be paid off. On being assured by the management that other measures would be taken to keep them employed, the situation was soon smoothed out and the anticipated benefits from the change were duly achieved. This instance illustrates very forcibly how necessary it is to examine every psychological factor attending an innovation either in the packaging process or in the actual design.

Evaluating The Package

Probably the most exhaustive foot-rule that has ever been evolved to evaluate a package is the Ullman check list. This is too well known to be quoted here, and my experience has been that it is too searching for most manufacturers to be sufficiently painstaking to go into the examination of detail which it demands. For all ordinary purposes I have found as a fair working basis that if the following characteristics are taken into account when considering either an existing or a proposed package, then the results are reasonably satisfactory.

1. The package must be easy to open and close.
2. It must adequately protect the contents.
3. The design must take into account three dimensions.
4. The design should be in as few colours as possible to save printing costs. Certainly not more than three colours should be used, and preferably only two.
5. The design must permit variations in the colours and in the illustrations to distinguish one product in the range from another.
6. The design should be simple and contain a minimum of copy. Usually instructions, etc., should be inserted inside the package or on the inner container.
7. The design must be adaptable to various shapes and sizes of container or carton.
8. It must be possible to reproduce the design effectively in advertisements.
9. The colours used must stand out in contrast with those of other products in window displays.
10. The typography must be legible and distinctive.
11. Well-known brands and trade marks should be included in the design.
12. The entire design must be distinctive and suggestive of the reputation and standing of the organization marketing it, it must be expressive of the product inside the container, and must harmonise with the surroundings in which it will be used by the consumer.

Changing the Package

With the new emphasis on package design, the danger often is not that the manufacturer is too hesitant but rather that frequently he is too anxious to change. Changing a package has many implications. New packaging machinery may be necessary and this is expensive. The possible gains should be considered against these costs. Often it is better to reject some design possessing unusual features for the sake of being able to use existing machinery in conjunction with a package which does not embody the unusual. Then the designer may know little of the chemical relations between the materials he proposes and the product that they are to contain. The research laboratory must be consulted. The efforts of competitors must be care fully studied so that any change must not simply be another addition to an already nondescript miscellany. The confectionery manufacturers have for years past been the worst sinners in this regard. Rowntrees,[68] under the guidance of their agents, J. Walter Thompson Co., Ltd., have introduced new ideas into confectionery packaging. Cadbury's began well by inviting the co-operation of Royal Academicians to develop designs and really deserved better than the failure many say they achieved.

It is a fundamental principle, but one too infrequently recognized, that no package design should be charged solely for the sake of change. The only real reason for a change should be that scientifically controlled tests show that a change is necessary. Many of these tests simply follow a technique developed as the result of combining logic and common sense. Others necessarily attempt to estimate the psychological factors involved. All such tests have not as yet been developed to a very advanced stage ; firstly because few at present even recognize their importance; secondly, because such tests take time and manufacturers are often too eager to act and are unwilling to take the time to make a careful scientific analysis of all the factors involved; thirdly, the tests increase the initial cost of the design and, in this, even if they are lavish in other directions, most manufacturers are shortsightedly grudging. Perhaps the styling department of the H. K. McCann Company has been as progressive as most advertising agencies in endeavouring to persuade their clients of the importance of scientific investigation as the prelude to packaging changes. On several occasions they have called upon the expert advice of the National Institute of Industrial Psychology either in making the necessary preliminary investigations or else in actually testing several proposed alternative new designs to assess the various psychological factors considered important. The results achieved have certainly justified the additional time and money spent.

[68] *Shelf Appeal*, Jan. 1934.

Factors Making a Change Necessary

One of the most frequent factors making a change in package design necessary is the continual alteration in the purchasing habits of the consumer. Financial depression, the development of new types of outlet, changing social habits, changes in the use to which the product may be put, are all important in affecting the trend of package design. Tooth paste is now retailed in sixpenny tubes. Forhans and other more conservative companies hesitated for a long time before packing a sixpenny unit for Woolworths. The same applied to Southall Barclay and Kotex with their sanitary towels. The drop in the price of raw materials enabled Pears' soap to be reduced to 4d. The invention of wax polish meant a transition from the old bottle of boot blacking to the tin of wax polish. The marketing of shoe cream has resulted in the tubes of Meltonian and Kiwi creams. An attempt to associate style and quality with shoe cream has resulted in the Kiwi[69] and the Lotus[70] Bakelite jar. The trend from the large family with servants to clean the shoes to the small family with out servants has meant a change from the large tin of polish at sixpence to the smaller tins at 3d. and 1d. Lifebuoy soap, once sold in large cakes in common place cartons, is now being increasingly sold as a toilet soap and the package design has been altered accordingly. Packages embodying novelty features rapidly become out of date. Other designs must be changed to keep pace with changing fashions. Jaeger have revolutionized modern drapery packing.

Methods of Changing the Package

Either one of two methods of changing the package may be employed according to circumstances. The design may be changed gradually over a long period of years; new features being included and undesirable ones eliminated until the package, at one time, when compared with that used some time previously, might be seen to be changed to a considerable degree, but so gradually that consumers have not, at any one time, been aware of it. This process is usually a simplification of an originally complex design by eliminating unnecessary

[69] *Shelf Appeal*, Nov. 1933.

[70] *Shelf Appeal*, March 1934.

features, by "cleaning up" the type and copy, shortening it, and perhaps leaving much of it out altogether. Since this has been done gradually there can be no loss of goodwill as the result of the changes. Lux is a classic example of this technique. During the last three decades it is said that over one hundred changes have been made in the original design to produce the present effective package.

The second method is much more drastic and involves a sudden change from one package to another entirely different. This type of charge may be, and often has been, attended with very disastrous results if it is not handled with a great deal of care. If handled effectively the change must be adequately merchandised by advertising, by canvassing retailers, and by securing displays, thus explaining to both retailer and potential consumer the reasons for the change, and at the same time pointing out the advantages of the new packing. The moisture-proof packing campaign for Craven "A" and the campaign for the large "Redi-fill" tobacco packets are good examples of this.

The Future of Package Design

Probably the next generation of designers will regard us with the same amused tolerance as we regard those of the pre-war years. To-day our designers appear to be favouring simplicity, lines, and lack of illustration. The designer of to-morrow may favour a return to the complex pictorial effect. To-day we are beginning to consider package design in three dimensions rather than the two of but a few years ago. The exploitation of three dimensions opens up vast possibilities. Improvements in the technique of reproduction open up others. The invention of new materials for containers and new packaging machinery open up still others. We are living in a 'scientific age and the package is becoming more scientifically planned. We are exploiting its possibilities as a sales aid. According to our standards we are making it more aesthetically pleasing. Let us hope that future generations will judge our efforts kindly.

How a Package Test was Made

Twelve designs of a new container for an established ointment put out by one of the oldest firms of manufacturing chemists in London were finally selected from nineteen alternatives prepared by the McCann Product and Package Styling Service.

The firm's present package design was included though the name of the product was disguised on this and other cartons.

These twelve final designs were turned over to the National Institute of Industrial Psychology with instructions to conduct a careful test on an adequate number of subjects, to determine that most generally preferred. In harmony with the market, middle and working-class groups were used, and more women than men, since women purchase most of the products used in the home.

Without going too deeply into the non-essentials of these results, Design N stood out as most popular, with K and Q next. "First impression" popularity was weighed with "Considered judgment."

Next, a fieldman took these designs round to fifty chemists in middle and lower-class neighbourhoods, displaying the designs (re arranged en different sequence each day), and obtained the opinions of these chemists in the same way.

N design again was the most popular, with O next and the manufacturer's own carton third. This last was due, of course, to the recollection of this design as belonging to a product already handled.

Before putting out the new carton, the client thus had clear evidence that its design would prove more popular than the old with both public and retailer.

New Problems in Advertising and Steps Towards Their Solution[71]

Henry King

I am not sure that it is not a little misleading to talk about new problems in advertising. For THE problem of advertising is still what it has always been—how to make it do the most effective job and pay 100 cents on the advertising dollar, bearing in mind that it is addressed to one of the most inscrutable audiences in the world— the human mind; and in the majority of instances, to the most inscrutable—the woman's mind.

Advertising used to be defined, rather inadequately, as "salesmanship in print." Perhaps that was true once, but now advertising is very much more than that. True, it includes printed messages in newspapers, magazines, trade papers, street car cards, posters, paperboard containers, and other such media. But modern developments have extended it to smoke signs above our heads, illuminated signs, counter displays, stentorian voices from the clouds, and of course the intimate voice of radio. Most advertising is concerned with direct selling, of goods and of services, but a good deal of it (and considerably more now than in older days) aims at what is known as institutional selling—a prestige-building campaign to explain how Company A works, and to prove that Company B is not the ogre that street-corner Pinks claim it to be, or (nearer home) a campaign to persuade the voters that their duty is to vote.

One distinction must be made clear from the beginning. There are two main forms of advertising: first, advertising that is looked for, and second, advertising that has to look for people. Of the first type are all the classified advertisements, of the type, for instance, appearing in our old English grammar book:

[71] From H.R. Kemp (ed.), *Canadian Marketing Problems*, Toronto: University of Toronto Press, 1939, pp. 72–85.

"Piano for sale by a lady about to cross the Channel with carved wooden legs in a solid mahogany case," and retail store advertising featuring spot light sales and specials at 3 for 19c. With this type of advertising the agency has little to do. The biggest problems in advertising are connected with the second type-advertising that has to force itself upon the attention of the reader and by its attention-value get itself read, remembered, and acted upon. The core of the problem is, "How can this be done most effectively and at the same time, of course, most economically?"

It is probably not necessary to convince readers today of either the achievements or the necessity of advertising under the existing economic order. What is making the various phases of the central problem more acute is the scrutiny to which advertising is now being subjected. What are the reasons for this? They are many. In the first place, we shall probably never return to the relatively easy-going and free-spending days of ten years ago. We have to watch our pennies, and the advertising manager must get his full money's worth from his budget; there must be full and adequate reason for every expenditure that he authorizes. Guesswork is not enough. Secondly, consumer movements, both governmental and privately sponsored, have focussed attention on all advertising and advertised products. Thirdly, advertising has often itself to blame—or to thank—for the present situation; it overreached itself with exaggerated claims, barrages of superlatives, and spurious testimonials. True, these practices were never universal, but they were sufficiently widespread to create at least a slight feeling of suspicion in the consumer's mind.

So what the advertisers and the agencies are crying out for today is FACTS. Bright ideas, hunches, and smart selling schemes by them selves are not enough; if you make a recommendation, you must be able to give a scientific reason (or as scientific as you can) for it. The advertising agency is continually building up a body of knowledge on all phases of its work. It is a never-ending process, the findings of which are frequently being modified as experience brings up more evidence but which is steadily advancing towards the goal.

At the outset let me briefly describe the development of the advertising agency, leading up to its present-day functions. The agency started merely as a buyer of space in the newspaper and magazine, and in England some agencies are still little more than space brokers. Having contracted for the space, it was responsible for seeing that the client's advertisements duly appeared. Soon it started to prepare these advertisements and to check them when they were published. Thus the creative department—the plans and copy department—began. The next step was in merchandising; the agency began to assist in drawing up the client's merchandising plans. This involves the study of such factors as salesmen's territories and remuneration, distribution, packaging, showcards, direct mail, and other phases of merchandising and selling. After that came the research department, which is concerned primarily with market research, but often turns its hand to a wide variety of other tasks. The work of an agency research department has been known to include such things as writing and presenting tariff briefs, research for new products, determination of factory locations, a laboratory study of the effect on fifty fat women of a certain diet. Such studies are only on the fringe of advertising proper, but they are a part of the service that the modern agency can and does give.

The most interesting method of treating this subject would probably be first to show, necessarily in outline only, what is being done in the way of research at each of the stages in the building and run-fling of an advertising campaign—that is, the marshalling of the facts which may be put generally under the heading of "taking the guesswork out of advertising,"—and secondly, to illustrate the general principles involved by the description of a market research job undertaken prior to an advertising campaign.

Part I

The questions to be decided in planning an advertising campaign may be outlined as follows:

1. The *appropriation,* or the amount of money to be spent. This is usually based on sales, their trend, past experience, and, to some extent, the job that has to be done.

2. *Determination of media—that* is, whether newspapers, magazines, trade papers, radio, posters, etc., are to be used; in what locations; and with what strength of coverage.

3. The *central theme—that* is, what the central appeal is to be.

4. *Treatment, layout, and copy,* including such questions as

number and size of individual advertisements, the predominance of illustration or copy, the tone of the copy.

To these may be added a fifth—the appraisal of the success of the campaign.

How is research applied during these various stages? In other words, by what means is the advertising agency building up its store of knowledge, as a specialist in its field, so that it can base its recommendations at each stage upon facts and not purely upon theory?

1. *The appropriation* need not here concern us. It is usually settled by the advertiser, though the agency will probably make a recommendation.

2. *Media.* The media man has in his files the circulation of every newspaper and magazine, and whether the trend is up or down. He also knows the class of reader to whom it appeals (that is, whether its circulation tends to be "class" or "mass"), and he also has a breakdown of circulation by territories so that he can tell how much overlapping occurs—how much duplication there will be, for instance, if he uses a local paper, in addition to the circulation already coming in from a neighbouring city daily.

He knows the effective day and night coverage of radio stations and also the proportion of total listeners in a given area that each station normally holds. This knowledge may be based partly upon engineering tests, but it is more effectively obtained by what are known as coincidental surveys—that is, telephone calls to a random sample of homes to find whether the people in them have a radio, whether it is turned on, and to what station they are listening. Though these surveys are usually made for a particular advertiser, to test the pulling power of his programme, the general results are usually made available. The media man also knows the limitations of various media. He will not allow the use of black and white for a job that needs colour; nor will he use radio, for instance, for house furnishings when the visual appeal is all-important.

His files also contain diagrams showing the location of posters and he can determine the necessary coverage of these. Parallel with the Audit Bureau of Circulations for newspapers, a Traffic Audit Bureau has been developed. This works on careful counts of traffic, subdivided into pedestrian, private automobile and public carrier, past poster (or shop window) locations. The compilation of traffic density figures past poster sites, combined with such factors as their visibility, height above ground, the angle at which they are set to the traffic, etc., makes rating of all such sites possible.

3. *The central theme.* Selection of the central theme is not so much a matter of research as of imagination and creative ability, as exemplified in the slogan of the Montreal Tourist Bureau, "Abroad without crossing the sea," and the Congoleum theme of depression days, "Brighten your home first." Psychologists, both professional and amateur, have discovered an almost endless array of appeals, some of them conscious, other subconscious. Everybody knows the characteristic exhortations to "keep up with the Joneses," and appeals to glamour-blinded youth. Dr. Laird, of Colgate University, has grouped all basic forces under four main heads: the desire to be more masculine (which he says is a potent though subconscious force even among women), the desire to be more adequate, the desire for romance, and the desire for life.

4. *Treatment, layout, and copy* are very different matters, and probably more original work is being done with them at present than with any other branch of advertising. Here the question is narrowed down from "How can advertising be made most effective?" to "What will make (or has made) this advertisement most effective?" There are three main elements: (i) something arresting that will catch the eye, (ii) something interesting that will make the mind follow the eye and read, and (iii) some incentive that will bring about action. These three elements have been well described as first surprise, then curiosity, then conviction. In the majority of advertisements this will mean (i) an attention-compelling illustration, (ii) a news-value heading leading to convincing copy, and (iii) a powerful argument to "do it now" or "buy a can tomorrow."

How then can we judge whether an advertisement meets this test? Of course we can wait to see the results, but as the effects of advertising are cumulative, we shall have to wait a long time, and meanwhile both money and time are being spent. There are several techniques that are now being used for such testing. These techniques can be broadly divided into two groups: those that are used before and those that are used after publication of the advertisement. The object of the former is to appraise the advertisements before they are run; the object of the latter is to add to the general body of knowledge about what is "a good advertisement."

The pre-publication tests can again be divided into two groups. The first group are those that take the prepared advertisements and either run them in test papers or test cities to judge the results, or put them before what is known as a consumer jury—a group of persons collected for this purpose-so that they may appraise each one from the point of view of their own reaction to them.

The second group consists of those based on definite formulae for the composition of an advertisement. These formulae are, for the most part, worked out from careful observations of the constituent elements in advertisements known to have been successful, the question asked being, "What are the physical properties of this advertisement that have made it good?" Various elements enter into such studies, which have been and are being carried out by a number of groups working independently. Among the more important factors are the relative size and position of the illustration, the position and character of the heading, the ease with which the advertiser or the brand advertised can be identified, and the particular appeal used.

Pre-publication tests are thus of two kinds—those that are applied to human beings and those that depend upon studies of the make-up of the actual advertisements. Post-publication tests are divided in the same way. The best known of the "human" tests is the aided recall or recognition test, in which readers are shown the advertisements to be tested in the magazine or newspaper in which they actually appeared, and questions are asked to show whether they noticed them, read them, remembered what they were about—and sometimes whether they acted upon them. Often the names of the advertiser and the brand are deleted, for if the reader can name the product or company advertised without being able to see the identifying words, there is much stronger proof that the advertisement has gone home than if he merely tells the investigator that he has read the advertisement. A variation of this test is what is known as the "unaided recall method," in which people are asked to identify the slogans used by advertisers entirely independently of the presentation of any advertisement in which these slogans are featured.

The oldest method of testing is, of course, the inquiry or coupon test, which is very satisfactory in certain cases—where for instance the coupon carries an offer of a booklet or other free presentation. It is, however, obviously impractical to include coupons in advertisements for every product, and the return of coupons to the advertiser may mean only that the advertisements have attracted the attention of that large class of people who always want something for nothing. Moreover, little indication of the attention-value of the advertisement is given; many people will not take the trouble to put pen to paper.

Post-publication studies of advertisements follow the same lines as those already outlined for pre-publication tests; that is, the advertisement itself is dissected either by pre-arranged and rigid formulae or by an analysis of its constituent parts.

Before commenting upon the values and limitations of these various tests, it may be mentioned that most of them are useful and are used for radio advertising. The coincidental telephone survey already described determines accurately the size of the listening audience, and also whether the listener knows the sponsor of the programme or the product advertised. Other tests on the lines of the "unaided recall method," outlined previously, show whether the advertising message has registered. Consumer jury and limited area tests are as useful for radio programmes as they are for publication advertising.

All consumer tests are subject to the normal drawbacks of sampling—e.g., the difficulty of choosing the part in such a way that it adequately represents the whole. (This difficulty can be and is minimized by taking the most careful precautions about the make up of the sample by age, income group, occupation, locality, etc.) Furthermore, human beings are not static; what they like today, they may dislike tomorrow. Their wants and desires are continually in a state of flux; last year's tests may not be valid for this year. Their tastes vary enormously in accordance with environment and standards of wealth, entirely regardless of the process of time. This is a very serious objection to any tests that depend upon a set of rigid formulae. Two instances will show what is meant. The January number of *Advertising and Selling* reports that in a series of advertisements for a correspondence school (note that the coupon test is fully valid here because it is possible to ascertain not only the response to the advertisements but also the number of sales closed) the advertisement that ranked first in 1936 ranked tenth in 1937, the same media being used. The second instance was given in a recent issue of *Printer's Ink Monthly*: an agency, discussing a new campaign for the coming year, wanted proofs of the most successful and the least successful advertisements of the previous year's campaign. When they were brought, the agency men were surprised to see that the most successful and the least successful advertisements were the same, the explanation being that it was particularly suited to the readers of one magazine in which it ran, while in another medium it received hardly any response at all. These instances emphasize the fact that no amount of working by formula can possibly take the place of creative imagination and hard thinking as far as the preparation of advertisements is concerned. Formulae can show what ought not to be left out; they cannot show what ought to be put in. Once we appreciate these limitations, we can see the value of all these tests.

Advertising agencies are working on these problems; they are continually building up their store of knowledge of what makes a good advertisement; they are more and more becoming specialists in all phases of their own business. It has been said, very unjustly, that an advertising man creates advertisements of which other advertising men will approve. This is strictly untrue, but it is not untrue that he sometimes has to create advertisements of which the client will approve. The time is not far distant when the client will co-operate with the advertising man by allowing him to use his professional judgment and have the last word in his own sphere, so that advertisements of the right kind will be built—of which the public will approve.

Before passing on to market research, a few words may be devoted to the fifth phase of the advertising campaign—the testing of actual results. The most obvious and oldest method of testing results is, of course, by an analysis of actual sales figures—by product, by salesman's territory, by city, etc. Owing to limitations of time, divergent channels of distribution, etc., this does not give the whole picture. Two techniques have recently been developed to bring the consumer picture immediately home to the manufacturer and to reflect changes as soon as they become evident at the crucial point— the point of sales. (In this they correspond with the Crossley method of radio programme testing and rating in the United States, which is a continuous process.) The first system makes continual tests in homes of the brands of certain products last bought, so that, with an adequate sample, changes in brand preference become quickly obvious. The second, which has been developed by A. C. Nielsen, involves taking the inventory of some 2,000 stores at the beginning of a period, the purchases by the stores during the period, and the inventory at the end of it. The value of this last method is its accuracy. Manufacturers' sales records cannot take account of either wholesalers' or retailers' inventory (for instance, when they are building up their stock in preparation for a heavy sales period) so that sales records do not accurately show the seasonal variations in retail sales. I heard the other day of a manufacturer who had changed the whole seasonal emphasis of his advertising on the basis of a Nielsen report. Furthermore, this method obviously gives an absolutely accurate picture of an advertiser's competition and its changing trend. Additional value comes from an analysis of competitive advertising during the same period, presented simultaneously with the sales analysis and correlated with it.

Part II

After this rather sketchy outline of what the advertising agency is doing and learning in the preparation of advertising campaigns, we may turn to my own field of market research.

Twenty years ago when agencies first took up market research, some enthusiasts thought it was going to solve all problems. It can never do that, but it is an absolutely essential adjunct of all advertising work. Advertising is concerned with and addressed to "the market," and unless we know in detail what the market is, we obviously cannot do a good job. Research into the market should be, and usually is, a continuous process—finding all about the market and noting trends and changes as soon as they are visible. The kind of question that market research answers is, "Who buys our product? Why do they buy it? Do the old buy more than the young? Is competition gaining or losing? What do the retail trade think of the product? Do they push it in preference to competing products? Why? Are our prices right? What is the trend, likely to be in the next twelve months?" In fact, any question bearing on the movement from the factory until the product is finally used up is the subject of market research. All possible sources of information are used—government and other published data, facts gathered from wholesalers and retailers, housewives, institutions, professional or trade associations, and others. ("If you get information from one source," said Leslie Henson in his recent London show, "it's called plagiarism; if you get it from two or more sources, it's called research.")

One of the most attractive aspects of this work is its variety. Most of this work is necessarily confidential; it is prepared solely for the use of the client and his advertising advisers. But a concrete illustration of its use will be the most interesting way of showing its function, and there is one report on which I worked recently that is not a private document and will therefore serve the purpose. This was a report on the marketing of apples made in 1936 for the British Columbia Tree Fruit Board. A few pages may therefore be devoted to an analysis of what this report contains and how it was worked out.

First a few words about the underlying situation. The California citrus growers had been organized since 1904; their marketing plans had been well developed and since 1907 they had spent $22,000,000 on advertising "Sunkist," not a little of it in the Canadian market. Apple growers here in the meantime had done practically nothing. In Eastern Canada apple-growing is usually a supplementary source of income to the farmer; in British Columbia it is his whole crop. Hence the agitation for some method of centralized control of shipments. Various co-operative schemes had been tried in the Okanagan Valley for some years, but none was wholly satisfactory. The Natural Products Marketing Act gave the growers their chance. A board was set up with authority to assess a small fee per box to pay for administration and with enough left for a modest advertising campaign. What plan should they use?

When we set to work on this problem, we had to learn about the British Columbia apple business from top to bottom in order to draw up an intelligent and constructive plan for the campaign.

The first job was on the spot. How were the growers organized? What were their relations with the shippers? How much did the various operations cost—growing, picking, storing, grading, wrap ping, packing, shipping, and brokerage charges? The findings on all such points were included in the report in order to give the back ground to our merchandising department. Also examined was the type of tree being planted; statistics showed that such varieties as McIntosh and Delicious were increasing very rapidly, while the less favoured varieties such as Jonathan and Wagner were showing an equally rapid decline. (This had to be compared later with consumers' preference for different varieties.)

From figures supplied by the Dominion Bureau of Statistics we made a study of the consumption of various fruits in the Dominion as a whole. We found that apples are still far in the lead with a five-year average of 274,000,000 pounds, but that oranges are steadily coming up with 161,000,000 pounds, and 132,000,000 pounds of bananas were also consumed. The per capita consumption of apples, however, had dropped from about 30 pounds in 1926-30 to 26 pounds in 1931-5.

We then examined consumption figures in the Prairie Provinces—the principal domestic market for British Columbia growers. (In this survey we were not concerned with export markets.) Of course some British Columbia apples are shipped to Eastern Canada, but the volume varies enormously from year to year depending upon the size of the eastern crop. As there is no commercial crop in the prairies, the Bureau's figures of freight tons unloaded in each of the three provinces gave us an accurate figure of the local consumption of fresh apples and also of other fresh fruits taken together. We found that during the ten-year period 1925-34 there has been a steady decline in apple consumption in Manitoba and Saskatchewan, and a very small increase in Alberta. So regular were the curves in each province that a trend line could be fitted mathematically to each. Other fresh fruits, on the other hand, showed a rapid increase from 1925-9, and an equally rapid falling-off from 1930 on. The per capita figure for the three provinces as a whole was even more disturbing. Though per capita consumption of apples is about 50 per cent higher in the prairies than in the Dominion as a whole, the ten-year period showed a steady falling off from a level of 51 pounds per capita in 1925 to 37 pounds in 1934—or a rate of about 1 _ pounds a year.

Next we looked into the factor of price, especially in relation to the price of oranges. As might be expected, the price of British Columbia apples varies inversely with the size of the crop in British Columbia; it has nothing to do with the size of the crop in Eastern Canada. Unfortunately when there is a big apple crop in British Columbia there is usually a heavy orange crop in California, so that the price of oranges also falls. We found that the proportion of money spent on apples out of total farm income was becoming steadily smaller from 1925 to 1939, though it has tended to increase since that year. The basic problem, therefore, was the decline in purchasing power in Western Canada, but the fact that a steady decline in consumption had occurred even in 1925-9 showed that the growers could not afford to wait for the return of better times to the western farmer.

Apart from some studies of seasonal fluctuations, this indicates the kind of data obtained from published statistics. We then turned to field work. We interviewed 10 brokers, 68 jobbers, 338 retailers, 101 restaurants, 3,148 urban housewives, and 1,603 farmers' wives. Most of these were in Western Canada, but we included six centres in Ontario and also Montreal.

Some of the findings in regard to the housewives may be quoted first. The basic questions were: "How often do they use apples? How do they use them? What do they think of British Columbia as opposed to eastern fruit?" We found that more than 90 per cent of the urban housewives had apples on hand almost all the time during the season, but that only 70 per cent of the farms at that time did so. The majority ask for particular varieties, but their knowledge of varieties and what they can best be used for is limited. The McIntosh is generally preferred throughout the territory covered, followed by Delicious in the West, and Northern Spy or Snow in the East. Flavour, juiciness, and firmness are the most generally desired qualities. (It may be thought that all this was known already, but a survey of this kind is required to give an accurate rating of the relative importance of variety-preference or desired qualities.) More than half of the housewives buy by the box, but the proportion falls with the size of the city, and it was less than one-quarter in Winnipeg. Apples are eaten raw more often than cooked, and we obtained figures showing the relative frequency of cooking methods. The more variety a woman uses in cooking methods, the greater the family consumption of the product: in this respect, the same thing is true of apples as we found, in a report prepared for the Department of Fisheries in 1931, to be true of fish. Professed dislike of raw apples was negligible, extending to only 10 per cent of the women, 8 per cent of the men, and 2 per cent of the children. Lack of purchasing power was the only important reason for not buying more apples, and this was advanced by more than 80 per cent of the farmers. Recommendations by a doctor to eat apples were admitted by 15 per cent.

Practically all the western housewives, and 70 per cent of those in Ontario, knew that they had eaten British Columbia apples. The corresponding figure in Montreal was only 26 per cent, however, and as the Quebec crop never lasts very far into the winter, it is obvious that little had been done to identify the British Columbia apple in Montreal retail fruit stores. Only in Ontario was any appreciable dislike of British Columbia apples expressed, chiefly on the ground of lack of flavour and juice. On the other hand, the better grading and packing of the British Columbia apple were much appreciated. Criticisms of the British Columbia apples were made by one out of five restaurants.

Information from retailers showed that eastern apples comprise less than 1 per cent of the stocks in Alberta, but rise to about 10 per cent in Manitoba. This Manitoba demand, they said, came mostly from persons who have moved west from Ontario; the eastern apple was not so satisfactory to handle owing chiefly to poor grading and packing. On the other hand, the retailer regards the citrus business as being more profitable than apples, the chief reasons being the smaller number of persons handling oranges, the less perishable nature of the fruit, and orderly marketing. We questioned each dealer as to whether he thought the putting up of a smaller than standard box would assist sales, and found that the suggestion was not generally favoured. Methods of increasing sales most emphasized by dealers were more advertising, better displays, lower prices (chiefly through reduction in distribution costs), and better regulation of the channels of distribution.

This is about the briefest summary that can be given of what amounted to nearly 300 pages of detailed findings. We followed this up with 67 pages of recommendations based upon the evidence gathered. In our capacity as merchandising advisers we made recommendations not only on specific merchandising policies but also on the general policies of the board. The advertising suggestions were concerned chiefly with keeping the apple before the public eye, including the important matter of display, and stressing a variety of cooking recipes. The campaign, as far as one can judge from a short time, may be considered successful. It would have been more so had the growers been able to combine with growers in other provinces for a joint campaign, perhaps with the assistance of the Dominion Department of Agriculture. The policy of the Department of Agriculture is, however, to advertise the grading regulations and their dependability. This is all to the good; but it leaves the task of publicizing the apple as such to the growers themselves.

One fundamental principle must be emphasized in conclusion. It is absolutely essential that all such surveys (including also the various other forms of research mentioned above) be scrupulously fair and honest. What we are after is the facts. We know the questions we want answered; we do not know the answers. We start with a large blank sheet of paper, with an important question at the head of it; the answer to the question will become clear only as the reports are analysed. If we adopt the attitude of setting up a case and then trying to prove it by research, we are wasting time and money; the inquiry must be honest. Some may imagine that all market surveys are conducted to prove a case for advertising or for more advertising. They are not; in our 1931 fish report, for example, we stated that any advertising scheme was premature until the fishing industry had set its own house in order, and Mr. Rhodes, the then Minister of Fisheries, mentioned this fact with approbation in the House of Commons as an illustration of the impartiality of the report.

In this brief review I have tried to give some idea of the lines along which advertising agencies are working. In Canada we are handicapped to a certain extent by the small size of the market and the consequent limited expenditure, which would make some of the methods above described uneconomical. At the same time, a great deal of work of this kind is being done in the Dominion today, and being done well, and many of the results worked out in the United States apply here.

If this description has carried some conviction that the agency is doing a solid and honest job, the writing of it has been worth while.

Recent Developments in Co-Operative Marketing[72]

J.E. Lattimer

Just a decade ago, numerous deputations from several European countries visited the continent of North America to inquire into the foundation of the prosperity that they believed to prevail here. Not long since, a deputation from this side of the water visited some of the European countries to find the formula which enabled them to regain a greater measure of recovery than was locally in evidence. One deputation visited Sweden, and on returning to Canada stressed recent developments in co-operation, which form the subject of the present paper.

The question that aroused the curiosity of the European visitors a decade since was mass production, or how workers on this continent could produce so much goods. The question arousing the curiosity of the recent delegations visiting European countries was how these countries have been able to keep their workers busy. The different directions travelled by these searchers for the larger life and the different subjects exciting their curiosity, suggest that a change has taken place in our own country during that time. That change has had a great effect on marketing policies in general, and it has led to an increasing interest in the subject of co-operation.

The nature of the change in Canadian economic conditions since 1929 is familiar to us all, and it need not be treated in detail here. Some of its more outstanding results may, however, be examined to establish a foundation for the present discussion. In the beginning of the tenth year of hard times and unemployment, it is per haps not too soon to glance at some of the results of these changed conditions.

[72] From H.R. Kemp (ed.), *Canadian Marketing Problems*, Toronto: University of Toronto Press, 1939, pp. 112–25.

One characteristic of the fourth decade of the twentieth century in North America is the prevalence of unemployment. Examination of various industries reveals where unemployment prevails to the greatest and also to the least degree. During this particular decade the production of food has continued almost as regularly as the vagaries of the weather would permit. The provision of shelter has been very irregular. Consumption goods have been provided fairly steadily. Producers' goods have not been coming forward in any thing like so steady a volume, and it is in the latter industries that unemployment is felt in the greatest degree and appears to be the most persistent.

The production of food is organized (or perhaps the word should be unorganized) in a different way from that of some other goods. The growing of food is carried on largely by people working for themselves. In the last census report (1931) about 1,132,000 people were recorded as engaged in agriculture, less than 200,000 of whom were working for wages. Farming is still organized on the basis of individual production. Even in Europe, with its many different political philosophies, it is claimed that one similarity is discernible, namely, an agreement that the most certain way of securing food is to allow the farmer to work for himself on his own farm.[73] Provision of food in plenty awaited the development of the family farm equipped with modern machines. The individual organization of farming works well in production, particularly with modern equipment. The difficulty of supervision and the inadaptability of piece work payment seem to prevent this business from becoming too much dependent on hired labour.

Production by people working for themselves may be advantageous in farming, but it does not necessarily follow that individual sale or marketing of the product is either necessary, advisable, or advantageous. Individual bargaining worked when all business was individually organized. Recently, however, business has developed other forms of organization. The partnership has been superseded by the corporation designed to provide three things, length of life, large amounts of capital, and limited liability. Labour organizations have achieved over a

[73] Karl Brandt, *Public Control of Land Use in Europe*. Address to the American Farm Economic Association, Annual Meeting, Detroit, Dec. 28, 1938.

considerable period of time a greater or lesser degree of collective bargaining power which has some influence on wages. Those working for them selves today are compelled to bargain directly with such corporations and directly or indirectly with organized labour.

Individual organization may make it possible to provide oneself with a job. It may be the only possible way to produce some lines of goods. At the same time it may furnish small remuneration to the worker who employs himself, if he markets his goods or services individually by dealing directly with large organizations with greater bargaining power and indirectly with labour which has collective bargaining power.

The next development that one might expect would be an endeavour to secure some measure of collective bargaining power for the disposal of the goods and services produced individually. This is co-operative marketing. The recent increased interest in this subject is on account of its necessity. Where specialists must exchange goods and services with each other it follows, as night follows day, that if those specialists with the greater bargaining power secure the greater portion of the returns, then those who receive the smaller portion cannot keep the others busy and unemployment prevails. Let us examine the evidence.

The following index numbers for various commodities have been published by the Dominion Bureau of Statistics:[74]

	1913	December *1929*	December *1932*	December *1938*
Food	100	161	96	113
Fuel and light	100	157	145	141
Rent	100	158	141	148
Clothing	100	156	114	117
Sundries	100	166	161	156

At the end of 1929, everything was on a comparatively even keel, and that period has been frequently described as one of good times. Since 1929, the significant thing, from our present point of view, is the extent to which food prices (which in some degree reflect the farmer's income) have fallen below the level of the

[74] *Labour Gazette,* Jan., 1939, p. 101.

other commodities. Some industries maintained prices to a much greater degree than others, indicating greater bargaining power in the market. Some of these industries succeeded in maintaining prices only by sacrificing volume of production. In such industries unemployment prevailed. The construction industry, for instance, which recorded a business of about $546 million in 1929, was down to $97 million in 1933 and has not even yet got well under way. By and large the production of food was maintained as well in volume as the vagaries of the seasons allowed, though the price was lowered. Farmers suffered, and where they had contracted to pay some $52 million for Farm implements in 1929, in 1932 they purchased only $6 million worth.[75]

The most interesting and complete record that I have seen of the various ways in which industries responded to depression conditions is a report by Mr. Gardiner C. Means of Washington, who in 1935 furnished the following figures of the percentage decline in prices and volume of production:[76]

Products	*Per cent fall in price*	*Per Cent fall in production*
Agricultural implements	15	80
Motor vehicles	16	80
Cement	18	65
Iron and steel	20	83
Auto tires	33	70
Textile products	45	30
Food products	49	14
Leather	50	20
Petroleum	56	20
Agricultural commodities	63	6

This table reveals the extent to which different industries reacted to the conditions in the first half of the period. Some took their punishment in low prices, others in lack of business or unemployment. This condition still prevails, and now we have

[75] Dominion Bureau of Statistics, *The Agricultural Implement Industry in Canada* (Ottawa, 1934), p. 1.

[76] G. C. Means, *Industrial Prices and Their Relative Inflexibility* (Report to Secretary of Agriculture, 1935).

idle men and idle money so far at variance that some are looking to co-operation as a means of replacing suspicion with confidence. Co-operation may do it by enabling more people to give themselves a job—individually where individual organization is suitable, co-operatively where the individual organization is unsuitable. Hence we see increased interest in consumers' co-operation—a combination of individual buyers—and also in producers' co-operation, where those who produce individually may sell collectively.

There are many operations in connection with farming that may best be done co-operatively. One of the oldest and most successful is the provision of fire insurance for farm buildings. This field of co-operative effort has been in operation so long and has been so successful that it is generally taken for granted and seldom included in any discussion of the subject. Recently this field has been broadened in some localities. In the state of Ohio, the Farm Bureau Federation decided ten or fifteen years ago to apply the co-operative principle to motor-car insurance. The savings resulting in this field have already prompted this co-operative association to purchase a controlling interest in a life insurance company.

Another field for co-operation is health insurance. Out in Saskatchewan recently a medical man announced that the people were either too healthy or too hard up to make it worth his while to stay in the town. When this rumour got abroad, two hundred men put up ten dollars each to have this medical man on call. He is still in the town and so started co-operative medical services in Saskatchewan. In a rural district of Quebec a similar arrangement is now in existence. Through co-operative credit local groups may do a great portion of their own banking. This has been demonstrated in Germany since about the middle of last century, through the Raiffeisen system designed to serve rural districts and the Schuize Delitzsch system designed for urban areas. Copied from this experience, the Caisse Populaire was started in Quebec province in the first decade of the present century, and by 1934 there were 177 of these banks in operation. This development in Quebec was the basis of the development of the Credit Unions in Cape Breton under the sponsorship of St. Francis Xavier University. The movement has also expanded in the eastern states with the financial assistance of the late A. E. Filene, the well-known Boston merchant, and it was claimed last year that there were credit unions in more than forty states of the United States.[77]

These co-operative activities are mentioned only to show possibilities in various fields. What we are interested in is co-operative buying and selling, especially in farm products and food products. It is in this field that co-operation has been most important. In 1844 a small group of Lancashire people whom we know as the Rochdale Pioneers started a consumers' co-operative association to provide themselves with unadulterated goods, ensure honest weights and measures, provide homes for working people, and prevent the exploitation of labour. The method of securing these ends was the fair treatment of labour and the payment of dividends in proportion to business done with the association rather than according to money invested in it. Within a century this association has grown to include several million members, and it now supplies an important part of the retail merchandise marketed in Great Britain. It employs some 200,000 workers, of whom about 110,000 are employed in the co-operative stores and about 90,000 are engaged in making goods to sell in those stores. This is the most important of all co-operative developments, not only on account of its own success and expansion but also because this association was the pioneer in establishing the principles of co-operation upon which the movement has been based wherever it has later successfully developed. One of the principles of the Rochdale Pioneers was absolute neutrality in regard to race, religion, and politics.

On this continent, we have devoted most of our attention in the past to producers' co-operation, which is also the outstanding form of co-operation in Denmark, and it is only recently that consumers' co-operation has received much attention. Recent developments have directed attention to both the buying and the selling of goods co-operatively. This is particularly true of farmers, among whom there is more need and opportunity of buying and selling today than there was in earlier times. It is not very long since, when the roads were blocked with snow in winter, a scarcity of food developed in the cities. Now the organization of production has changed in such a way that blocked roads threaten a scarcity of food in the country. The surplus crops that were once stored on the farm are now carried in terminal elevators and cold storage plants. The flour once milled by local mills is now made

[77] R. Bergergren, *Cuna Emerges* (Madison, Wis., 1937).

in large cities, and the bread once baked at home is largely made by city bakeries and delivered (ready sliced) to country districts. There are exceptions to this centralization, yet in almost every product this is the trend. Even fluid milk is being shipped into large centres in excess of local requirements for use in fluid form, and York County is credited in Canadian dairy records with the manufacture of upwards of ten million pounds of creamery butter, most of which is made in Toronto and some of it by the United Farmers' Co-operative.

This change has paved the way for the development of co-operative purchase of farm supplies, which in the eastern states and in the eastern provinces include no small amount of feed for live stock. With the specialization that has recently developed in farming it is possible for a farmer in Western Canada to purchase his raw materials of seeds, feeds, fertilizers, and equipment at retail prices and sell his product, grain, at wholesale prices. It is also possible for those who purchase these grains wholesale to process them into chicken feed and dairy feeds, and to sell them to farmers in live stock, dairy, and poultry sections at retail prices. These farmers may turn these raw materials into manufactured products of meat, milk, and eggs and sell them again at wholesale prices. Naturally some of these meat animals may be processed into unexcelled fox food and again sold at retail to the fur farmer.

It was to prevent this possibility that a number of thoughtful people including farmers, manufacturers, bankers, ministers, and professors started in 1918 the Eastern States Farmers' Exchange. This association was started in order that farmers might purchase at wholesale the raw materials used in providing milk, eggs, and crops which they sell at wholesale. There are no membership fees required to belong to this association, and there is no capital stock. A man becomes a member by purchasing from the association, and he is carried as a member for two years after his latest purchase, after which his name is dropped from the list. The bankers, merchants, and manufacturers who were the first directors of this association later withdrew, leaving 48 members of the Board. Among these 48, there were 46 farmers, the other two being an ex-manager of the association and the financier who assisted it in its early stages.

Financed first by the credit of its founders, it became enabled to carry on by itself in five years. By 1935 the capital of the association amounted to a million and a half. From 1926 to 1933 the

Exchange distributed $557,000 in patronage dividends. By 1934 the membership exceeded 50,000 scattered over several of the eastern states, and the association possessed feed and fertilizer plants at Buffalo, Boston, and Wilmington, though its headquarters are at Springfield, Massachusetts.

The Eastern States Farmers' Exchange is not here mentioned because it is the most important in membership or business done, but as an instance of an organization first provided by disinterested people and later turned over to the farmers to run. This represents an approach to the idea that exploitation is a rather short-run policy. Evidently those who started it are reaping rich returns in improved prosperity of their area, especially on account of the educational and research activities carried on in providing a better quality of seeds, feeds, and fertilizers.[78]

A larger, older, and better known association catering to a similar demand is the Grange League Federation of Ithaca, New York, familiarly known as the G.L.F., a combination of three early associations of co-operative activity, namely the Grange, the Dairymen's League, and the Farm Bureau Federation. The roots of co-operative activity in this instance go back many years. The G.L.F. has had its ups and downs, but now with its huge feed and grain plants at Buffalo and Albany and 250 rural co-operative associations, it is in business in a large way. It is interesting to note that the annual meeting brings an attendance of twelve to fifteen hundred. Preceding a recent annual meeting some 50,000 members of locals took part in selecting the delegates.

It has sometimes been assumed that Canada has neglected co-operation. Any who are of that opinion should read Dr. J. F. Booth's address at the recent conference at Guelph, which is avail able in the *C.S. T.A. Review* of December, 1938. Before the frontier of Canada was extended beyond the Great Lakes, the co-operative movement began to receive some fitful attention in Ontario under the Grange and the Patrons of Industry. The latter body elected one member to Parliament—Mr. Jabell Robinson—and thus violated one of the early principles of the Rochdale Pioneers already mentioned. It is necessary to refer to these as early principles, as the C.W.S. now has a small number of members in the British House of Commons.

[78] Quentin Reynolds, "Cooperative Buying of Farm Supplies" *(Journal of Farm Economics,* Feb., 1935, pp. 157–66).

As we are here dealing with the recent development of co-operation, perhaps it may be sufficient to point to the recent increase in interest, leaving aside for the moment the question whether this represents a new development or simply a revival.

In the province of Quebec, the census reported for 1930 that some eight thousand farmers sold a million dollars' worth of goods co-operatively, while some ten thousand farmers purchased almost three-quarters of a million dollars' worth of goods. Last year the Cooperative Fédérée de Québec reported a business of around ten million dollars. This is a rate of expansion that gives the warmest friends of the movement considerable concern.

The recent expansion at Antigonish has received much publicity. My remarks about this movement will be confined to what was learned from a visit there. Before 1930 the young people of Cape Breton left for Boston when they grew ready for a job. After 1930 this way of getting work faded. Other jobs had to be found for the people. Capital was made available through the credit unions. Lobster marketing furnished the opening for the use of the capital required. The fishermen and the miners have proved good co-operators, but it is conceded at Antigonish that the farmer is a harder man to interest. This is because he frequently has little to co-operate with or for. Recent specialization in farming, however, makes co-operation among farmers at the same time more necessary and less difficult.

Integrated Marketing

The most successful co-operative on this continent is no doubt the Cooperative Citrous Fruit Growers of California and Arizona. This association with its 16,000 members, 210 local associations, 25 district exchanges, and central exchange has been operated over fifty years. In 1886, it shipped 2,000 carloads of fruit. In 1936, 100,000 carloads were marketed in 800 markets of the world—an increase of fifty times in fifty years. This is a good example of integrated marketing. Canadian consumers who now buy oranges by the case may form their own opinion as to its success.

The balance sheet of the Citrous Fruit Growers for 1936 shows \$30 million paid out for labour. Of this \$30 million, \$18 million was spent in the groves for spraying and heating orchards and picking the fruit. The co-operative organization has found by experience that it is not advisable to have the grower spray the trees or pick the fruit, let alone grade it. This point should be particularly noted, as it will be mentioned again. The balance of the $30 million was laid out in the packing houses. It is interesting to note that of the entire labour bill of this organization three-fifths was spent in the groves and the other two-fifths in the packing houses. This association at one time tried retailing its own products. That was given up, and the association now takes the fruit from the tree and sells it to the retailer. The association does the advertising. The advertising bill varies from one million to two and a half million dollars, depending on the size of the crop.

The price policy of this organization has been described by the late G. H. Powell, author of *Co-operation in Agriculture,* who successfully managed the association for many years. After finding out the annual supply, that total is divided by 52, and if any week has failed to move one fifty-second of the total, then the price is modified until it does. This is a fairly simple system of what is termed orderly marketing.

This association is not only a good example of integrated marketing: it is also a good example of a federated system of organization as contrasted with a centralized organization. The members elect the boards of directors of the 210 locals, the locals elect the boards of the 25 district exchanges, and the exchanges elect the board of the central body. It is representative control, as contrasted with direct control of the centralized type where each is a member of the central association.

Recent Expansion in Canada

Farm business organizations report their amount of business of selling farm products and farm supplies as totalling $174 million in the year 1936-7, as contrasted with $116 million in 1932, an increase of 50 per cent. In 1936-7 these associations reported 451,231 patrons. As there are about three-quarters of a million farms in Canada, the number of patrons equals about 60 per cent of the number of farms. This does not mean that 60 per cent of the farms do business co-operatively, as some of the farms may do business with more than one association. Yet it is some indication of the importance of this form of doing business in the country.

Naturally the proportion of co-operative patrons varies among different provinces. The proportion of patrons to farms, based on the number of farms reported in the census of 1936 for the three Prairie Provinces and 1931 for the others, varies from 97 per cent in Saskatchewan to some 12 per cent in New Brunswick. The complete comparison is as follows:

Proportion of Patrons to Total Farms

	Per cent
Canada	62
Saskatchewan	97
Manitoba	85
Prince Edward Island	72
Alberta	68
British Columbia	62
Quebec	29
Ontario	21
Nova Scotia	15
New Brunswick	12

The bulk of the business is done in the selling of farm products, the patrons of selling organizations numbering almost 400,000, and the patrons of purchasing associations 52,000. The expansion of this method of doing business has been rapid during recent years. Since 1932 the expansion in the various provinces has been as follows:[79]

Incresse in Money Value of Business Done by Farmers' Co-operatives in 1936–7 as Compared with 1932–3

	Increase Per cent
Canada	50
Prince Edward Island	91
Nova Scotia	23
New Brunswick	35
Quebec	106
Ontario	65
Manitoba	65
Saskatchewan	88
Alberta	6
British Columbia	31

[79] A.E. Richards, *Farmers' Business Organisations in Canada* (Department of Agriculture, Ottawa, 1935).

An increase of 50 per cent in five years is rapid expansion. The province of Quebec more than doubled the value of co-operative business done during that time. The rate of expansion has given considerable concern to many, and we may well examine some of the limitations of the movement.

Summary And Criticism

Much has been learned about co-operation in the century during which it has developed. The citrus fruit growers, for example, found from experience that growers could not satisfactorily spray, pick, or grade their own fruit. It was essential to have an unbiased grader. If this is necessary among such staunch co-operators, how may any individual organization or corporation satisfactorily pro vide dependable grading? The same association found that the necessary price policy for a commodity regularly consumed through out the year was to adjust the price in such a way that one fifty second of the total crop would be sold each week. This may be appropriately called orderly marketing. It is an effective price policy, a policy that moves the goods so that employment may continue.

Some have expressed the view that the recent expansion in interest and activity in co-operation has been a result of inequality of bargaining power. If and when this inequality is lessened, there is a very great danger that this bargaining power may be used to exact higher prices and thus reduce volume of business and employment. To avoid this a better understanding between producer and consumer is essential. The best means of arriving at this objective is integrated marketing, which may be provided by various agencies. The United Fruit Company is a corporation that grows and markets bananas. The Atlantic and Pacific Tea Company shows a movie film that starts with growing lettuce in the field and concludes with the display in the store windows. The C.W.S. has its own tea plantations as well as manufacturing establishments that provide many of the goods sold in its stores. The C.W.S. also acquired some thirty odd thousand acres of land in Great Britain, but after a few years' experience decided not to extend its operations in general farming. Integrated marketing has possibilities, but whether it should be provided by consumers' co-operatives, producers' co-operatives, or other agencies is a question worth discussion.

Other questions of current interest in connection with co-operation include the following: Are co-operatives now securing too much encouragement and assistance? Are taxation policies favouring this form of business organization over other organizations? Why is it that during the five years from 1931 to 1936 the urban population of the three Prairie Provinces declined while the
rural population increased? Why was it that the farmers reported over one hundred thousand more animals home slaughtered in 1935 than in 1930? Was it because the marketing agencies, which in this country now employ about half a million workers,[80] are exacting too much for their services?

The manufacture of materials of Canadian farm origin has been recorded since 1924. In that year the percentage of the gross value of product that was paid for raw materials was slightly over 65 per cent. In 1932 it was around 56 per cent, and in 1935, the last year for which the figures are now available, it was less than 62 per cent.[81]

The percentage cost of distribution of ten foods in the United States, including bread, flour, butter, cheese, potatoes, beef, pork, poultry, eggs, and milk has increased in recent years as the following figures show.

Cost of Distribution

Period	*Farm value*	*Retail value*	*Per cent margin*
1910–14	$9.18	$16.30	43.7
1915–19	14.34	23.72	39.5
1920–4	13.27	16.41	49.8
1929	13.59	27.13	49.9
1932	6.04	17.30	65.1
1934	7.34	19.06	61.5

Apparently that part of the provision of food, which is now carried on largely by organized industries in the city and which used to be carried on by farmers or not done at all, is at present the most remunerative. In 1938 the total volume of field crops produced in Canada was about 40 per cent greater than in the

[80] L.G. Reynolds, "Distributive Trades in Canada" (*Canadian Journal of Economics and Political Science*, Nov., 1938, p. 538).

[81] *Canada Year Books.*

previous year, while the farm value of the total was some $30 million less. If some, other industries could or would provide 40 or even 25 per cent more goods, and charge less for them, would unemployment be so prevalent?

The leading points brought out in this paper may be summarized as follows:[82]

1. Specialization may provide plenty only if exchange of goods and services is allowed to proceed.
2. At present some goods and services are provided by organized groups, others by unorganized individuals.
3. Some of the groups that produce goods for exchange have control over production, limited liability, and collective bar gaining power, while others have limited control over production, unlimited liability, and limited bargaining power.
4. The result is sometimes unbalanced production, unequal prices, buyers' strikes, and unemployment.
5. Such a result has prevailed in Canada for almost a decade.
6. Such conditions were relieved in former times by migration of unemployed to virgin land.
7. With the passing of the frontier and restricted migration, new conditions have arisen, and it is more difficult to bring idle men and idle money together.
8. This condition has made co-operation more necessary, interesting, and applicable.
9. It is necessary to provide limited liability and collective bar gaining power for those industries which do not yet possess them, in order to equalize their bargaining power with those who do.
10. Such a policy would enable more individuals to give themselves a job.
11. A century's experience shows that this may be done.
12. The recent expansion of co-operation is partly due to the fact that some other methods of doing business have failed to function, thus allowing unemployment to develop.
13. Co-operation may apply to many fields such as insurance, health, credit, and marketing.
14. It permits the development of integrated marketing.
15. It may improve quality by allowing the grading of goods by unbiased parties.

[82] *Consumer's Guide* (U.S. Government Printing Office), April 8, 1935, p. 7.

16. It provides a means of education of both producer and consumer.

17. It may provide a greater chance of securing an economy of abundance rather than one of scarcity.

18. It may provide the maximum of freedom with the minimum of regulation, since it allows the maximum number to work for themselves.

19. It deserves study as an alternative to the trend towards increasing governmental activity in business.

Retailing From the Consumer's Point of View[83]

Walter Thompson

In the most recent edition of McNair, Gragg, and Teele's *Problems of Retailing,* the authors quote from Daniel Defoe's *The Complete English Tradesman,* published in 1726:

> Trade must not be entered into as a thing of light concern. It is called business very properly, for it is a business for life and ought to be followed as one of the great businesses of life. Trade must, I say, be worked at, not played with. He that trades in jest will certainly break in earnest, and this is one reason indeed why so many tradesmen come to so hasty a conclusion of their affairs.
>
> The sum of the matter is this. It is necessary for a tradesman to be subject, by all the ways possible, to his business; his customers are to be his idols; so far as he may worship idols by allowance, he is to bow down to them and worship them; at least, he is not in any way to displease them or show any disgust or distaste at anything they say or do. The bottom of it all is, that he is intending to get money by them, and it is not for him that gets money by them to offer the least inconvenience to them by whom he gets it, but he is to consider that, as Solomon says, "The borrower is the servant to the lender," so the seller is servant to the buyer.

These words were published two hundred years ago. At the present time, word comes back from Russia which gives us some idea of the present state of retailing in that country. A commentator suggested that at least two signs should be conspicuously

[83] From H.R. Kemp (ed.), *Canadian Marketing Problems*, Toronto: University of Toronto Press, 1939, pp. 46–60.

placed in all retail establishments there. These should say:

If you don't like this store, go to some other store.
The public is always wrong.

The same commentator told the story of a burly Russian forcing his way to make a purchase in front of a line-up of prospective customers. The man at the head of the line objected. The aggressor, however, produced a card which seemingly allowed the holder to buy merchandise without standing in line. "Oh," said the injured party, "this is the line where holders of such cards line up."

Before going too far in the subject of the consumer and his relation with his retailer, it is well to give some background for the typical individual's attitude toward business in general. Our modern individual has still some of the attitudes of his ancestors, so far as this subject is concerned. Miriam Beard, in a recent book, *History of the Business Man*, relates some interesting anecdotes regarding early antipathy to traders. The author repeats an experience of Odysseus in one of his wanderings. He found himself a stranger in a foreign land. He was immediately accused of being a business man. Words failed him under this dastardly accusation. His contempt could only be expressed by throwing the largest boulder available a great distance. This feat was followed by spitting upon the ground. Immediately he was accepted as a gentleman.

An early school of economists held with considerable tenacity to the opinion that the only real producers were those who extracted goods from the soil. Service industries were, under such lines of thought, drones on society. Many of our early ideas of value were closely tied to labour expended on particular articles. Some believed that any individual selling an article for more than it cost was stealing. The motives behind monopoly investigations are at least partially tied up to this background. Attempts to establish cooperative stores, to some extent, reflect distrust of retailers. The establishment of the business man as a reputable member of society has been, of course, accomplished for some time. It is well, however, for us to keep in mind at all times that this status has not always existed. It is well to remember, too, that respect must be transformed into appreciation by doing a difficult job well.

Forces Affecting Retailers

The pace in present-day business is a fast one. Retail stores, as we know them, are absorbing the force of a number of factors which should be kept in mind. The purchaser relies upon two individuals when an article is purchased. He relies on either the man who sells him the article or the manufacturer who made it, or on both. With the rise of advertising to the consumer by manufacturing, packaging, and branding, the typical consumer has tended to fall back on the manufacturer for assurance of good value. Properly planned advertising should give information to the buyer. In this development the retailer's function has been somewhat reduced. The growth of heavily advertised lines has done much to make possible our large self-serve chains in the grocery trade.

The list of factors affecting the retailer's position is a long one. A bare mention of these should establish the point that our present retailing structure is a changing one. Some of these movements are: tendencies to develop greater centralization; chain store taxation; price maintenance legislation; continued emphasis on price by large sellers; the movement of the variety chain into smaller centres; the rise of stores handling high unit value specialties; the break-up of the traditional "types" of retail stores; the large part played by style in the sale of goods, and the change in the character of variety chains.

All these and others are points which are affecting the retailer's position. As business men we should not lament change. With change comes risk, and with risk-taking we find possibility of profit-making. The elimination of the possibility of risk-taking means, ultimately, a destruction of the motive for our present business structure, namely profits. The business man must understand the forces affecting him. With this understanding he is able to perform his function of risk-taking with minimum adverse effect.

At this point it may be well to recall that Canadian retailers, generally speaking, have done their job well. Canadian manufacturers have found that, foreign subsidiaries operating in Canada offer potent competition. There has undoubtedly been a strong urge for United States manufacturers to come into Canada—such as the protection of markets established under a more favourable tariff. On the other hand, the Canadian retailer has kept his field substantially with a Canadian complexion. One large retail grocery chain in Canada has been operating on an expense ratio of approximately 13 per cent of sales, while similar organizations in the United States were operating on an expense ratio of around 20 per cent. The strength of Canadian retailers must have been a factor in the decision of large American retail units to stay out of the Canadian market.

Interest of Manufacturers in Retail Problems

It is through the retailer that the manufacturer meets his final customer. A product which is sold must give satisfaction, The ordinary customer is not interested in buying so much leather or so much cloth. He is interested in what a specific article will do for him. Greater satisfaction in actual use comes with more intelligent selling by retailers.

One large department store in Boston, Massachusetts, has gone so far as to publish, on tags attached to the merchandise, the advantages and limitations of all products sold, so that each customer will have a better knowledge of articles purchased. A few years ago an outstanding advertising executive in the food field intimated that his firm was disregarding the retailer so far as it was possible. His theory was that consumers clamouring for a particular product, because of consumer advertising, rendered dealer work unnecessary. Fortunately this attitude is not general. Sound executives are realizing the necessity of co-ordinated sales programmes. These programmes include dealer education and assistance along with constructive consumer advertising. Profitable repeat business done by manufacturers to retailers must be based upon mutual confidence. This confidence can be established by the manufacturer when he has a thorough understanding of retailer problems.

About a year ago a retailer with whom I was working at the time was called upon by a representative of a leading hosiery company. The first reaction of the retailer was that he did not need any more hosiery. The salesman, while he left his sample case still open, immediately stopped talking about hosiery. Observing that the retailer had some time available, he lectured on the subject of retail pricing strategy. The substance of his little talk was that every retail store should price some articles with utmost care. There are a few articles which are bought with high frequency by the average consumer. In these goods price is quite important. When these prices are higher than average, a store is likely to get the reputation of being a high-priced store. He mentioned an example of a successful merchant in Western Ontario who regularly priced articles of this type at a low figure, and thereby developed a reputation for having a very fair price policy. On items of less, frequent purchase, the same merchant put a price slightly above the regular price. Goods of the latter type are often highly styled merchandise, carried with considerable risk, and the merchant must therefore have a higher-than-average original mark-up. He pointed out that too many retailers were setting their prices by simply adding a uniform 50 per cent to billed cost. This salesman's understanding of the price problem was a sound one. Incidentally, he got an order for hosiery that day.

There is considerable evidence that a large number of our manufacturers are realizing their responsibility when they sell merchandise to retailers. I know of one wholesaler who does a substantial manufacturing business as well, who has a unique policy. When ever he adds to his line an item which has questionable consumer acceptance, the article will be stocked in sufficient quantity to allow for calls on one-half of the accounts. Several stores may be unable to move the new item. The wholesaler's policy is to accept returns from these customers. The sales force then calls on the remainder of the customers who have not been solicited with that particular item. This particular firm has been able to move a large number of novelty lines, and at the same time it has maintained excellent relations with retailers. The feature of the manufacturer-retailer relation which should be kept uppermost is that, over a long period of time, the manufacturer and the retailer, as well as the consumer, must work together in such a way that all will be satisfied.

Consumer Attitude to Retailers in London, Ontario

Two years ago, during a series of lectures to retail merchants in London, the following questions were discussed:

1. How loyal are customers to particular stores?

2. How long does the average customer trade with his favourite store? What does the typical consumer like about his favourite store?

3. For what reasons do customers switch from one store to another?

4. What are the specific characteristics of a store that cause the individual to look on it as an undesirable place to buy?

5. What are the characteristics, from the consumer's point of view, of a good retail clerk?

6. On the other hand, what actions, if any, have annoyed customers?

7. Just how important are special sales?

With the help of the London merchants, a questionnaire was devised to throw some light on these questions. A group of senior students in Business Administration at the University of Western Ontario interviewed a cross-section of London consumers, including 8 wealthy people, 33 well-to-do, 69 of medium purchasing power, and 32 in a lower purchasing power classification. Hardware, shoes, dry goods, department stores, and furniture stores were investigated.

Most of the progress made in connection with such surveys, in which the sampling technique is used, may be attributed to advertising agencies. Such men as Cherington, Gallup, and Weld have been or are engaged in research work for advertising agencies. Where men's wear popular surveys have failed, it has often been because they have not used a particularly scientific sample. The *Literary Digest's* election poll, to quote one of the best-known instances, failed because the sample used was not representative. Other previous polls had been highly accurate. In this instance, their difficulty seems to have been that they made too much use of telephone directories as a means of choosing people to question. This meant that they ignored the great mass of individuals in the lowest purchasing power groups, who obviously cannot afford to be listed in a telephone directory. Their erroneous forecast of the probable election of Landon was due to this faulty sampling.

Some surveys do not reflect true conditions because they ask questions which rely to too great an extent on memory. Other surveys are faulty because of the wording of questions. It is very easy to get 95 per cent of the people to agree with you that today is a very fine day if the wording of the question is, "Today is a fine day, isn't it?" Bias can enter questionnaires. The survey technique used by the bulk of our commercial organizations is good, but we must constantly be on our guard against bias either in the questions asked or in the selection of those who are to answer them. In this way we may be able to use the survey tool in shaping sound marketing policy.

In the London consumer survey here described, we tried to give fair representation to each economic class in the community, and to present the questions in such a way as to avoid any tendency to bias in the answers. Some of the principal findings of the survey are briefly set forth below.

The statements of London consumers with regard to the length of time during which they had dealt with the retail stores now patronized are summarized in Table I.

Duration of Preference

Years	Department stores	Furniture stores	Men's wear	Dry goods	Shoe stores
	%	%	%	%	%
Under 1.....	1.6	....	8.6	9.1	11.1
1-5.........	42.6	0.29	46.5	9.1	66.6
5-10........	24.6	0.17	24.1	36.4	5.6
10 and up...	31.2	54	20.8	45.4	16.7

One of the surprising features in this table is that there seems to be a definite tendency on the part of London customers to deal with their favourite store for only a short period of time. Merchants are perhaps inclined to pay too much of their attention to getting customers from a competitor, and more effort devoted to pleasing existing customers would probably be profitable. It would seem that a store can assure itself of a very substantial growth if it can Reduce the number of customers lost. Even a small reduction in the loss percentage will assure such growth.

After stating the name of their favourite department store, London customers were asked what they particularly liked about that store. Many mentioned more than one thing. Table II presents a summary of the answers received.

As one might expect, quality and good assortment stand out as the most significant factors. This may explain to a very great extent the importance of the buyer in the success or failure of large department stores.

It is noted that exchange and refund policies come fourth in the features liked about the favourite store. Mr. Tom Faust is investigating customer returns of merchandise in London at the present time. One of the questions that he asks in this questionnaire is: "Do you know of any article returned by an acquaintance of yours that has been unfair to the store?" Some of the examples reported are interesting:

A hat made to order, worn to a wedding and returned.

TABLE II

Things Liked about Favourite Department Store

Number of persons reporting

What they liked:	Class A (Wealthy)	Class B (Well-to-do)	Class C (Middle)	Class D (Lower)	Total
Quality: good stock assortment	5	18	33	12	68
Service	3	6	11	5	25
Value: price attractive	1	1	8	9	19
Exchange and refund	1	6	9	1	17
Clerks	2	4	7	2	15
Dependable	1	5	6	2	14
Charge account		2	4		6
Habit			2	3	5
Latest goods		2	1		3
Clean			2		2
Satisfaction		1	1		2
Best in town				2	2
Discount		1			1
Advertising			1		1
Order desk			1		1

A coat taken home and used for a pattern and design, from which another coat was made.

A rug ordered especially for a party and returned afterwards.

Lace table-cloth used for an afternoon tea and returned.

Boy's suit used to have a boy's picture taken by a photographer and then returned.

A pyrex dish bought in Detroit and returned to a store in London.

China used for a trousseau tea, for display purposes.

Silk lingerie kept for four months and never worn and then returned.

Rug ordered especially for a social function and then returned.

An unknown article which was returned to a store from which it was never purchased.

Furniture for newlyweds, used for display purposes and returned after the wedding.

Dance accessories used and returned.

Jewelry worn and returned. (This must have been a few months ago because now most stores will not take costume jewelry back.)

There were also many cases of dresses and hats worn and later returned without any reason.

Retailers have probably gone too far in allowing customers to return merchandise. From a practical point of view, however, liberal policies must often be continued. Competitive conditions are often the controlling factor.

In summarizing the reasons for preferring a department store, it was found that about 40 per cent of informants mentioned some aspect of store policy: about 30 per cent liked the goods themselves, about 15 per cent mentioned prices, 10 per cent

TABLE III

Why Did You Switch Stores—All Types of Stores

Percentage of persons reporting

Reason stated:	All stores	Classes of consumers: Higher purchasing power	Classes of consumers: Lower purchasing power	Types of stores: Men's	Types of stores: Department	Types of stores: Dry goods	Types of stores: Shoes
	%	%	%	%	%	%	%
Attitude of salespeople	38.0	34.0	42.0	31.7	43.0	36.6	58.6
Poor service	19.0	13.4	25.3	19.0	17.2	23.3	20.5
Inconsistent quality	15.9	22.0	13.3	20.1	14.4	20.0	8.3
Returns	8.7	8.5	6.0	8.8	8.1	13.6	12.6
High price	7.9		6.0	7.7	5.7	6.5	
Misrepresented goods	6.5	10.2	3.0	7.7	7.3		
Attempted substitution	4.0	1.7	3.0	5.0	4.3	0.6	

preferred a certain store because of its clerks, and the remaining 5 per cent mentioned a variety of considerations.

In investigating the motives that had led customers to change from one store to another, the best questions for obtaining information were: "Have you recently switched stores?" and "Why did you switch stores?" Table III gives a summary of the answers to these questions.

The outstanding criticism indicated in the above table is the attitude of salespeople. It is also interesting to note that this factor is more important in the lower purchasing power groups. It seems that many of our retail clerks are not sufficiently careful in selling to customers in the lower purchasing power classifi-

TABLE IV

Least Desirable Shoe Stores and Reasons

Number of persons reporting

Reason stated:	Wealthy	Well-to-do	Middle class	Lower class	Total
Cheap merchandise.........	5	10	26	12	53
Poor service..............		2			2
Surroundings cheap........		1			1
Not dependable............		2			2
Poor appearance...........		1	3		4
Poor advertising..........			1		1
Poor clerks...............			5		5
Price cutting tactics........			2		2
Poor fit..................		1	4		5
Not enough clerks..........			2		2
Low salaries, poor principles.			1		1
Try to substitute..........			1		1
Poor style................			1		1
High price................			4		4
Too flashy................			1		1
Totals...........	5	17	51	12	85

cation. Many salesmen have the conviction, when a sale is lost, that the price is too high, but according to the statements of all classes of consumers the relative unimportance of price is surprising. One fact that emerges from a study of the above figures is that practically all those inter viewed had a definite reason for switching from one store to another.

Replies to the question, "Which shoe store do you believe to be the least desirable in London? Why?" are summarized in Table IV.

TABLE V

Reasons for Preferring a Particular Shoe Clerk

Times mentioned

Reason stated:	Wealthy	Well-to-do	Middle class	Lower class	Total
Considerate Obliging Tries to please Courteous		6	1	3	10
Good fit	2	2	5		9
Intelligent Knows shoe buy Knows business	1	3	4		8
A friend		4	2	2	8
Judgment good Capable Efficient		6		1	7
Knows personal requirements		3			3
Won't sell poor buy		2		1	3
Personality			2		2
Service			1		1
Truthful			1		1
Takes time			1		1
Patient			1		1
Enthusiasm			1		1
Shows styles quickly			1		1

In the response of customers to the question, "Which shoe store do you believe to be the least desirable in London, and why?" cheap merchandise is a reason frequently mentioned, while poor clerks seem relatively unimportant. Often an individual is convinced that a store is not desirable without ever actually dealing with that store. People may get the impression that a particular store has "cheap merchandise" from advertisements and displays. The table indicating reasons for switching stores is probably far more significant for our purposes, since it is based upon the actual experiences of customers who have dealt with the stores in question.

Preference for Particular Clerks

Among all the types of stores investigated (shoe, hardware, department stores, men's clothing, and furniture) preference for a particular clerk seems to be most marked in shoe stores. There is a reason for this situation. The shoe clerk performs a distinctly personal service. He can contribute a great deal to the shoe buyer. In view of this fact, a summary of reasons for preferring a particular shoe clerk is given in Table V. Of the reasons given,

TABLE VI

Criticisms of Shoe Clerks

	Number of times mentioned
General Inefficiency	
Forces sale	10
Does not pay attention to buyer	3
Slow	3
Poor salesman	2
Does not know goods	2
Dislikes to show unseasonable goods	2
Too busy to show goods	1
Inattention	1
Does not correct mistake in measure	1
Total	25
Personality Faults	
Discourtesy	5
Smug, smart	5
Talks too much	2
Does not try to please	2
Lazy	2
Displeased when customers go elsewhere	1
Dictates needs	1
Untruthful	1
Total	19

45 per cent had to do with the clerk's personality, and 55 per cent related to his ability to fit shoes well. The majority of shoe buyers prefer a particular clerk because he renders a proper fitting service.

Table VI contains a summary of replies to the question, "Have you ever been displeased with a particular clerk? If so, what caused your displeasure?"

Many of these faults could be corrected by proper sales training and proper consciousness of the situation on the part of retail store managers.

Many retailers are considerably concerned over the question of "sales." To throw some light on this subject, we asked customers, "What proportion of your purchases are made at special sales?" As might be expected, the groups having lower purchasing power show a far greater interest in this subject, but many well-to-do and wealthy people also are not averse from buying at special sales. As confirmation of this result, it may be mentioned that an earlier survey made for the *Mail and Empire* in Toronto showed that many well-to-do Toronto citizens regularly purchase from certain grocery chains to take advantage of advertised specials.

Sales Procedure From a Customer's Point of View

A number of years ago an auditor acquaintance arranged for me to assist in the closing out of an electrical specialty store. Formerly one of the leading stores of the district, the store had got into difficulties as a result of health and personnel troubles and the business depression. Before asking for help, the managers themselves had tried without success to sell out. They had marked the prices of their stock down to cost and below, but the net result of their action was that unit sales remained substantially the same and dollar sales were substantially reduced. An unsuccessful attempt was also made by the auditor to sell the store as a going concern. We decided that the stock must be sold to the general public. To facilitate this task the store was first operated for a month in the usual manner. During this period, all merchandise was repriced at normal retail levels. At the end of this interval a small notice in the press announced that the auditor had been placed in charge and would sell the stock to the general public. The price reductions necessary to sell the merchandise were not as great as those previously made by the proprietors, and the stock was sold out in about three weeks.

This experience illustrates that the public must be given some specific reason for a sale. They must believe that there is a *bonafide* reason for a reduction in price. Otherwise they refuse to believe that merchandise offered is a bargain.

The same auditor had another client in a small town who was in financial difficulties. The store owner had experienced a poor spring season, and his creditors were asking for money. Some business acquaintances of the proprietor in neighbouring towns had instituted summer sales, but these had resulted in but three or four days of good business, after which business generally receded to former levels. In this case, it was necessary to have a successful sale and to make that sale last for a period of at least four weeks. To assure success, drastic steps had to be taken. The plans for carrying out this assignment, which were made in co-operation with the advertising manager of the *London Free Press*, Mr. Walter Gunn, may be briefly described.

We believed that the store had an important announcement. In order to convince the buying public of that area that it was a significant event, we thought it necessary to use about four times as much newspaper space as was customary for that store. The town was small and we hoped to receive the benefit of a certain amount of gossip. For this reason, the store was closed for one day prior to the sale. All items advertised were in general demand, and the price tags were attractive. In order to keep the sale talked about in the town, a midnight sale was held. This was advertised in the local theatre.

The last week-end (the town happened to be a "week-end" town) presented a problem. In order to assure good business, an announcement was made that a free gift would be given to every purchaser, regardless of the amount of his purchase, after seven o'clock on Friday and Saturday nights. Although the gift cost but seven cents, it was a lady's handkerchief of high quality. The final week end was the second largest during the four-week period.

After the sale was over, there were still considerable odds and ends left, and we used the following week-end to run a rummage sale in the basement. Sales volume during the first two days of this sale was equal to that of the previous month. A great number of the things done might be classed as high-pressure salesmanship, but the situation was acute and called for drastic action.

Summary

By way of summary, emphasis may be laid on the following points:

1. We must be aware that the consumer is not a completely friendly creature. He must be carefully handled by retailers.
2. While the quality of merchandise is always important, unsatisfactory retail clerks are reported to be the most important reason for loss of customers.
3. Space advertising and window display should not give the impression that "cheap" merchandise is handled: if they do, the establishment runs the risk of being regarded as an "undesirable store."
4. Customer turnover in stores is spectacularly high. Even a small reduction in the loss of customers will improve long-term results.